Booth's Confederate Connections

Booth's Confederate Connections

Sandy Prindle

Foreword by
Steven E. Woodworth

PELICAN PUBLISHING COMPANY
GRETNA 2019

The word "Pelican" and the depiction of a pelican are trademarks of Pelican Publishing Company, Inc., and are registered in the U.S. Patent and Trademark Office.

Library of Congress Cataloging-in-Publication Data

Names: Prindle, Sandy, author.
Title: Booth's Confederate connections / by Sandy Prindle ; foreword by Steven E. Woodworth.
Description: Gretna, Louisiana : Pelican Publishing Company, [2019] | Includes bibliographical references and index.
Identifiers: LCCN 2018030315| ISBN 9781455624737 (hardcover : alk. paper) | ISBN 9781455624744 (ebook)
Subjects: LCSH: Lincoln, Abraham, 1809-1865—Assassination. | Booth, John Wilkes, 1838-1865. | Surratt, John H. (John Harrison), 1844-1916. | United States—History—Civil War, 1861-1865.
Classification: LCC E457.5 .P875 2019 | DDC 973.7092—dc23 LC record available at https://lccn.loc.gov/2018030315

Printed in the United States of America
Published by Pelican Publishing Company, Inc.
1000 Burmaster Street, Gretna, Louisiana 70053
www.pelicanpub.com

Contents

Foreword 7

Preface 11

Acknowledgments 15

Chapter One   Justification. 19

Chapter Two   Building the Intelligence Road . . . 27

Chapter Three   The Canadian Connections. 31

Chapter Four   Black Flag Warfare Turned Serious . 49

Chapter Five   Booth Arrives in the Story 55

Chapter Six   A Plot Develops 64

Chapter Seven   A Plan Comes Together. 75

Chapter Eight   The Drama Begins 86

Chapter Nine   The Alibi 102

Chapter Ten   The Final Days 107

Chapter Eleven   The Great Tragedy 119

Chapter Twelve   The Pursuit of Justice. 133

Chapter Thirteen   The Trial of the Century 157

Chapter Fourteen   The Final Hours. 181

Chapter Fifteen   After the Executions 190

Chapter Sixteen   Off the Hook 202

Chapter Seventeen   A Story Revised. 218

Notes 227

Index 235

Foreword

Abraham Lincoln has for decades been America's most beloved president. His steady leadership through the nation's darkest crisis, his eloquent expressions of the meaning of that crisis and that nation, and above all his death at the very moment of triumph have secured his place in America's secular pantheon. Conversely, the man who shot Lincoln, actor John Wilkes Booth, gained a well-earned and permanent place in the nation's hall of shame, somewhere between Benedict Arnold and John Gacy. Americans, at least those who pay moderate attention to history, realize Booth did not act alone. Didn't they hang three other people along with him? Yet it continues to be amazing how little the American public, even the history-reading part of it, knows about who and what ultimately lay behind the Lincoln assassination. No, this is not one of those conspiracy theories that require wearing a tinfoil hat, and, no, we're not talking about the Vatican, the Jesuits, or space aliens. The real story of the Lincoln assassination conspiracy is sober history, based on sound evidence—just as real and raw as any other part of the Civil War, which is what it is, and just as fascinating and full of suspense as a spy story, which is also what it is.

Even though some historians have begun to unravel the connection between Lincoln's assassination and the Confederate espionage network in Maryland and northern Virginia, the depth and importance of that connection remain not fully grasped by most students of Civil War history. The fact is that the Lincoln assassination was an operation of Confederate espionage directed from Richmond with authorization from the highest, or nearly the highest, level of the Confederate government. Booth's executed co-conspirators, Lewis Powell, George Atzerodt, David Herold, and Mary Surratt, carried out their roles in the assassination plot as part of their duty to the Confederate government. So too did some of those who escaped the hangman's noose—the ostensibly innocent doctor who set Booth's leg, Samuel Mudd; Mary Surratt's adult son John, who apparently knew when to leave town; and several others—all following orders as good agents of the Confederate States of America. And whence came those orders? From Richmond—in short, from Confederate president Jefferson Davis—or *perhaps* from someone very close to him within the Confederate cabinet. No wonder the public has had difficulty believing it.

Now to lay the case before the reading public comes this book by retired Texas judge Sandy Prindle. Who better to sort through the evidence and present a case clearly than a judge? Who better to tell the story with all the flair and suspense that a good (and true) tale of espionage deserves than a writer of novels? Yes, Judge Prindle is both. And that makes this book especially well suited to bring these events to life and to explain how something actually happened that we never thought could have happened on our shores.

Perhaps the most intriguing aspect of the judge's account is his identification of the man who may have been the true mastermind of the plot, a man who may have known more about its workings, and had more to do with its direction, than did Jefferson Davis. Those of us who have studied Davis over the years have tended to balk at the idea of his authorizing an assassination. Jeff Davis would shoot you soon enough, but in the face, not in the back of the head, and it has been hard to imagine that he commissioned someone else for such a deed. Judge Prindle's account shows that he may not have. He may not have been aware that an operation aimed at capture had turned into a plot to kill, and that the transformation had been conceived in an office not very far from his own. That decision may have been taken by the president's right-hand man, his top supporter within the Confederate cabinet, and the chief of the Confederacy's secret espionage organization.

With the courier John Surratt's admission a year later and the volume of events and circumstances submitted in this book, this may be the best that we historians will ever manage for a conviction. It is well worth a careful reading.

Steven E. Woodworth
Civil War history professor,
Texas Christian University (TCU)

Preface

Your high-school history books didn't spend much time telling you the story of the first murder of an American president. You would think that it would be a more important story than that. There were many reasons why it went on the back burner at the time. Lincoln's murder was something that the divided nation wanted to forget and put behind them. In 1866, Congress canceled its investigation. Why? Perhaps it was because of political embarrassment over perjured testimony. A military tribunal rather than a civil court tried civilians. A woman was hanged. Was the verdict in her case fair? Was she even guilty? Did Pres. Andrew Johnson ever see the plea for leniency for her from five of the nine members of the tribunal? Johnson swore that he never did. The prosecutor, Benjamin Holt, swore that Johnson did. The Union had both Jefferson Davis and Clement Clay (a Confederate agent in Canada), along with other Confederate leaders, imprisoned and publicly charged with complicity, but they were never tried. The Union could have pursued the evidence but didn't. This book will suggest reasons why. The Union's handling of the affair of the conspirators, both real and alleged, was quite a mess. The North didn't want to talk about it, and for thirty years, they didn't.

The South had no reason to investigate the murder. Their whole culture had just been turned upside down. Their political and social structure was in ruins. Just as important, they did not consider Lincoln their leader. Almost everyone in southern Maryland knew of John Wilkes Booth's kidnapping plot. The Union government announced that aiding and abetting Booth would result in a death penalty. Hardly anyone in the South talked about Lincoln's murder. Bringing up the subject didn't help their cause in the least. The radicals in Congress were imposing a harsh reconstruction on them, and they were using Lincoln as one of the excuses. Lincoln was a political embarrassment to them too.

The South remained proud in their defeat, extolling many of their war leaders for their steadfast ethics. In doing so, they denied that the assassination was part of their effort. This began immediately with George Sanders exposing Charles Dunham, aka Sandford Conover, and James Merritt as frauds and perjurers after they claimed to the military tribunal to have sat in on meetings in Montreal with Confederates discussing plans to kill Lincoln. The Confederate plan developed in 1864 to kidnap Lincoln was either downplayed or quashed, protecting many Southerners, including Col. John Mosby and perhaps Robert E. Lee himself, who was consulted about the plan. This book will reveal what many historians have known for generations. Lee shifted his Virginia cavalry troops to conceal the fact from Union intelligence that men were deployed in Virginia's northern neck to aid the kidnappers when the event took place. Confederate covert actions were well organized in the last nine months of the war, but the details have remained hidden from view of the American people.

Years went by before much was discussed about Abraham Lincoln or his murder. In the early 1880s, George Alfred Townsend wrote a few short articles on the assassination. He was the youngest war correspondent during the Civil War and wrote news articles on the assassination. His prominence rose to the level of a Samuel Clemens (Mark Twain) with his novels and short histories of Washington, D.C. He had charisma and fame. In his Lincoln stories, he uncovered Thomas Jones and Thomas Harbin. While his stories caused sensation, they did not carry the impact of historical accounts. For the most part, history is not considered history for at least a generation. The historians didn't arrive until 1895. They were John Hay and John Nicolay, Lincoln's secretaries. They published a seven-volume set on his presidency. The last chapter, on his assassination, was very brief. John Surratt, Jr., Sarah Slater, Thomas Nelson Conrad, Thomas Jones, Samuel Cox, Thomas Harbin, Jefferson Davis, the Canadian Confederate agents, and Judah Benjamin were hardly mentioned, if at all.

A Lincoln assassination researcher and author, Otto Eisenschiml, in the 1920s discovered that the War Department, under Edwin Stanton, had classified most of the documents. This kept many researchers and authors from the turn of the twentieth century from examining the evidence. Apparently, the documents were suppressed to hide greed regarding the reward money and the mishandling of prosecution of Booth's co-conspirators. We have Eisenschiml to thank for getting those records declassified. But Eisenschiml apparently misinterpreted Stanton's motives for the suppression, and his message for the next twenty-five years was that Stanton instigated the assassination itself. A few of Eisenschiml's disciples survive to this day, but modern historians have debunked his theory. Secretary Stanton was indeed hiding a skeleton, but you will find out in this book what it was.

Nicolay and Hay's brief chapter about Booth and the eight convicted co-conspirators became the accepted source in American history books, even today. This story is not nearly as brief as that. Those were tumultuous times. One part of our society clashed with another, and it was a fight to the finish. Afterwards, our nation was never the same. Old traditions can die hard, and feelings can become intense. Social revolution causes that, and it did in this case.

Down through the ages, historians and scholars have researched the Lincoln assassination as thoroughly as possible. These historians usually fall into one of two categories: Civil War historians and Lincoln assassination historians. Few, if any, were both, but it would have been beneficial if more had been. Military conditions, political events, and prevailing sentiments of the times affected the players in this drama. Few scholars had their fingers on the pulse of all three. But many were good, and many were thorough, at least in a particular field. These authors include, but are not limited to, Clara Laughlin,

David Dewitt, Lloyd Lewis, Douglas Southall Freeman, and Shelby Foote. The better ones on the assassination are some of the most recent ones: William Hanchett, Edward Steers, Roy Chamlee, Jr., and William Tidwell, James O. Hall, and David Winfred Gaddy in their comprehensive book, *Come Retribution*. In 2015, Michael Schein authored *John Surratt: The Lincoln Assassin Who Got Away*. These authors had more information and less bias.

The interested scholar of today has learned or confirmed from these recent authors that dozens of people were involved in a war plot to kidnap Abraham Lincoln and take him to Richmond. This became a major Confederate project in the last nine months of the war and for several reasons. The agent in the Confederate Secret Service in charge of this plan in Washington, D.C. was none other than John Wilkes Booth. We have learned that on March 17, 1865, he gathered his band to attempt the kidnapping, and we have pictorial evidence that all or most of that band was in place at the second inauguration on March 4. We've always known that the Confederates evacuated Richmond on April 2, so taking Lincoln there was pointless. Maybe Booth, as the project leader, made the decision then to murder Lincoln instead of kidnapping him, but *maybe he didn't*.

This book will shine light on the probability that the change in plans from kidnapping to murder happened in the last week that the Confederates occupied Richmond. This plan changed in a meeting in Richmond with four people present, *and none of them was Booth or Jefferson Davis*. They were some of *Booth's Confederate connections*.

Acknowledgments

More friends have contributed than I can list here, but I am grateful nevertheless. My friends at the Surratt House Museum have helped with this book. Laurie Verge, director; Joan Chaconas, history specialist; John Stanton, a noted member; and Colleen Peterbaugh, librarian, will always be gratefully remembered. There were many good folks at the National Archives whose names I didn't get. Prof. Steven Woodworth at Texas Christian University, another friend, generously provided his expertise and wrote the foreword. *Dallas Morning News* columnist Dave Lieber introduced me into the Speakers Bureau in Dallas and East Texas. Joe Kennedy, from Bradenton, Florida, provided me with a lot of background material on Judah Benjamin. A special friend, Jennifer Guertin, saved me with setting up formats. Sheri Blaney, a photo specialist from Lake Worth, Florida, deserves special kudos for organizing and developing the photos for this book. I couldn't have made it without her. Most of all, my wife, Linda, patiently helped me meet the deadlines.

Booth's Confederate Connections

CHAPTER ONE

Justification

The story of Abraham Lincoln's assassination didn't begin with John Wilkes Booth staring out of a hotel window, riding on his horse along the back roads of southern Maryland, listening to Lincoln's speech on April 11, 1865, or even meeting with Confederate agents in Montreal, Canada, in October 1864. It began in the White House on February 12, 1864,[1] with a meeting between Lincoln and Union cavalry general Hugh Judson Kilpatrick. In that fateful meeting, Lincoln approved Kilpatrick's plan to raid Richmond to free Union prisoners of war at Libby prison and on Belle Isle.

Recent newspaper reports had painted a sordid picture of the treatment of the prisoners there. Resources were getting scarce in the Confederacy. Caring for its own armies and people was becoming more challenging. Feeding the prisoners was becoming increasingly difficult. Union officers were dying every day from the neglect. Lincoln's concern was genuine, but also public opinion was rising.

Kilpatrick had conceived a plan to penetrate the weak home guard defenses of Richmond and free the prisoners. Tragically, Kilpatrick was the wrong man for the job. He was young, brash, reckless, vain, ambitious, glory seeking, and lacking somewhat in empathy for his men. His camp was unclean and he openly entertained prostitutes there. His men called him "Kill Cavalry" because he drove his men and horses into the ground and ordered suicidal charges. He was not a popular commander with either his own troops or his fellow officers.

Kilpatrick had only graduated from West Point in 1861,

finishing seventeenth out of forty-five graduates. His aggressiveness, as well as his fearlessness, garnered him rapid promotion. His career and personality closely paralleled George Custer's. Kilpatrick is credited with being the first Union officer to be wounded in the war. He was struck in the thigh by canister fire at the skirmish at Big Bethel on June 10, 1861. By the Battle of Gettysburg, he commanded a division. Two months earlier, he had been part of a raid during the battle of Chancellorsville. The newly formed cavalry corps under George Stoneman had virtually encircled Robert E. Lee's army, wrecking trains and destroying supplies. During this raid, Kilpatrick came close to penetrating the Richmond defenses, prompting Lincoln to exclaim, "He could have destroyed Richmond and brought us Jeff Davis."

During the Battle of Gettysburg, Kilpatrick ordered Col. Elon J. Farnsworth to attack the anchored right flank of the Confederate army. Farnsworth balked at this order. Those Confederates were part of Longstreet's corps, the best defensive troops in Lee's army, and they were well dug in. Cavalry troops seldom, if ever, attacked infantry. Kilpatrick cursed Farnsworth, calling him a coward in front of his troops.[2] He threatened to personally replace Farnsworth and lead the attack himself. Farnsworth bristled and led the attack, killing himself and most of his troopers in the process.[3]

The consequences of Kilpatrick's order came to the attention of the new Union commander, George Meade. Meade was old enough to be Kilpatrick's father. Not only was he an experienced soldier but he, by nature, was conservative and cautious too. Kilpatrick's personality and style were the opposite of Meade's. Meade took notice of Kilpatrick's recklessness and never forgot it.

Kilpatrick's reputation didn't improve when he was arrested in Washington during a drunken spree, and poor administrative performance after the battle didn't help either. In addition, a recent similar raid had failed miserably. So when Kilpatrick submitted a plan for a cavalry raid on Richmond, Meade wasted no time in turning it down.

Disappointed, Kilpatrick wrote to Michigan senator Jacob

Howard. "Kill Cavalry" was not above going outside the accepted channels to get what he wanted. Senator Howard, known by history as the early architect of the Whistleblower Act, no doubt showed the missive to President Lincoln. Lincoln was always on the alert for aggressive commanders. So far in the war, his armies had been woefully deficient in competent, aggressive officers. Kilpatrick's idea caught his imagination and he invited Kilpatrick to a meeting, again bypassing Meade. After hearing Kilpatrick's plan, he had only one question: Would Kilpatrick distribute amnesty leaflets as he traveled on this raid? Kilpatrick readily assented and Lincoln approved the plan. Lincoln then sent him to Secretary of War Edwin Stanton to work out the details.

Eleven days later a young officer named Ulric Dahlgren showed up at Kilpatrick's headquarters and requested a part in the raid.[4] History does not disclose who sent him or how he found out about the raid, but there are clues. Dahlgren, who had lost part of his leg at Gettysburg and walked on an artificial foot, claimed

Hugh Judson Kilpatrick. (National Archives)

friendship ties with the president, and his father, John Dahlgren, was a rear admiral in the navy. Kilpatrick bypassed his own division's officers and named Dahlgren his second in command of the expedition. A plan was developed directing Dahlgren to take a five-hundred-man contingent and sweep around to the south of the James River and attack from a different direction while Kilpatrick attacked Richmond from the north. Dahlgren only had a week to organize his men and train for the mission. Since he was new to command, he wrote detailed plans in a notebook. He met with Gen. George Custer, who was to feign an attack on the Union right to distract the Confederates.[5] Gen. John Sedgwick was to provide infantry as well. The results of that meeting were also in the notebook. At least two officers provided intel from the Bureau of Military Information, Capt. John McEntee and John Babcock. In addition, these two were part of the raid.

The four-thousand-man raid left the Union lines on February 28 but did not escape the eyes of Gen. Wade Hampton of the Confederate cavalry.[6] Hampton's troops were soon dogging the heels of the raiders. After crossing the Rapidan River, Dahlgren's command separated from Kilpatrick and veered to the west. Kilpatrick continued south, damaging railroads and distributing the amnesty leaflets as he went, but Dahlgren soon ran into trouble. Recent rains had flooded the James River, making a crossing difficult if not impossible. A free black named Martin Robinson guided them to a ford at Dover Mills. There, the Union command found a raging river. Dahlgren, his fiery temper exploding, hung Robinson for supposedly tricking him.[7] Now behind schedule and out of position, Dahlgren headed east, trying in vain to rendezvous with Kilpatrick.

Kilpatrick had found the Richmond defenses much stronger than expected. He abandoned the plan and headed southeast toward the sanctuary of Gen. Benjamin "Beast" Butler. Half of Dahlgren's men followed, a day behind Kilpatrick. Dahlgren and about a hundred men turned slightly north of east, running from an aroused group of cavalry and home guards. In the late evening hours of March 2, Dahlgren ran headlong into an ambush by the Ninth Virginia Cavalry and was killed.[8] Most of his remaining men were captured.

During the night, a thirteen-year-old member of the home guard named William Littlepage rifled through the pockets of Dahlgren's uniform. Finding the notebook and two folded papers, he turned the items over to his officer, Capt. Edward Halbach. Halbach opened the papers and discovered two documents on official Army of the Potomac stationery. One was a signed order by Dahlgren, issuing directives to his men for the raid. The other was unsigned but in the same handwriting and included the words, "The men must be kept together and well in hand, and once in the city it must be destroyed and Jeff. Davis and Cabinet killed."[9] Halbach immediately turned over the papers and notebook to his superior, Capt. Richard H. Bagby. Bagby, recognizing the importance of the documents, used Lt. James Pollard as a courier to deliver the papers to Col. Richard L. T. Beale of the regular Confederate cavalry. Beale, keeping the notebook for further intelligence, sent the two papers on to the Confederate cavalry commander, Fitzhugh Lee, a nephew of Robert E. Lee. Lee personally delivered the

Lt. Col. Ulric Dahlgren. (Public domain)

two letters to Pres. Jefferson Davis, who was meeting with Secretary of State Judah Benjamin. It had taken a little more than forty-eight hours to get the papers from Littlepage to President Davis.[10]

Davis read the message aloud. Smiling, he turned to Benjamin. "That means you, Mr. Benjamin," he teased.[11] Benjamin was far from amused. Davis sent the papers to Secretary of War James Seddon, who immediately photographed the papers and released them to the press at 5:00 P.M. that very day. Dahlgren's notebook was retrieved later.

The letters caused an immediate sensation in the South. These terms of engagement were not acceptable under their military rules. Cabinet members called for hanging the prisoners caught in the raid, but cooler heads prevailed. Robert E. Lee knew that guerilla fighters and Confederate soldiers under the command of John Mosby had been captured. Mosby held other Yankee officers, and Lee certainly didn't want to start a hanging contest. Lee sent a copy of the papers to General Meade under a flag of truce, asking if these orders had indeed come from the Army of the Potomac and demanding an investigation.[12]

Meade called in Kilpatrick and ordered him to investigate. That was putting the fox in the henhouse. Kilpatrick claimed the papers were forgeries. Arguments and debates have raged on this subject until modern times. General Meade denied any official complicity, but in private correspondence to his wife, Meade said, "Kilpatrick's reputation, and collateral evidence in my possession, rather go against this theory."[13] What was this collateral evidence? It could have only been the testimony of intelligence officers McEntee and Babcock.

Those claiming forgery certainly had support for their argument. Dahlgren's name appeared to have been misspelled. Confederate general Jubal Early claimed the so-called misspelling was caused by ink bleeding through the folded pages. Dahlgren's apologists, as well as the entire Federal government, denied this possibility. It wasn't until 1999 that Lincoln scholar James O. Hall had handwriting experts examine the copies. In 1959, an earlier handwriting expert, Ira Gullickson, examined the papers and concluded that the documents were authentic. The experts confirmed that the controversial language was in fact written in Dahlgren's handwriting. Furthermore, the timeline was investigated to see if the Confederates had enough time to forge writing into the document, and it was clear from the investigation that the Confederates had neither time, means, or opportunity to forge anything before turning over copies to the press at 5:00 P.M. on March 4.

At first glance, this raid might seem unconnected to the assassination of Abraham Lincoln. But to the Confederates and Judah Benjamin personally, this raid changed the rules of engagement. Gone were deeds of chivalry. Many of the leaders on both sides knew their counterparts from before the war. Respect and, in some cases, fond friendship lingered in spite of the conflict. Southern leaders, with few exceptions, were taught to be gentlemen with impeccable manners. In August of 1862 a young Union general named Philip Kearny was killed in a skirmish near the Chantilly plantation following the Second Battle of Manassas.[14] General Lee sent Kearny's body back to the Union lines under a flag of truce with the comment, "Poor Kearny deserved a better fate than this." Such was the sentiment of professional soldiers and those in the governments during the early phase of the war. But to the South, the Dahlgren raid changed the rules and spirit of the participants. The Civil War was about to degenerate into as dirty a business as the mind could imagine.

Judah Benjamin, the secretary of state since mid-1862 and personally in charge of the Confederate Secret Service, a network of spies and agents, intensified the intelligence war on the Yankees. We can't read Benjamin's mind, but one must wonder what impact the Dahlgren raid had on him. Did he take personally the fact that four thousand men came to town to kill him? Did he change the rules of engagement because of the raid? All evidence and circumstances suggest that to be the case.

Did Stanton send Dahlgren to Kilpatrick with secret orders, and in so doing sign the death warrant of his own leader? Following the capture of Richmond, Francis "Franz" Lieber was charged with maintaining and organizing the Confederate

Union Secretary of War Edwin Stanton. (Brady-Handy Collection, Library of Congress)

records. Later in 1865, Stanton ordered Franz Lieber to bring him Dahlgren's original papers. Those papers were never seen again.[15] No one disputes the theory that Stanton destroyed the papers. Why would he do this unless he had his own complicity to hide?

The authenticity of the Dahlgren papers has been debated for the last one hundred fifty years and the debate may continue for decades. We need not concern ourselves with that. What is important and clear is that the South believed they were authentic and reacted accordingly. The espionage operations under Judah Benjamin escalated from this point forward. The actions of the Confederate Secret Service and their agents included, but were not limited to, a bank robbery in Vermont, organized arson in New York City, the distribution in Northern cities of clothing thought to be infected with yellow fever, and, above all, the kidnapping of Pres. Abraham Lincoln.

CHAPTER TWO

Building the Intelligence Road

In the early days of the war, Abraham Lincoln had his hands full keeping Maryland from joining the Confederacy. This would have put the Federal capital inside the Confederacy, an unacceptable premise. The Maryland population was split on the issue of staying in the Union, and Lincoln had only received 2.5 percent of the state's popular vote in 1860. Maryland was clearly sympathetic to her Southern sister states.

Shortly after the war began, Baltimore residents seized the railroads and cut off troop transportation to the capital. In addition, they tore down the telegraph lines and destroyed bridges north of Baltimore to prevent Northern troops from crossing their territory to get to Washington, D.C.[1] This caused some anxious days for President Lincoln, underscoring how easily the Union could lose Maryland. There were crisis days in Kentucky and Missouri too, but Maryland was his biggest strategic worry. Lincoln was pressured to refrain from moving more troops through the inflamed city of Baltimore and for a short time did so.

Things changed when Gen. Benjamin Butler carried his Massachusetts troops via ship into Annapolis, bypassing Baltimore and providing a commanding presence in the Maryland capital.[2] Governor Hicks called for his assembly to convene to consider secession on April 26. They were ordered to meet in Frederick instead of Annapolis to avoid the intimidation of Butler's troops. Ignoring their constituents' wishes, the assembly voted overwhelmingly on a bill stating that they had no authority to take any action to secede.

General Butler then moved quickly, without orders, to seize and occupy unruly Baltimore.

Butler would gain fame—or infamy—a year later as the occupying commander in New Orleans. After his officers suffered insults and snubs from the ladies of New Orleans, he ordered that women abusing his soldiers were to be treated as common streetwalkers. The South bristled with fury. Decades later, commodes were manufactured with "Beast" Butler's face painted on the bottom.

The Confederates were working to secure Maryland for their side too. As early as the first week of the war, Virginia governor John Letcher began making moves to recruit Maryland to the Confederate side. On April 20, 1861, Maj. William S. Barton wired Governor Letcher, "A line of express may be established to Baltimore from opposite Aquia Creek—a reliable man here will assist."[3] This proposal marked the genesis of Confederate communications in southern Maryland that evolved into the Confederate Signal Corps and its secret line.

E. P. Alexander, a bright and promising West Point graduate from Georgia, first used a flag method at Manassas to warn Col. Nathan Evans of a Federal flank attack on the Confederate left. This quick thinking saved the day for the Confederate forces.[4] Alexander was one of the heroes of the hour. He was also the first officer to train the men in the signal stations in Virginia and Maryland. Alexander would eventually attain the rank of brigadier general, commanding the artillery of Longstreet's corps.

Others, including James F. Milligan and William Norris, would change the signals to align more with the naval system by employing a Confederate cipher. Pres. Jefferson Davis had served on several boards while he was secretary of war for the U.S. He had looked into signal systems to help commanders during battles and was a believer in their efficacy. Under his guidance, the Confederate Signal Corps was established in April of 1862 with William Norris in command.

Ten captains, twenty lieutenants, and various enlisted men were authorized, and they started setting up camps from the Virginia side of the Potomac River across from Port Tobacco,

Maryland, all the way to Richmond. Sgt. Charles H. Cawood, later to make lieutenant, was stationed in the camp farthest north and figures later in the story.[5] An adjacent signal group sprouted up and operated in the same area under the command of Sgt. Harry Brogden. Messages were flashed across from Maryland by agents there and were quickly forwarded to the Confederate capital. This line was soon given the tasks of exchanging mail with people in the North and sending spies and couriers to and from Washington.[6]

By the summer of 1862, the South had a very efficient method of gathering and sending intelligence to its leaders. The Union never duplicated this system, opting to use the telegraph instead. This method of communication required extensive laying of wire on cleared telegraph roads lined with sunk telegraph poles. The Union added to their telegraph network as its armies progressed across the country.

Soon Cawood, E. Pliney Bryan, and later Benjamin Franklin Stringfellow were traveling across the Potomac River to move people and mail as well as to gather intelligence in southern Maryland. They had many helpers in Maryland. Thomas Jones was the main Confederate mail agent and lived on a bluff in Port Tobacco overlooking the Potomac. His next-door neighbor was Maj. Roderick Watson, the father of R. D. Watson, who would become a major New York agent for the Confederacy. His sister, Mary, had a signal arrangement with Sergeant Cawood across the river. When Union soldiers were in the area or a Union boat was patrolling the river, her window on the second floor was empty. If the coast was clear, she positioned a mannequin in a dark dress by the window, easily seen with a spyglass used by Cawood. Those signals controlled the flow of Confederates across the river. Despite the Union patrol boats on the Potomac and periodic cavalry patrols, Confederate activity flourished south of Washington, D.C.

Most of the local postmasters, including John Surratt's father, participated in the exchange of communication. The postmasters would receive letters addressed directly to them. Inside the envelope was a smaller envelope addressed to the intended recipient. The postmaster would put a stamp on the inside letter if there wasn't already one and forward it on. Thus, the federal postal system was used effectively by its own enemy. When John Surratt, Sr., died in the fall of 1862, his son John, Jr. took his place as a federal postmaster.

Newspapers followed a reverse delivery route. One of the *New York Times'* most avid readers was Robert E. Lee himself. All of the Northern newspapers carried needed intelligence such as troop movements and ration requirements of the various military units.

Agents, messages, mail, newspapers, and needed war material moved easily along this route from North to South. The North tried a few times to break up this system but never succeeded. The Confederate sentiment in southern Maryland was just too strong. No one knew it then, but this information highway would become a major factor in the plot to kidnap Lincoln in the years to come. Some of the people involved in this clandestine activity would become players in that kidnap plot and ultimately the assassination.

CHAPTER THREE

The Canadian Connections

To expand the reach of their intelligence circles, Canada was attractive to the Confederates from the very beginning of the war. Its geography and transportation system allowed rapid movement of Confederate agents from Chicago to Maine. From America's northern border, agents carried dispatches to Europe.[1] Clandestine operations could be carried out in proximity to the Canadian border, and the men necessary for the jobs could move rapidly by rail.

The Confederate presence north of the United States seems to have emanated from Halifax, Nova Scotia, which was a separate British colony from Canada until July 1, 1867, when Premier Charles Tupper negotiated a union called the British North America Act. As the war progressed, the Confederate presence in Canada grew. The North housed Southern prisoners of war close to the Canadian border. In addition, there was a strong peace sentiment in the Midwest for the Confederates to encourage, nourish, and support. The South hoped to organize these anti-war Northerners, or "Copperheads," in establishing uprisings to draw Federal troops away from the Southern fighting theatre.

In early 1862, the Confederate government hired two agents in Halifax, the B. Weir Company and Alexander Keith, to aid in their efforts.[2] These agents supported the South throughout the war in routing men and supplies in the right directions and the right locales for clandestine operations. Blockade runners appeared there as early as August 1861 to refit, re-provision, and choose the right time to run the Union blockade. Halifax was on the direct route from Europe. From Halifax, the blockade runners would travel to Bermuda or the Bahamas for the quick dash to the Southern ports.

In August 1862, Robert E. Coxe, a wealthy Georgian, moved from Europe to a house in St. Catherines,[3] a few miles north of Niagara Falls on the Welland Canal. This house was strategically situated near a major railway. In addition, Copperhead leaders could meet with Coxe and others in Niagara Falls or nearby Clifton without being privy to the exact whereabouts of Coxe's base of operations. Confederate agents blended with the many tourists who visited the falls and stayed in Clifton's hotels. The Barnett Museum kept a visitor's register, which modern historians believe may have allowed Confederate spies and agents to announce their arrival. After signing the register, they would be contacted by Coxe or his agents.[4]

In the same month, George Sanders arrived in Niagara Falls and met former Kentucky governor Charles Moorehead at the Clifton House Hotel.[5] Sanders would move on to Europe at that time but would return later to Canada as a full-time Confederate agent. He was the most acrimonious of all the Confederate agents. He had a radical revolutionary background[6] and was embittered by the treatment of his son in a Yankee POW camp, where the younger Sanders died of disease and neglect. Before the war George Sanders traveled Europe representing the Democratic party and the pro-slavery interests in the South. There he became an advocate of assassination as a way to solve political problems, even advocating the assassination of Louis Bonaparte. An ally of Pres. James K. Polk, Sanders was appointed U.S. consul in London but was never confirmed by the Senate. He stayed in Europe, becoming an embarrassment to the U.S. for consorting with anarchists. Historians suspect that he planted the seeds of assassination in Booth's mind, but the only evidence that ever surfaced against him was tainted.

Another Confederate operative in Canada in the early years was Patrick C. Martin. Martin was originally from Baltimore, Maryland.[7] A friend of Police Marshal George P. Kane, he figured prominently in the Baltimore riots in early 1861. It

George Sanders. (Public domain)

is unclear if he was involved in the pre-inauguration plot to assassinate Lincoln as he traveled through the city, but Martin left for Canada as soon as General Butler restored order in Baltimore. Martin soon established himself as a successful blockade runner and traveled often from Halifax to Montreal as an agent for the Confederacy. In late 1863, he and Kane participated in a plan to free Southern prisoners at Johnson's Island, Ohio, located in Sandusky Bay on Lake Erie. This plan, which attracted more than four hundred Southern agents and soldiers, was a poorly kept secret and quickly thwarted by the Federals before many of the operatives could even arrive.[8]

This plan was spurred by the grievous losses Southern leaders were facing on the battlefields by the end of 1863. Vicksburg was gone. The South was split in two. Transferring General Longstreet's corps to the West had not led to victories, thanks mostly to Gen. Braxton Bragg's command bungles. The South's best soldiers were buried on battlefields from Gettysburg and Sharpsburg to Knoxville, Chattanooga, and

Chickamauga Creek. Survivors languished in Camp Douglas in Chicago, Fort McHenry in Baltimore, Fort Delaware in Delaware, Camp Morton in Indianapolis, Fort Warren in Boston Harbor, a large camp in Elmira, New York, and Fort Lafayette near New York City.

With casualties growing, Pres. Jefferson Davis considered alternatives to battlefield victories. To mobilize the rising anti-war sentiment in the Midwest, he sent two of his best diplomats, Jacob Thompson and Clement Clay, to Canada to coordinate the Copperhead movement and use it against the North. In addition to sending Thompson and Clay, he allocated for this purpose the huge sum of one million dollars in late February 1864. Thompson was the senior commissioner and controlled the money, but Clay was the more aggressive.

Jacob Thompson owned a plantation in Oxford, Mississippi, and was secretary of the Interior in the Buchanan administration. When the war broke out, he resigned and joined the Confederacy, becoming the inspector of the Confederate army. He served as an aide to General Beauregard at Shiloh and was present at several other battles in the West.

Thompson was no political lightweight. It was his job to collaborate with Clement Vallandigham, the leader of the Copperhead movement's inner circle. The Confederates had received intelligence that there were more than 340,000 dissidents in the Midwest. They hoped these Copperheads would arm themselves and create a second front against the Yankees. However, the anti-war dissidents had no stomach for actual fighting. This did not become apparent to Thompson for several months. Meanwhile, Vallandigham was banished from Congress, lost the election for governor of Ohio, was charged with treason, and ultimately deported to the Confederacy in 1863. By July 1863, Vallandigham was back in Canada.

Thompson, along with his secretary, William Cleary, moved in with Robert Coxe in St. Catherines. Thompson met with leaders of the Copperhead movement, directed the Confederate repatriation of Southern soldiers, and convened with various anti-war leaders from the North. Thompson and Cleary then moved on to Toronto and established headquarters

Jacob Thompson. (Brady-Handy Collection, Library of Congress)

there. Soon a plan emerged—one in which Clement Clay was also active—to send arms into several states to arm the Copperheads, release Southern prisoners, seize Federal arms in Louisville, and start an insurrection in the North.

After two delays, the date of the operation was set for August 29, 1864. The Confederate agents sent sixty-two men to Chicago to help free the prisoners in Camp Douglas. But plans went awry. The Sons of Liberty, part of a secret organization within the Copperhead circle, had been infiltrated. The Federals were warned and ready. In addition, an Indiana newspaper editor, Joseph J. Bingham, who was also chairman of the Indiana Democratic Party, called in his allies in the Sons of Liberty and forced them to cancel the project. Without Indiana, the neighboring states backed out as well.[9]

Clement Clay was a former U.S. senator from Alabama, an attorney, and a former judge. He operated under James Seddon, the Confederate secretary of war. Clay arrived in Halifax with

Thompson and Cleary but when they moved on to Toronto, Clay stayed in Nova Scotia an additional two weeks, getting the lay of the land from the B. Weir Company, Alexander Keith, and another agent named James P. Holcombe.

During that time, Clay met a Confederate soldier trying to get back home named Bennett Young. Young had been part of a cavalry raid commanded by the famous John Hunt Morgan that made it almost as far as Cincinnati the year before. The raid had been aided by members of the Sons of Liberty, but Morgan finally became trapped and had to surrender. He and some of his officers were placed in a criminal penitentiary instead of a military prison camp. This treatment was an intentional insult, but it worked in Morgan's favor because he was able to escape due to substandard security. Bennett Young was taken to Camp Douglas in Chicago but he escaped as well.

When Young met Clay, he presented an intriguing plan. From Canada, he could raid locations in the Northern border states, wreaking havoc and burning homes and businesses in

Clement Clay. (Library of Congress)

retaliation for the current burning of the Shenandoah Valley, before escaping back over the Canadian border. Jefferson Davis and Judah Benjamin summoned Young to Richmond for a personal interview. Impressed, they promoted him to first lieutenant and approved his plans. Upon returning to Halifax, he followed Clay to Montreal and set to work. He was one of the sixty-two men sent to Chicago for the August 29 attempt to rescue the prisoners from Camp Douglas. When that plan failed, he returned to Canada. Clay then sent him to scout Burlington and St. Albans, Vermont, as possible raid targets.

While he was absent, Clay received a letter from Jacob Thompson stating that such raids would cause the Canadian agents much embarrassment with the Canadian government. Clay must have taken this sentiment under consideration, for he then sent Young to scout Camp Chase, Ohio, to see if he could free the Confederate prisoners there. Young reported that the plan was feasible and set to work recruiting and training thirty men to do the job. On October 6, he reported back that he was unable to secure the quality of men necessary. The inference is that he tried to use local Copperheads and found them wanting. So he and Clay decided that St. Albans should be the first target.[10] The plan called for robbing the banks and burning the town with the newly discovered "Greek Fire" incendiary weapon.

Throughout the spring and summer of 1864, Jefferson Davis and Judah Benjamin had used Confederate Secret Service agent Thomas H. Hines to contact and analyze the strength and resolve of the Copperhead movement. Like Young, Hines came from the Ninth Kentucky Cavalry Regiment under the command of John Hunt Morgan. Morgan first used Hines to establish a liaison with the Order of American Knights, the inner circle of the Copperhead movement, during his raid into Ohio in mid-1863. At the end of their incursion, Hines was captured and imprisoned along with Morgan. The two men also escaped together.[11] Benjamin then sent Hines back north to examine the strength of the Copperhead organization. He returned with a favorable report before leaving for Kentucky to visit his fiancée. Then the Dahlgren raid occurred, and Hines was summoned back to Richmond.[12] On March 16, he was ordered to Canada and reported to top agents there to organize a Copperhead uprising in the Federals' rear. At that time, Thompson and Clay had not been selected nor the money allocated for the large operation. He was transferred from the War Department to the State Department under the supervision of Benjamin. When Jacob Thompson arrived in early 1864, Hines operated under his command as a matter of course.

R. C. Bocking, a Dutch chemist from Cincinnati, arrived in Windsor to teach the Confederates how to use the new fire enhancer referred to as "Greek Fire." Greek Fire was probably a mixture of petroleum (naphtha), lime, and tallow, with sulphur and pitch added.[13] What wasn't known then was the necessity of oxygen to create a healthy fire, which would play an important role in the effective use of the Confederacy's newest weapon. No one knows for sure who discovered Bocking, but since his home was in Cincinnati, it is likely that Hines is the one who discovered him. During the summer of 1864, he worked with Confederate agents in making and stockpiling this incendiary device. In addition, he developed several other explosive weapons. Some included delayed fuses. No doubt, both Hines and Young met with Bocking sometime during the summer.

On October 18, Bennett Young and about twenty men arrived in St. Albans, Vermont. They traveled in twos and threes to avoid suspicion and checked into local hotels. At 3:00 P.M. the following day, October 19, 1864, they assembled in the town square, shedding their overcoats, revealing Confederate uniforms and navy Colt pistols. The locals thought it was a joke or a masquerade until Young started firing at those who moved too slowly or refused to obey his orders. Young sent teams of threes to relieve the banks of their money and others to set some of the buildings aflame with Greek Fire. In the sealed rooms, with their windows and doors shut tight, the incendiaries didn't work very well. The lack of oxygen starved the flames, but Young and his men managed to escape the fifteen miles back to Canada. Shedding their uniforms, they began to lay low. When they counted the loot, they had seized more than two hundred thousand dollars. The Northerners took little note of the aborted fires and announced the incident as a bank robbery—one of the first in American history.[14]

Fourteen raiders were arrested in Canada along with ninety thousand dollars. Lengthy legal and political maneuvers followed over the course of about four months. Although Canada had imprisoned these men, its government refused to extradite them back to the U.S. The fourteen men were eventually released and the money returned to them. At a hearing in February 1865, the defense attorneys presented documents from Jefferson Davis stating that the defendants were Confederate soldiers on a mission. In all probability, those documents were sent by a new courier from Richmond. The perfect spy, she was a dark-haired twenty-two-year-old beauty with a slim figure and a widow's veil. A young woman, fluent in French, smart, resourceful, and somewhat quiet, she could pass any gate guarded by a man or carry papers that no man would ever dare to search for. She was Sarah Gilbert Slater, aka Kate Thompson, aka Kate Brown, aka A. Reynaud.[15]

While the St. Albans project was under way, more soldiers were sent to New York City and Chicago with a supply of Greek Fire. Col. Robert M. Martin and a team converged on New York City to work with Capt. Emile Longuemare and his team to set New York ablaze. Martin had arrived in Canada with Lt. John W. Headley in late September to assist Jacob Thompson in his efforts. Martin was also under orders from Thompson to work with James McMasters, the local leader of the Order of the American Knights. The fires were supposed to occur in both cities just before the November elections. McMasters, like the other Copperhead leaders, was much talk and no action. Due to his lethargy and the increased presence of Federal troops, the election came and went without any action being taken. Finally, on the day after Thanksgiving, November 25, the Confederates took matters into their own hands. They set fires in twenty-two hotels and in P. T. Barnum's American Museum. Once again, the doors and windows were kept shut to avoid detection, and the fires just smoldered from a lack of oxygen. Greek Fire had failed again as far as the Confederates were concerned.

Two weeks later, Jacob Thompson heard that seven general officers were to be moved from Johnson's Island to Fort Lafayette in New York. He quickly assembled a team to intercept the train and rescue them. The plan failed and two of the South's best Secret Service agents were captured. One was the intrepid John Yates Beall. Beall would have found himself atop the North's most wanted list if there were one. He had caused them grief everywhere. Beall's companion, George S. Anderson, turned state's evidence, and Beall was tried and convicted as a guerrilla and a spy and sentenced to hang. The sentence was carried out sixteen days later, on February 24, before any efforts to save him could be organized. It is unclear whether Booth ever knew Beall, but he later complained bitterly about his execution. Some legends have him trying to intervene with Lincoln for Beall's life, but there is no record to substantiate that.

By the fall of 1864, Jefferson Davis had set up four separate operations in Canada. Jacob Thompson had the job of stimulating a Copperhead uprising in the North designed to draw Federal troops away from the Southern war zones. George Sanders was working with Northern Democrats to enhance anti-war sentiment and even bring Lincoln to a peace table. Clement Clay was in charge of military operations to raid into the North from Canada. Another top-level agent, Beverly Tucker, was in charge of moving badly needed supply items from Canada to Halifax so the supplies could be sent to the South by blockade runners.[16]

All things considered, it was a sophisticated strategy. Raids had achieved only mixed results, but Clay had succeeded in making the North nervous about its border. Sanders had made some progress in enlisting the aid of Northern Democrats to urge a peace settlement. George McClellan, the Democratic nominee, had even made peace negotiations his political platform. Tucker was doing an adequate job of getting the necessary supplies to Halifax. This author can only conclude that Davis and Benjamin were dissatisfied with Jacob Thompson's efforts to stimulate a Copperhead uprising. His primary charge had been to encourage the Copperheads into a second secession or to defeat Lincoln. Sabotage was not to his liking and, failing the uprising, the Richmond authorities now wanted to go in that direction. Once Lincoln was reelected, Jacob Thompson had no meaningful role to play in Canada. In December 1864, Thompson received a letter from Judah Benjamin recalling him to Richmond and turning over his funds and operations to the bearer of the letter. The bearer of the letter was Brig. Gen. Edwin Gray Lee, nephew of Robert E. Lee.

Edwin G. Lee was not just a nephew of Robert E. Lee benefiting from nepotism. Edwin Lee had served on Stonewall Jackson's staff at First Manassas, saw action in the Shenandoah Valley Campaign of 1862, and fought in the Seven Days Battles, Second Manassas, and Cedar Mountain. He was the commander of the Stonewall Brigade at the Battle of Fredericksburg. Poor health forced him to the sidelines in early 1863, but he was appointed colonel of cavalry in Robert Ransom's brigade on November 12, 1863, serving in the Shenandoah Valley. He was promoted to brigadier general under Thomas Rosser on November 12, 1864. Then, in January, he was sent north to Canada on his secret mission.[17]

Directing these operations behind the scenes was Judah Benjamin. Many historians have downplayed or overlooked Benjamin. A closer look shows that Judah Benjamin was a brilliant man in his own right. Jefferson Davis did not choose him lightly or negligently keep him in the cabinet when the hounds of hell were screaming for his Jewish head. He was dismissed from the office of secretary of war because he failed to furnish the Roanoke area with adequate gunpowder to oppose McClellan's army, which was driving up the Virginia peninsula in early 1862. The truth came out twenty-five years later that Jefferson Davis had faced a dilemma. He could admit that there was no gunpowder to send or sacrifice Benjamin and put him elsewhere in the cabinet. A gunpowder shortage would get back to the Yankees. That was intelligence that the Confederates could not afford for the North to know. The blockade was working, and the Confederates were struggling to manufacture enough powder to defend the capital without a

Gen. Edwin Gray Lee. (McCord Museum, I-17038.1)

supply from Europe. Benjamin was better suited for secretary of state anyway. Benjamin understood this as well as Davis and loyally suffered Congressional censure rather than give up the secret of the gunpowder shortage.[18]

Less than a year after the war started, everyone in the cabinet realized that Benjamin was the smartest of them all. Benjamin proposed at the very first cabinet meeting that the South buy up all the cotton that it could afford and send it to England. He proposed that at least 100,000 bales be sent overseas. Some would be exchanged for the purchase of 150,000 small arms, artillery, and ammunition. The rest of the cotton would be held to secure credit for the government. Davis and the rest of the cabinet voted him down, but they regretted the decision within a year.[19]

Davis had chosen Benjamin for his cabinet because he had shown great leadership skills as a U.S. senator as well as an amazing work ethic. His oratory skills were becoming legendary. Benjamin's talents were in his DNA. His ancestors

Judah Benjamin. (Library of Congress)

were prominent Sephardic Jews in fifteenth-century Spain who had escaped the Spanish Inquisition by fleeing to Portugal. The Benjamin ancestors were named Mendes.[20] Two hundred and fifty some-odd years later, one of the Mendes men migrated to the Netherlands, where he married a Dutch Jewish woman and they moved to London. They had three daughters, of which the one named Rebecca would become Judah's mother. Rebecca's two sisters married wealthy planters from the Caribbean while Rebecca married a small Sephardic Jew from a family of more modest means in London. His name was Philip Benjamin. Together, Philip and Rebecca opened a dried fruit shop in London. The shop struggled, and the couple soon followed Rebecca's sisters to St. Croix. Judah was born there on August 11, 1811. His favorite sibling was his older sister, Rebecca, who went by the nickname of Penny.

St. Croix was seized in 1807 by the British during the Napoleonic Wars. The island, along with other nearby islands, was occupied by the British until 1815, and Philip Benjamin was a taxpayer of record in Christiansted. This fact enabled Judah Benjamin to claim British citizenship after the Civil War and avoid extradition back to the United States for war crimes. The United States, however, had little interest in pursuing Benjamin. As far as they knew, there was no proof against him at that time.

In 1813 the Benjamin family sailed to the United States in hopes of financial success. They settled in Fayetteville, North Carolina, at his mother's uncle's home. This uncle, named Jacob, owned a small grocery store, but it was too small to support two families. After a few years in Fayetteville, the couple and their children moved on to Charleston. They arrived there in 1822, just in time for a slave rebellion led by Denmark Vesey. Many slaves were involved and almost one hundred were hanged, leaving quite an impression on the eleven-year-old Judah.

His mother opened a fruit store on the docks, which she kept open even on the Sabbath. Rebecca had her family's determination for financial success. Judah's father never had a head for business, instead spending time with the orthodox leaders of the local synagogue and debating the state of their religion. Soon, he joined the church's reform movement, which called for shorter services and prayers in English.

Thus, Judah inherited his father's love for books and study and his mother's work ethic and financial drive. He was also the brightest student among his Jewish community. His academic qualities caught the attention of one of the Jewish leaders in Charleston, Moses Lopez, president of the local Hebrew Orphan Society. Lopez offered to send Judah to Yale College.[21] His mother was reluctant to accept charity but could not turn down the offer. Although most of the funds for Judah to attend Yale appear to have come from Lopez's society, a woman from Massachusetts helped as well as his parents. This detail probably led to Judah's downfall at the university three years later.[22]

At age fourteen, Judah arrived at Yale, where he flourished for two years. Through hard work, he gained the respect of his professors and the grudging admiration of his fellow students. Judah studied his fellow classmates, learning the manners and protocols of the rich and privileged. He learned business law and economics, excelling in Horace, the Greek orators, philosophy, and astronomy. As he rose to the top of his class, he became increasingly estranged from his jealous classmates. Then early in his third year, disaster struck, and he had to leave school.

There are two stories about what happened. The first story was that his family didn't pay a school bill of something just over fifty dollars, a significant sum in those days, but which could have been paid by his benefactor, Moses Lopez. The other, and more credible story, was that his fellow students caught him stealing from them and he promised to withdraw from school if they would not turn him in to the faculty.[23] Lending credibility to this tale is the fact that Judah sent a letter about six weeks later to Yale asking to be reinstated and referencing his improper conduct. Back in Charleston, Judah Benjamin had to endure shame for his dismissal.[24]

Soon, he left for Louisiana and arrived in New Orleans with five dollars in his pocket. New Orleans was a wide-open town where religion didn't count as much as deeds and success. There he met the prominent Creole St. Martin family, who hired Benjamin to teach their sixteen-year-old daughter English. Benjamin negotiated the deal so that the daughter, Natalie, could teach him French at the same time. He needed French to study the Napoleonic Code. In 1832, Benjamin passed the bar as romance bloomed with Natalie St. Martin. Natalie was mature and adventuresome for her age. She had the instincts of a courtesan. She was audacious, unafraid, and experimental. They were married on February 12, 1833, and spent their honeymoon at her parents' home due to financial limitations.

Judah became law partners with Tom Slidell and E. A. Bradford. New Orleans was a city with an expanding economy, but competition was fierce. To increase his legal credibility, in 1834, Benjamin published a digest of Louisiana cases that would guide attorneys in their practices. It was comparable to the Southwest Seconds and Thirds or Westlaw in modern law and told the story of past cases that attorneys could cite to support their clients' positions in court.

Benjamin soon came to the attention of the leading lawyer in New Orleans, John Slidell. Slidell was politically powerful and the older brother of his law partner. He made Benjamin his protégé and enhanced his career in many ways: helping him ascend the social ladder, sending him his overflow cases, and pushing him towards public office. Slidell was the political boss of New Orleans with all of the benefits of patronage. He was a forerunner of the Tammany Hall of New York City, which would emerge fifty years later. His tactics were similar, and he was not above ballot stuffing or using repeat voters to get his candidates elected.[25] Elected U.S. senator after two unsuccessful attempts, he could deliver votes at the national conventions and in 1856, he was the chief patronage distributor at the Democratic convention for James Buchanan. Buchanan rewarded Slidell by appointing him ambassador to Mexico. This led four years later to an appointment as ambassador to France to lobby Louis Napoleon for Confederate recognition and support.

As Benjamin's legal career grew, his marriage with Natalie withered. Natalie was a lady who would not accept neglect, and Benjamin spent most of his time buried in his work. As his financial condition improved, they moved to a plantation outside of New Orleans called Bellechasse. This allowed them to entertain in true Southern style, but Natalie still was unhappy. In 1843, ten years into their marriage, they had a daughter they named Ninette. Her nickname was Nettie. Benjamin brought his mother (his parents were separated by this time) and favorite sister, Penny, to Bellechasse, wrote a small book on raising sugar cane, and worked hard at his career. Planters from all over the South visited to see the improvements the brilliant Benjamin brought to raising sugar cane. He was on top of his world.

But Natalie did not flourish in Benjamin's paradise. She felt isolated from New Orleans and her social world there and developed depression after the baby was born. In 1844, she suddenly announced that she was leaving for Paris and taking Ninette with her.[26] Benjamin must have been devastated over losing his daughter and wife but believed that Natalie would

John Slidell. (Library of Congress)

soon come home. She never returned to the U.S. and the state of Benjamin's relationship caused him a lifetime of humiliation.

Despite his wife's departure, Benjamin plunged ahead with plans for a new house on the plantation and built a splendid mansion with twenty rooms and hallways sixteen feet wide. The house featured a marble fireplace, crystal chandeliers, a spiral mahogany staircase, and a verandah that surrounded the entire house. He was hoping the magnificent home would entice Natalie back from Paris, but to no avail.

Benjamin was admitted to practice in the U.S. Supreme Court in 1848 and he went to Washington as a Whig elector for Zachary Taylor. While in Washington, he earned substantial fees in some landmark cases of the time. In addition to money, he gained a reputation as a grand orator with an incisive mind.

In 1852, Benjamin was solidly entrenched with the various factions in Louisiana politics and won a seat in the U.S. Senate. He was the first Jew practicing the faith to be elected to the Senate. An earlier Jew, David "Levy" Yulee of Florida, had converted to Christianity before his election. Benjamin was joined that day in the Senate by Sam Houston and Stephen A. Douglas, fiery orators of deep principles who were replacing the great compromisers Daniel Webster, Henry Clay, and John C. Calhoun.

Benjamin was sworn in as senator the same day Franklin Pierce was inaugurated as president. Pierce appointed Jefferson Davis as his secretary of war. At first, Davis and Benjamin were rival Southern leaders. But Benjamin's eloquent arguments and oratory and his capacity for hard work gradually began to earn Davis's respect and esteem. His speeches were printed in Southern newspapers, gaining him even more credence and enhancing his reputation, and he gained the title of the champion of states' rights while debating Sen. William Seward on the slavery issue in intense and emotionally charged arguments. Seward was the only senator for whom Benjamin ever showed a dislike.[27] By the time Jefferson Davis was elected president of the Confederacy, Davis was not at all reluctant to appoint Benjamin as attorney general. Their friendship and alliance were just beginning.

CHAPTER FOUR

Black Flag Warfare Turned Serious

By the summer of 1864, the Southern attitude toward "black ops" warfare had changed dramatically. Not only had the Dahlgren raid changed the mindset of Confederate officials, but military victories had become a thing of the past. Ulysses S. Grant and George Meade had the Army of Northern Virginia pinned to the trenches of Petersburg. William T. Sherman was approaching Atlanta and it looked like it was impossible to stop him. For the South to win the war, they would have to win another way.

In many cases, historians are far more tolerant than most modern readers. Historians understand that those who lived during the Civil War grew up in another time with different values and traditions. Slavery was all the South knew and its citizens saw nothing wrong with it. It was a widely held belief at that time that the white man was superior to the black man and slaves were property. This was backed up by the famous Dred Scott Supreme Court case in 1857. In most cases, Southerners thought slaves were treated fairly well. Treatment varied from true fondness for their servants to, at the very least, care for their property. Few slave owners treated slaves harshly without reason because it was not good business to abuse property. Southern plantation owners generally considered themselves caretakers and benefactors to the slaves they owned, and resentment toward "radical abolitionists" was strong and bitter. In their view, Harriet Beecher Stowe's book of 1852, *Uncle Tom's Cabin,* totally misrepresented Southern culture.

In addition, state law generally was supreme over federal

law. States' rights was the law of the land. In our modern times that is nearly inconceivable, but to an antebellum Southerner, both custom and law were on his side. Therefore, as the war progressed, his bitterness and hatred grew as his family and friends were killed by the "hated invader foe," his farms were destroyed, and his property confiscated. That property included slaves after the Emancipation Proclamation came into effect. As the war dragged on, Southerners grew increasingly desperate. Most Southerners would do just about anything to save their culture and way of life. Historians understand that. The average citizen of today does not.

However, the story of Dr. Luke P. Blackburn turns the stomach of even the most neutral historian. Dr. Blackburn did his best to wage biological warfare against the civilian population of the North. He was truly the first American terrorist in American history, and his actions are made all the more egregious because he had to disregard his Hippocratic oath in his undertakings.

Dr. Blackburn was born in 1816 and graduated from Transylvania University in 1835.[1] The young doctor moved to Natchez, Mississippi, and established his medical practice in 1846. He became an expert in treating yellow fever, traveling to Europe and studying hospitals and yellow fever treatment. By the beginning of the Civil War, he was considered one of the foremost experts on yellow fever treatment in the United States.

In the early years of the war, he served on generals' staffs and held various medical positions in the Confederate army. Dr. Blackburn came to Canada in November 1863. That was at least six months before the arrival of the Confederate commissioners Jacob Thompson and Clement Clay and their cohorts. No evidence exists to tie the genesis of his plan to any Confederate authority. His plan seems to be his own, but it was later embraced by the Confederate Canadian leaders.

Once Dr. Blackburn arrived in Canada, he recruited an associate named Godfrey J. Hyams, a former resident of Little Rock, Arkansas. Dr. Blackburn left Hyams in Toronto with instructions to await his orders while he traveled on to Cuba. There, he wrote back to Hyams, in April 1864, to proceed to Halifax and report to Alexander Keith. Keith, as you recall, was one of the first Confederate agents hired in either Halifax or

Canada. Hyams traveled to Halifax in the company of a young man named W. W. Haynes after being funded by Confederate agent William L. McDonald in Toronto. Hyams and Haynes arrived in Halifax on June 22, 1864. Agent Alexander Keith put them up in the Farmers Hotel to await Blackburn, who arrived from Bermuda on the ship *Alpha* on July 12.[2]

Blackburn then laid out the rest of the project to Hyams. He was to unload several trunks from the ship *Alpha* and arrange to have them shipped to Washington, D.C., Norfolk, Virginia, and New Bern, North Carolina. These last two were Southern cities under the control of Federal troops. The trunks contained infected clothing from a yellow fever epidemic in Bermuda, and the plan was for the clothing to be sold at auction in those cities and therefore spread the infection.[3] Blackburn also gave Hyams a valise of fancy shirts and instructed him to travel to the White House and present them to Lincoln as gifts. According to the statement Hyams gave to federal authorities on April 12, 1865, he refused to follow Blackburn's directives. No one would know for another thirty-five years that yellow fever does not spread from infected clothing but from mosquitoes.

After shipping the trunks to Boston, Hyams forwarded the trunks to Philadelphia. From there he took some of them to Washington and arranged with a Philadelphia sutler to take the remaining clothes on to New Bern, North Carolina. Coincidentally, a yellow fever epidemic did break out in New Bern, so the conspirators believed their mission to be a success.

Hyams returned to Canada on August 13, 1864, and ran into Clement Clay and James P. Holcombe in Hamilton, where they congratulated him on his successful trip.[4] Tragically, this implicates the Confederate government. It appears that knowledge of this project went all the way to the top at some point. On November 30, 1864, Jefferson Davis received a letter from Rev. K. J. Stewart saying in part, "the yellow fever project had no other effect than to disgust good men and anger the Almighty."[5]

Dr. Blackburn not only tried to wage war on the civilians in the North but also intended to expose his fellow Southern civilians in the same process. No one knows today why the cities of Norfolk and New Bern were selected. The motivation behind the attacks would have been easier to understand if only Northern cities had been chosen. The mission also would have been easier to accomplish. This author can only conclude that the object of the mission was to force an evacuation of the Federals from these two port cities in the case of a widespread epidemic. Dr. Blackburn was never prosecuted for this conspiracy and would later become the governor of Kentucky.[6]

Having already demonstrated that the South was willing to pursue unconventional means with Blackburn's biological warfare, the next phase of Southern conflict also took place outside the battlefield. The Northern election was looming in November, and Northern Democrats had not only nominated Lincoln's arch-enemy Gen. George McClellan but had put a negotiated peace plank in their platform. In the summer, the Democrats' future looked bright. If Lincoln lost the election the South could still negotiate for their independence if they could hold out until the following spring.

The same theory applied if he could be removed from office, and Jefferson Davis was no longer saying "no" to kidnapping Abraham Lincoln. Col. Bradley T. Johnson presented a plan to take two hundred men and conduct a rapid raid into Washington and seize Lincoln at the Soldiers' Home. He gained the approval of cavalry general Wade Hampton and started collecting and training men for the mission. General Hampton never would have allowed such a mission without approval from the top. Wartime fate intervened, however.[7]

Union general David Hunter invaded the Shenandoah Valley and began implementing a scorched earth policy. Lee could not afford to lose his food supply and sent Gen. Jubal Early from the Petersburg trenches to stop him. Colonel Johnson was in his command and his raid was put on hold. During the battles in the valley, Gen. William E. "Grumble" Jones was killed on June 5, 1864,[8] and Bradley Johnson was promoted to brigadier general and placed in command of Jones' brigade. That ended the plans for the raid. General Early then took his whole army north down the valley and conducted a breathtaking invasion that came within one or two days of penetrating Washington itself. General Wright's Union Corps hurried north from Virginia to turn back Early just in time.

On September 17, 1864, Davis dispatched a secret agent to scout Washington, D.C. to see if kidnapping Lincoln was feasible. That agent was Thomas Nelson Conrad. Conrad took several men and traveled to Washington, staying at the home of Thomas Greene, located a few blocks from the White House.[9] From this location, Conrad could monitor Lincoln's movements. He returned to Richmond with a report stating that it would be possible to seize Lincoln and escape with him through southern Maryland and down the courier trail.

As plans for kidnapping Abraham Lincoln were developing, a group of Confederate agents met in Boston. On July 26, 1864, around the same time Dr. Blackburn's yellow fever trunks reached the city, several men met at the Parker House Hotel. All but one used an alias: alias Charles R. Hunter—Toronto, alias A. J. Bursted—Baltimore, alias H. V. Clinton—CW (Canada West), alias R. A. Leech—Montreal, and one J. Wilkes Booth.[10]

It is doubtful that Godfrey Hyams was a participant in any meeting that occurred at the Parker House. He was using the

Thomas Nelson Conrad. (Surratt House Museum/ MNCPPC)

alias J. W. Harris at the time and confessed his involvement with the yellow fever affair to Union officials in a sworn statement on April 12, 1865, just two days before Lincoln's assassination. He later testified to the same at the conspiracy trial. No part of his story includes a meeting with Booth.

A Boston port official named Cordial Crane read about Hyams' testimony in the papers and checked with the local hotels looking for the name J. W. Harris. He found the names from Canada and Baltimore, including Booth's, registered at the Parker House and notified Secretary Edwin Stanton by letter dated May 30, 1865. Stanton took no action at the time. The omission is puzzling. Perhaps Stanton and Joseph Holt, the prosecutor in the assassination trials, thought the fraudulent testimony from Sandford Conover and James B. Merritt would be sufficient to tie Booth to the Confederates. They certainly knew better by January 1866, but they still didn't follow up. At that point, Jefferson Davis and Clement Clay were still in custody. Ostensibly, Northern prosecutors were desperate to tie them to the murder.

Recent historians investigated this Boston hotel registration by the late 1980s. They combed the records in the cities listed on the hotel register for the individuals named and found nothing. They were obviously false names. One name did reappear though. H. V. Clinton—St. Louis checked into the St. Lawrence Hotel in Montreal on May 28, 1864, and again on August 24. The St. Lawrence Hotel was the headquarters for the Canadian agents and St. Louis was a frequent city used by Confederate agents using aliases.[11]

Perhaps agents unknown were in Boston at the same time as Hyams and met with Booth, who had been smuggling quinine into the Confederacy. Perhaps these agents were involved both with Hyams and setting up a contingency plan for capturing Lincoln. Perhaps their presence in Boston at the same time the infected clothing shipment was due to arrive was a coincidence. But that would be quite a coincidence.

It is probable that Hyams never knew about a plan to kidnap Lincoln. By late November 1864, the Canadian agents suspected he was a double agent.[12] It turned out that they were right.

CHAPTER FIVE

Booth Arrives in the Story

We don't know who the men at the Parker House in July of 1864 really were or where they were really from. We don't know why they used aliases and John Wilkes Booth did not. Perhaps Booth was so well known that using an alias would bring more attention to himself than if he had used his own name. We can't even be sure that the four men met with Booth. If they did, we don't know what was on the agenda. If a plan was set in motion, we don't know if it was a contingency plan or if it was to be enacted. We don't know if it was in the infancy stage or seriously thought out in detail. We don't know if several plans were discussed or if only a kidnapping was considered. There is, however, one thing of which we are certain. Within three weeks of that date, Booth's lifestyle changed and so did his purpose.

By the middle of August, Booth had checked into the Barnum Hotel in Baltimore. From there he summoned two of his childhood friends, Samuel Arnold and Michael O'Laughlen. Arnold arrived first. Samuel B. Arnold was twenty-nine years old and met Booth while they were students at St. Timothy's Hall school in Catonsville, Maryland. O'Laughlen arrived shortly thereafter. He had grown up across the street from the Booths' home on North Exeter Street in Baltimore and had known Booth all of his life. Although he had never met Arnold, they quickly learned that they had both served in the same Confederate regiment, the First Maryland Infantry, early in the war. They had been honorably discharged due to disabilities.

The three young men conversed pleasantly over cigars and

Samuel Arnold. (Library of Congress)

Michael O'Laughlen. (Library of Congress)

brandy for some time until Booth got down to business and told them why he had sent for them. The South was running out of manpower and Booth proposed that they join a plot to capture Lincoln while he was en route to or from the Soldiers' Home, where he stayed in warm weather, and hold him hostage to effect a prisoner exchange. Booth pointed out that Lincoln often traveled unguarded and the capture should be easy. A captive Lincoln in Richmond could be used to trade for many Southern prisoners. Both men agreed to join the team.[1]

Booth's detailed information on Lincoln's habits and movements are a clue to his involvement in the meeting at the Parker House. Booth himself had not been to Washington since November 1863.[2]

With the first two team members on board, Booth traveled to Philadelphia to visit and stay with his sister, Asia Booth Clarke. His sister Asia would later write of the visit, detailing that her brother John slept in his clothes on the sofa in the parlor, received visitors at odd hours, and spoke in whispers. Because of an illness, he stayed there for more than a month. As soon as he could travel, he went to Franklin, Pennsylvania, and began disposing of his oil investments. Perhaps Booth knew that anyone charged with treason forfeit their property to the government. By September 28, 1864, he had transferred his oil assets to members of his family or sold them for cash.[3]

On October 16, he crossed the Canadian border. On October 18, he checked into the now well-known St. Lawrence Hotel in Montreal, staying there for ten days. He brought a large trunk with his acting costumes and many personal items. We will return to this fateful trip a little later.

Booth's early life and family history are well chronicled elsewhere so will be touched on only briefly here. John Wilkes Booth was born May 10, 1838, the second youngest of ten children born to Junius Brutus Booth and Mary Ann Holmes. Only six of the children lived to maturity. His parents did not marry until John Wilkes's thirteenth birthday. Junius was a well-known actor in England with a wife, Adelaide, and a son named Richard. He escaped the marriage by coming to America with his pregnant mistress, Mary Ann. They stepped

John Wilkes Booth. (Library of Congress)

off the ship *Two Brothers* on June 30, 1821,[4] in Norfolk, Virginia. After their first two children were born, they settled down on a farm in Hartford County, Maryland, about twenty miles northeast of Baltimore. Mindful of inheritance problems, Junius acquired the land via a thousand-year lease for $733.20. He paid a single cent a year in rent. A humble cabin was soon moved onto the property. Over the years substantial improvements and additions were made. The Booths named the farm Tudor Hall. It eventually included barns, stables, slave quarters, and even a pond for swimming for John Wilkes and his siblings. In 1845, the Booths acquired a house, again by long-term lease, at 62 North Exeter Street in Baltimore.[5] They spent the winters there.

Booth's early childhood was rather unremarkable. He was the family favorite, receiving little discipline and much independence. His father named him after John Wilkes, a man much admired by his parents. John Wilkes was an eighteenth-century political agitator and champion of the American

Revolution. The young Booth often used his name for theatre billing and as an alias. He received his initial education at the Milton School for Boys in Sparks, Maryland; Bel Air Academy in Baltimore; St. Timothy's Hall in Catonsville, where he met Samuel Arnold; and Bland's Boarding Academy in York, Pennsylvania.

Booth's two brothers Junius Jr. and Edwin went on to achieve stardom in acting careers, as did John S. Clarke, his sister Asia's husband. By the time John Wilkes was seventeen, his two older brothers were well established. His future brother-in-law, John S. Clarke, helped him obtain his first acting job in 1857 at the Arch Street Theatre in Philadelphia, where he played under the name of John Wilkes. His career there was undistinguished. He was inexperienced and lazy, missing lines and queues, and drawing poor reviews. The next season, his brother Edwin got him a job at John Ford's Holiday Street Theatre playing Richmond in the play *Richard III*. Under his brother's tutelage, John slowly improved. John Ford was a partner with George Kunkle in the Old Marshall Theatre in Richmond, Virginia. Booth moved there for two seasons in 1859 and 1860. Southern audiences were not as sophisticated as their neighbors to the north and John received better reviews.

John fit in quite well with Southern society and as he matured, he embraced the Southern political point of view. According to the statements of two fellow actors, Samuel K. Chester and George Wren, Booth joined the Knights of the Golden Circle, the secretive inner circle of the Copperhead movement.[6]

While living and acting in Richmond, Booth received the electrifying news that changed the course of the nation. On the night of October 16, 1859, a band of men led by John Brown attacked the U.S. Armory at Harpers Ferry, Virginia. These eighteen men, including five blacks, took thirteen hostages.[7] Then they retreated from an outraged crowd and local militia to the engine house of the armory. They holed up there, exchanging a slow fire with the local inhabitants.

Pres. James Buchanan sent a company of marines under the command of Col. Robert E. Lee and assisted by Lt. J. E. B. Stuart to Harpers Ferry. At daybreak on October 19, the marines stormed the building. The marines suffered two casualties but killed a number of Brown's men, including two of Brown's sons, and wounded John Brown himself. No hostages were harmed, due to Lee's care to use bayonets only in the charge. The uprising was put down in three minutes.[8]

The news flashed around the country, identifying John Brown as the instigator. He was already famous for his anti-slavery position in Kansas and as leader of the massacre at Osawatomie Creek. The South shuddered as it became clear that Brown had intended to begin a slave uprising. They remembered the Nat Turner rebellion almost twenty years earlier when many plantation owners were killed by their slaves. Southern emotions were inflamed and they blamed Northern abolitionists for supporting this plot. To them, it wasn't just politics, it was a plot to take their lives. It was also an invasion.

Booth's Southern sympathies solidified at that time. Virginia governor Henry Wise activated the Virginia militia and sent them to Charles Town, where Brown and the other

John Brown. (Library of Congress)

conspirators were jailed and awaiting trial. These militia units included the Richmond Grays. Booth talked his way onto the train with the Grays even though he was not a member.[9] Several people saw and recognized Booth as he shadowed the trial and managed to be on the front row of the Grays during the hanging of Brown on December 2, 1859.

Booth returned to Richmond and played another season at the Old Marshall Theatre. In the fall of 1860, Booth got his first starring role in *Romeo and Juliet* with Matthew Channing's company in a tour of the South. He was billed as John Wilkes. Large crowds and rave reviews followed, and the tour flourished until disaster struck. Channing accidentally discharged a pistol that wounded Booth in the thigh. While he healed, Booth missed many performances and played less taxing roles when he could.

Once the tour was over, Booth returned home to Baltimore to spend the Christmas of 1860 with his family. A bleak Christmas it was. Families as well as the Union were splitting in two over politics and secession. John clashed with his brother Edwin over secession and slavery. His brothers both scolded him and laughed at him over his "patriotic froth." But this was no longer a laughing matter. South Carolina had seceded on December 20 and the second state, Mississippi, would secede on January 7. During the following weeks, one Southern state after another would leave the Union, bringing the nation to a crisis stage as Abraham Lincoln's inauguration day approached.

During this time John Wilkes Booth prepared a fourteen-page position paper, intending to deliver to a theatre audience a speech in defense of the South and its right of self-determination. Booth never made the speech but his sister Asia kept the paper for years. It was a closely guarded secret not made public until 1938. The still unpublished manuscript is kept at the Walter Hamden Library in New York City.[10]

Booth's home city of Baltimore was a hotbed of secession prior to the inauguration. Its citizens destroyed bridges north of the city, rioted, activated local militias, and threatened to prevent soldiers from the North from traveling through their city to protect the capital. Even worse, a serious assassination plot developed. To prevent his taking office, Lincoln was to be murdered while he traveled through the city. Hundreds, if not thousands, of local citizens rose up in rebellion. It is unclear whether John Wilkes Booth participated in any of this, but there is a clue that he was involved. He may very well have been arrested but later released upon taking a loyalty oath.[11]

The rebels in Baltimore were no ordinary rabble. They included some of the city's leaders, including George P. Kane, the police marshal. Kane was arrested on June 27 but later released and became a leading member of the Confederate Secret Service in Montreal, Canada. He would take leading roles in plots ranging from the freeing of Southern prisoners of war to the arson attempts in New York City in November of 1864. It is unclear if he ever met Booth. No documents linking the two are known to exist, but Kane lived at times with Patrick Martin and his wife, who did work with Booth. It is also possible that George P. Kane was the Baltimore man registered at Boston's Parker House Hotel on July 26, 1864, for that meeting with Booth. Kane was also credited with a kidnap plan that was examined by Gen. Robert E. Lee two months prior. General Lee mentioned the "Marshal Kane Plan" in a letter to Jefferson Davis on June 26, 1864.[12] If this was the case, Booth never came up with a kidnapping plan of his own. He was recruited for Kane's plan.

By the time Lincoln's train arrived in Philadelphia in 1861, news had come to him from several reliable sources that a hostile reception awaited him in Baltimore. The city had sent no delegation to arrange an official welcome and planned no ceremonies at all. Bands of toughs called Blood Tubs roamed the streets threatening to kill Lincoln if he showed his face. General Winfield sent Lincoln written warnings. Senator Seward, slated to be appointed secretary of state, sent his son with documented evidence. Allan Pinkerton sent news that his operatives had infiltrated the gangs, who had taken blood oaths to kill Lincoln. This had become a serious matter.

Lincoln, with his best bodyguard, Ward Hill Lamon, boarded a special train and traveled to Baltimore, arriving in the early hours of the morning. Anxious minutes passed as his private car was horse drawn through the streets to another station whose tracks led to the capital. The switch was safely made as his enemies slept, and Lincoln arrived in Washington, D.C. about daybreak disguised in a plaid overcoat and Irish soft cap. Lincoln had to endure derision from some hostile newspapers about disguising himself in a woman's cloak and running from imaginary threats from the Blood Tubs, but the insults were brief and a dangerous incident was avoided.[13]

By late 1863, Booth began acting in starring roles. He traveled the nation drawing better and better reviews from audiences that were hungry for entertainment and had the money to pay for it. Booth was soon earning twenty thousand dollars a year.[14] He expanded his roles to include Pescara in *The Apostate,* characters in *Hamlet* and *Richard III,* and the roles of Phidias and Raphael in *The Marble Heart.* On November 9, 1863, he played both roles before President Lincoln at Ford's Theatre. By now Booth could compare with any star in the acting field.

Booth was hungry for more than just fame. He took a shot at some real money, forming a wildcat oil drilling company with two acting friends, John Ellsler and Thomas Mears. They formed a partnership called the Dramatic Oil Company. They drilled a well on the Fuller farm near Franklin, Pennsylvania, early in 1864. Booth was in Franklin often during those months, occasionally staying at the McHenry House Hotel in Meadville, Pennsylvania. Someone etched an inscription on a window pane in room 22 that said, "Abe Lincoln Departed This Life August 13th, 1864 By the Effects of Poison." Booth never stayed in room 22 and was not at the hotel on August 13. Whoever wrote that message remains a mystery.

Booth moved on to Cleveland and for the next three weeks dropped out of sight as far as historians are concerned. But on July 26, he arrived in Boston for that fateful meeting at the Parker House. That seems to be the turning point for the remaining ten months of his life.

CHAPTER SIX

A Plot Develops

After securing two of his friends as accomplices in the plot and divesting himself of assets subject to seizure, John Wilkes Booth arrived in Montreal with his personal effects and acting costumes on October 18, checking into the St. Lawrence Hotel. The hotel was a favorite of Europeans as well as Confederates. It was modern and posh, covering a whole block of St. James Street. It had a main lobby barbershop, two hundred well-ventilated suites, a billiard parlor in the basement, a grand piano in the ornately furnished second-floor lobby, and a dazzling dining room under chandeliers.[1]

St. Lawrence Hotel, Confederate headquarters in Montreal. (McCord Museum, MP-1975.36.5.1)

During the ten days that he stayed in Montreal, Booth attended a meeting with New Yorkers and Confederate agent Beverly Tucker to secure a secret deal to trade Northern pork for Southern cotton.[2] He also met with various agents, including George Sanders and his associate Patrick Martin. Sanders was called away part of the time to help the raiders of St. Albans after some of them were arrested following the bank robbery on October 19. Although the fraudulent testimony of Sandford Conover, who testified that he saw Booth and Sanders together, can be discounted, the Union did find three credible witnesses who saw the men together on more than one occasion: Hosea B. Carter of New Hampshire, John Deveney of Maryland, and William E. Wheeler of Chicopee, Massachusetts.[3]

George Sanders not only was an anarchist advocating assassination but also was bitter over losing his son, Maj. Reid Sanders, in a prisoner of war camp in Boston just six weeks prior. Sanders hated all things Yankee and no doubt found a kindred spirit in Booth. What they discussed we will never know for certain, but their visit was likely a follow-up to the July 26 meeting at the Parker House Hotel. In all probability, Sanders and Clement Clay had not heard back from Richmond on the feasibility study being made in Washington, D.C. by Thomas Nelson Conrad. Conrad had not yet reported back to James Seddon that a kidnapping was possible if Lincoln could be nabbed on his way to the Soldiers' Home and transported through southern Maryland. Without knowing the specifics of Conrad's report, it is likely that Sanders and Booth discussed how to acquire the necessary items, equipment, and personnel to begin the project. These details would have brought Patrick C. Martin into the discussion.

Patrick Martin was a New York native and a liquor dealer in the rebel hotbed of Baltimore before the war. Martin and his wife appear in Confederate reports in several places, making it clear that he was a Confederate insider and helped the Southern cause in several ways. Martin had arrived in Canada in late 1862, forming a loose partnership with Alexander Keith in Halifax and beginning a blockade-running operation shortly thereafter. His wife, along with George P. Kane, helped Robert D. Minor in an attempt to free prisoners on Johnson's Island, Ohio.

With an introduction from Martin, Booth opened a bank account with Ontario Bank. Jacob Thompson also used this bank for Confederate enterprises. Booth deposited $455 in the bank and secured a bill of exchange for about £61 that could be cashed anywhere with proper identification. A month later, Booth deposited $1,500 in the Jay Cooke and Company bank in Washington, D.C. This money apparently came from the Confederates, as Booth was not working at the time. It may be inferred that Booth received the money from Patrick Martin,[4] but the funds were probably released by George Sanders, a more senior and direct agent.

Booth then left his wardrobe with Martin for shipment to Richmond aboard his blockade runner, the seventy-three-foot schooner *Marie Victoria*. At that time, Martin provided Booth two letters of introduction to leaders in the southern Maryland underground: Dr. William Queen and Dr. Samuel Mudd. Two weeks later Martin's ship foundered in the St. Lawrence River during a storm. All hands were lost, including Martin.[5]

His business finished, Booth left Montreal for New York on October 28. He only stayed a day or two in New York, where he concluded some details with his oil venture. He then moved on to Baltimore to update Samuel Arnold. He next surfaced at Dr. William Queen's house with the letter of introduction from Patrick Martin.

John Chandler Thompson, Dr. Queen's son-in-law, was very vague on Booth's arrival date in his testimony before the military tribunal.[6] He said that Booth arrived on a Saturday evening with Dr. Queen's son, Joseph. The date could have been anywhere from late October to November 12 as Dr. Samuel Mudd traveled the eight miles to St. Mary's Catholic Church to meet Booth on November 13. Thompson could very well have been covering for his family with this potentially important testimony. If Booth had arrived as late as November 12, the Queen family would have had to scramble to get the message to Dr. Mudd so that he could meet Booth at their church the next morning. Had he admitted that Booth arrived a week earlier, on November 5, questions would arise as to Booth's and Dr. Queen's activities for seven days. Did Booth explore the lower end of the southern Maryland peninsula to learn the condition of the roads, discern the width of the Potomac there, and meet the people who might assist the kidnapping party in several ways? Dr. Queen and his family were not prosecuted by the federal government; Dr. Mudd was. That could have been important testimony.

Booth next appeared back in Washington three days later, depositing $1,500 in Jay Cooke and Company's bank[7] before traveling on to New York City to rehearse with his two brothers for the play *Julius Caesar,* scheduled for November 25 at the Winter Garden Theatre. A benefit performance to raise funds for the Shakespeare statue fund, it was the only time the three brothers appeared together on stage. Ironically, fires set by agents of the Confederate Secret Service from Canada briefly interrupted the play. The Lafarge Hotel next door to the theatre was one of the hotels targeted by the Confederate agents.

While Booth was in New York, he acquired two Spencer repeating rifles, three pistols, a dagger, and ammunition.[8] The seven-shot repeating rifles were state-of-the-art technology at the time and would have been very hard to come by. Booth had to have influential contacts to procure them. Later, on his trip back to Washington, he dropped off most of the weapons and ammunition with Arnold and O'Laughlen in Baltimore.

On his way down to Baltimore, he stopped at his sister Asia's home in Philadelphia. He left a packet of papers in her safe, including a farewell letter to his mother and a letter to Asia's husband, John Sleeper Clarke. He probably intended for this letter to be published after the kidnapping or his death. The long letter was a defense of the Southern cause and of Booth's service to it. The letter began "To whom it may concern," a jab at Abraham Lincoln's response to those trying to establish a peace conference in Canada the previous summer. Lincoln's opening to their inquiry for a peace conference was artfully written to avoid officially recognizing the Confederacy. Southern leaders and citizens as well were angered by this official slight.

Booth's letter went on to read:

> The very nomination of Abraham Lincoln four years ago spoke plainly war—war upon Southern rights and institutions. His election proved it. . . . In a foreign war, I, too could say, "Country, right or wrong." But in a struggle, such as ours (where the brother tries to pierce the brother's heart), for God's sake, choose the right. When a

country like this spurns justice from her side she forfeits the allegiance of every honest freeman and should leave him, untrammeled by any fealty so ever, to act as his conscience may approve. People of the North, to hate tyranny, to love liberty and justice, to strike at wrong and oppression, was the teaching of our fathers. The study of our early history will not let me forget it, and may it never.

This country was formed for the white, not for the black man. . . . I thought then, as now, that the abolitionists were the only traitors in the land and that the entire party deserved the same fate as poor old [John] Brown, not because they wished to abolish slavery, but on account of the means they have endeavored to use to effect that abolition. . . . The South can make no choice. It is either extermination, or slavery for themselves (worse than death) to draw from. I know my choice. I have studied hard to know upon what grounds the right of a state to secede has been denied, when our very name, United States, and the Declaration of Independence, both provide for secession.

But there is no time for words. . . . My love (as things stand today) is for the South alone. Nor do I deem it a dishonor in attempting to make for her a prisoner of this man, to whom she owes so much of her misery.

A Confederate, at present doing duty upon his own responsibility.[9]

Booth may have written the words "upon his own responsibility" for a number of reasons. The most obvious one would absolve all higher-ups of any blame. It also could have been ego (Booth had plenty of that) or that Canada had not yet received approval from Richmond to proceed. Knowing the identity of the participants of that meeting at the Parker House would have helped immensely in understanding his meaning and motivation. As far as historians can tell at this time, the Canadian agents were only aware that Richmond was considering the kidnapping option. No decision had been made yet. We may never know when Richmond approved this plan, but we can look for clues, and there are clues aplenty.

We pick up Booth once more around December 17 as he visits Dr. Mudd again. Booth had made no progress in expanding his action team. It was still a small band of three. Leaving the weapons with Samuel Arnold, he had continued on to southern Maryland. On December 18, 1864, by arrangement, Mudd introduced Booth to a major member of the Confederate

Secret Service named Thomas Harbin at the Bryan Town Tavern.[10] Booth held a private meeting with Harbin. We can easily infer that three things resulted from that meeting. First, Harbin gave Booth the name of John H. Surratt, Jr. Second, Harbin joined in the plot himself but not as a member of the action team. Third, the Confederate government had approved plans for the kidnapping. Harbin, by nature, was cautious. He also commanded a signal camp across the river in King George County, Virginia.[11] To agree to join Booth's venture, he must have known the minds of the government's leaders and that they had been considering this move for some time. Over the course of the following month, events would make that clear.

On the same trip, Booth would buy from one of Dr. Mudd's neighbors a fast horse with just one eye for the discounted price of eighty dollars. The one-eyed horse would later prove distinctive and would indirectly lead to the early identification and arrest of members of the Booth action team. Booth rode this horse back to Washington, D.C. on December 22.

Dr. Samuel Mudd. (National Archives)

Thomas Harbin. (Surratt House Museum/MNCPPC)

Booth and Mudd obviously had agreed to meet in Washington, D.C. the following day. The next evening, December 23, 1864, would be a red-letter day for the conspirators. Dr. Mudd agreed to introduce Booth to another major player in the Confederate Secret Service, John H. Surratt, Jr.

Around 6:30 P.M., Booth met Mudd at the National Hotel and headed toward the Surratt boarding house.[12] On the way, they met Surratt himself, accompanied by fellow boarder and long-time friend Louis Weichmann. The four men then retired to Booth's room at the National Hotel. Booth ordered milk punches and cigars for the group. Mudd and Surratt briefly went out in the hall for a private conversation lasting no more than three minutes. Booth was then summoned to join them, leaving Weichmann alone in the room. According to Weichmann's later testimony, the three men returned to the room but sat apart from him and began an earnest conversation in whispers. Booth then began to draw lines on an envelope as he whispered. Mudd and Surratt watched

John H. Surratt, Jr. (Library of Congress)

Louis Weichmann. (Public domain)

and listened intently. The men then rejoined Weichmann and apologized for the private meeting. On the way home, Surratt told Weichmann that Booth needed a neutral party to help Booth buy Mudd's farm. This lie is obvious today but Weichmann had no reason to disbelieve it. It is impossible to know whether Surratt joined the plot that night or after subsequent meetings. But that he did so we know from the actions he would take, Booth's frequent visits to the Surratt boarding house, and Surratt's own statements in a lecture to a Rockville, Maryland, crowd in 1870.

In less than three weeks, Surratt had recruited three more members of the action team: George Atzerodt, a Potomac River pilot who ferried passengers and mail across the river; David Herold, a young man unemployed at the time but familiar with the back roads of southern Maryland; and Lewis Powell. Powell was the muscle for the group. Someone obviously had to handle a very large kidnapped president. Almost magically, Surratt was able to recruit the large, strong private from Col. John Mosby's command.

Surratt's ability to connect with Colonel Mosby (directly or indirectly) carries several implications. Powell was a valuable member of Mosby's Forty-Third Battalion. All the men were brave, disciplined, and capable soldiers. The Union was scared to death of them. For Mosby to relinquish one of his valued men speaks volumes about the progress of this plot. Mosby must have received orders from those in high command. Surratt's ability to recruit Powell implies that his connections were very strong with Richmond, that Richmond was now focusing on this action team headed by Booth, and that communication between the parties was exceedingly swift. It is possible that Thomas Harbin was the conduit to Mosby.

On January 13, 1865, Powell made his way into a Union camp at the Fairfax County Courthouse and claimed that he was a neutral citizen trapped in Virginia and wished to go north to avoid service in the Confederate army. He offered to take a loyalty oath. Powell, now using the alias Payne, was given a pass to Alexandria. He took a loyalty oath there and headed to Baltimore to his sweetheart Maggie Branson's home. He then

Lewis Powell aka Payne, Booth's muscle man.
(Public domain)

John Singleton Mosby. (Library of Congress)

Booth's action team. (Surratt House Museum/MNCPPC)

checked into Miller's Hotel. Branson had helped him escape from Federal custody in Baltimore in late 1863 when he was convalescing from a wound suffered at Gettysburg while serving in the Confederate army. Maggie Branson had been a nurse at the hospital where Powell, a prisoner of war, was recovering.

In many respects Baltimore was still a town loaded with Southern sympathizers. Southern agent Preston Parr, a china dealer in Baltimore, then notified John Surratt that Lewis Payne (Powell) had arrived. When Surratt arrived in Baltimore, he was accompanied by Weichmann, whom he left at their hotel, saying that he had to meet privately with a man.[13] Surratt met with Powell, gave him expense money, and instructed him to stand by for further orders.[14]

Now the team was set. It had seven members, muscle to handle Lincoln, a good guide to get them through southern Maryland, a river pilot to ferry them across the Potomac, and the necessary contact (Harbin) to meet them on the Virginia side.

CHAPTER SEVEN

A Plan Comes Together

On January 14, 1865, John Surratt and Thomas Harbin arrived in Port Tobacco, Maryland. After recruiting river pilot George Atzerodt, the two men purchased a fifteen-passenger boat from Richard Smoot for three hundred dollars and paid him another hundred dollars to hide it at a chosen spot in the deceptively named Nanjemoy Creek.[1] Larger than the name implies, this inlet from the Potomac River was actually the size of a large lake. The men paid half the money in advance and placed the rest in escrow with attorney Frederick Stone, who held the money with instructions to release the funds to Smoot when the use of the boat was consummated.[2]

Two weeks earlier, Surratt had obtained a job at Adam's Express Company in Washington, D.C. Surratt began this job just prior to meeting Booth. A veteran employee of two whole weeks, Surratt asked his employer for a leave of absence, citing unexpected but important personal business. His boss denied his request. An employee of only a fortnight couldn't expect this type of favor. When Surratt insisted, his boss informed him that if he left, the job would not be there when he got back. Inexplicably, Surratt's mother, Mary, also appeared before his employer. She explained that John's important business was critical to the success of her family. Mary received the same response from John's boss. Undaunted, John left the employ of Adam's Express Company. He never returned for his paycheck.

Surratt and his mother both knew of the impending Confederate plan. Circumstances imply that Booth intended to kidnap Lincoln at Ford's Theatre on January 18. That plan, however, would fail. Lincoln never attended that play.[3] However, in preparation for the plot—and the suspected reason behind his requested leave of absence—John Surratt probably had to report to Richmond to assess the completed action team and conduct last-minute training.

The week after Surratt and Harbin purchased the boat and hid it in Nanjemoy Creek, covert activity in conjunction with the kidnapping plot increased directly south across the Potomac River. The rebel scout and spy Thomas Nelson Conrad operated a signal camp called Eagle's Nest on the bluffs above an old ferry landing called Boyd's Hole.[4] At Conrad's request, Jefferson Davis had approved funds for his past and future activities. In addition, under orders from Secretary of War James Seddon, Lt. Beverly Kennon, Jr. had arrived from Richmond to lay mines in the two creeks on both sides of Boyd's Hole.[5] Thomas Harbin probably had a hand in this.

Both Chotank Creek and Passapatanzy Creek were very large, like Nanjemoy Creek across the river. The placement of the mines in shallow water, not in the main channel, was defensive in nature. It was expected that when the boat from Nanjemoy Creek brought the captured president across the river, it would be pursued by Union gunboats loaded with soldiers and horses. Mines would prevent the pursuers from landing close to Boyd's Hole, where the kidnappers intended to land.[6] Although the plan to lay the mines was approved around Christmas of 1864, due to bad weather and raids from Union gunboats, the mine laying wasn't finished for several weeks.

According to any detailed plan, the kidnapped president would have to be shifted to a land conveyance once he reached Virginia soil. Whether the kidnappers intended to use a carriage, wagon, or horses to transport Lincoln is unclear, but beginning in late October 1864, an elaborate ruse to place troops in the immediate area was enacted. In the coming months, approximately half of the Ninth Virginia Cavalry, who were from the area, were furloughed home for supposed medical reasons. By early January these troops were in position. Great pains were taken to conceal their movement from Union eyes, as the Union army kept careful records of the location, strength, and condition of known Confederate units. Many units were shifted around to conceal Confederate intentions to place additional manpower in an area of light military activity.[7]

For the kidnapping plan to work, the critical segment of getting Lincoln to Richmond would be the overland trip between Boyd's Hole and Milford Station, where Lincoln could be transferred to the railroad and spirited down to the Confederate capital. It appears that a great deal of thought and planning went into this leg of the journey. It would have been obvious to all planners that Union cavalry would be rushed to the area, not only from Washington but also from the Dimmock Line, where Ulysses S. Grant's troops were stationed. The Confederacy needed a force to guard Milford Station, but most of that was already in place.

With the details of the kidnapping already firmly established by mid-January, the Confederacy was suddenly distracted from its plot by the possibility of peace. The seventy-three-year-old Francis P. Blair, an advisor to presidents since the Jackson administration, dreamed up a plan to end the Civil War. He saw a chance to perform a final and grand service to his beloved country. Mexico had brought the exiled Emperor Maximilian from Italy to rule the unruly nation. Maximilian was the younger brother of the Habsburg emperor Franz Joseph, who ruled Austria and Hungary with an iron hand. While Maximilian may have been attractive to the leader-starved Mexicans, he possessed far fewer abilities than his brother. He was an outcast from his own family, living in exile in Italy, when he was invited to Mexico. The hatred and distrust between the brothers seemed to be without limit. Once in Mexico, Maximilian started rattling his saber towards a weak and divided United States. Mexican dreams of restoring territories lost in the war of 1846 to 1848 were rekindled, concerning American leaders on both sides of the Mason-Dixon Line. Blair saw a way for both North and South to lay aside their quarrel: invade Mexico once again and dispense of the troublesome so-called emperor.

In mid-December 1864, Blair approached Lincoln for permission to visit Richmond. "Come to me after Savannah falls," responded Lincoln. Blair returned to the White House on December 28 and received a card that read, "Allow the bearer, F. P. Blair, Sr. to pass our lines, go South and return. A. Lincoln." Blair left at once and on December 30 sent Davis two letters from Grant's headquarters at City Point. The first letter was a request to enter the South to search for some title papers missing since Jubal Early had visited his home in Silver Spring. The second letter was longer and explained that the first letter was just a cover for his real purpose, which was to "unbosom my heart frankly and without reserve" on matters regarding the state of affairs of the country. The letter admitted that Blair was wholly unaccredited, but he hoped to offer certain suggestions he believed would be of interest.[8]

Blair was a lifelong friend to both Davis and his wife. Davis was suspicious but did not dare to refuse the visit. There were delays but Blair arrived on January 12 and, unregistered, obtained a room at the Spotswood Hotel.

Blair arrived at the Confederate White House that evening and was greeted warmly. He laid out his plan for the cessation of hostilities. The united North and South would drive the European ruler out of Mexico, possibly with the army headed by Davis himself, and thus preserve the Monroe Doctrine. With the return of a triumphant army, the two sides could sit down calmly and work out a solution with dignity. After reassuring a distrustful Davis that William Seward had nothing to do with the plan, Blair helped the Southern leader draft a letter to Lincoln wherein Davis stated that he would commission conferees for a peace conference if Lincoln would do the same to "secure peace for the two countries."

Back in Washington, on January 18, Blair had a second conference with Lincoln. After showing Lincoln the letter, Blair commented on how many Southerners he had met who were war weary and strongly desired peace. Lincoln gave Blair a return letter telling Davis that he too yearned for peace and "would receive anyone sent by parties resisting federal authority to secure peace to the people of our one common country."

Notice the fundamental difference between the two letters. The South's letter stated, "our two countries." The North's letter stated, "our one common country." The two leaders would never back down from that original position.

Davis allowed agents to represent the South who were not zealots and who earnestly desired peace. Without comment he gave written instructions charging Vice President Alexander Stephens, former Supreme Court justice John Campbell, and Robert Hunter, who presided over the Confederate senate, to proceed to Washington for the purpose of securing peace between the "two countries." No one in the Confederacy under cabinet level knew the details of Davis's written charge.

The three Southern peace commissioners moved through both cheering army lines to Grant's headquarters. The prospect of peace had excited both armies, enlisted men and officers alike. The excitement was exhilarating and contagious. The general was just returning from an inspection tour at the time and made them comfortable on a headquarters steamer at City Point. Things went downhill from there.[9]

That afternoon they were greeted by Maj. Thomas Eckert, Secretary Edwin Stanton's administrative aide. That was an obvious insult to the ranking Southern leaders. Eckert had instructions to forward the men on to Secretary of State William Seward at Fort Monroe if their written charge was acceptable. Eckert saw immediately that there could be no common ground on the fundamental issue of one country or two and told the disappointed envoys that they could not proceed. The commissioners then proceeded back to City Point. Upon their return, Grant fired off a strongly worded message to Stanton, stating his disappointment that the commissioners seemed sincere in their desire for peace yet Lincoln would not meet with them. Grant closed the communiqué by emphasizing how bad their treatment would look and the negative consequences of the president's dismissal of their mission.

Lincoln gave in and immediately traveled with Secretary Seward to City Point on the steamboat *River Queen*. On February 3, Lincoln met with the three commissioners. After the usual pleasantries, with Lincoln lauding Stephens for his service in Congress, they got down to business. Lincoln was diplomatic but plain. The Union must be restored as part of any process to secure peace. Further, Lincoln promised to grant amnesty to all rebels where and when Congress allowed him to do so. That was a scary thought to the Southern envoys. They would have to return to the Union as traitors and hope that Lincoln could garner congressional approval to pardon them. The negotiations dragged on for four hours. The talks dealt with many issues, such as who would be allowed to represent the Southern people, the status of the two Virginias, and wartime confiscation of property, including slaves. The Southern leaders learned that Lincoln would not repeal the Emancipation Proclamation, and Seward broke the news of the passage of the Thirteenth Amendment, which would free all slaves. The meeting finally ended, leaving the South no better off than when it began. All they accomplished was the return of Alexander Stephens' son, who was a prisoner of war.[10]

Davis, however, was not disappointed in the outcome at all. He had understood the basic difference between the two sides from the beginning. Now the South clearly understood its future under Union control. They would all be treated as traitors. Galvanized, the South continued the war with no further illusions.

But continuing the war during the winter month of February wasn't easy. Beverly Kennon, Jr. was still at the Eagle's Nest, Conrad's camp, struggling with laying mines in the frigid waters of Chotank and Passapatanzy Creeks. Apparently, the mines were considered critical to the plan. The Confederates were reluctant to continue without its completion. With the fifteen-passenger boat hidden just across the river and Boyd's Hole the ideal landing site, it is easy to understand their commitment to that river crossing point. From the bluffs above, Conrad could look north up the Potomac River for miles to spot any pursuing gunboats. In the other direction Lt. Charles Cawood, in the adjacent camp, could see miles to the south as he kept an eye out for approaching Union vessels. Perhaps a signal system existed between the two camps.[11]

The weather wasn't the only thing causing delays. The Union navy in the area grew inexplicably frisky. In early January, they raided the creeks and seized several torpedoes along with the large boat Kennon used to sink the mines. He had to redraw supplies to finish the job. On March 3, the navy raided Chotank Creek and followed up two days later with a crippling raid in Passapatanzy Creek, again seizing a large boat and capturing more mines. This time Kennon's sailors fought back with their meager arsenal of pistols. The Federal navy reported back that they were engaged by Mosby's men, never suspecting the identity and purpose of the Confederate sailors. As a result, Kennon could not finish the project until sometime in March.[12] The exact date is unknown, but Kennon found time later that month to lay mines in the Rappahannock River before returning to Richmond. Kennon and his men were transferred to Lee's army upon the retreat from Richmond and Petersburg on April 2 and were paroled with the Army of Northern Virginia at Appomattox.

The mine project's completion date is significant when you consider Booth's movements on the other side of the Potomac. Booth had his team together on inauguration day, March 4. They were caught in photographs made by Alexander Gardiner at the inauguration. Booth stood behind Lincoln on the stage above and to the president's left while Lewis Powell stood just twelve feet below Lincoln as he gave his speech. Others in the band have been identified by the author, but the identification is not certain.[13] Yet Booth attempted no action that day. The reasons for their inaction would have been many: Lincoln was too well guarded. There were thousands of people around. Just as important, perhaps, his line of retreat was not ready. One thing is certain. He had no plans at that time to assassinate Lincoln, Andrew Johnson, or William Seward. Those three would have been together for most of the day. When such a plan developed and, more importantly, who developed that plan will be examined later.

How could the progress of the plan be transmitted so quickly and by whom? Could Booth and/or Surratt have known when everything was ready across the river? Who would send him this information? There are several possibilities. Conrad could signal this information to Lieutenant Cawood at the next camp, and Cawood could transmit the message across the river in one of two ways. He could use the old flag system, or he could send written messages in code across the river by boat. After the assassination, letters from a Southern cipher machine were recovered in George Atzerodt's room at the Kirkwood Hotel along with other items belonging to Booth. Booth could have received messages in code from a number of agents in southern Maryland, including Augustus Howell, who showed one of these machines to Louis Weichmann.

The Confederates used a cipher system known as the "court" cipher. It was reasonably secure, and each user could use a private matrix and code. Key words and phrases established the current code for the message.[14] These messages could be telegraphed or sent by courier. The couriers in this case could have been many, but the most logical choice would have been Augustus Howell. He operated in southern Maryland and knew the Surratts well. He also possessed a machine and a matrix.

One of the couriers with whom Howell worked in the last five months of the war is one of the most intriguing players in this story. Her name was Sarah Antoinette Slater and she was the best spy you never heard of. She was born Sarah Antoinette Gilbert on January 12, 1843, at Middleton, Connecticut. Her parents were Joseph Marie Gilbert and his wife, Antoinette Reynaud. Her grandfather, Ebenezer Gilbert, married Desire Boutin from the French island of Martinique. Sarah had several siblings, perhaps as many as nine, but six lived to maturity. The Gilberts moved from Middleton to Hartford in 1858. The eldest son, Eugene Francis, moved to Kinston, North Carolina, in 1858, establishing a jewelry business there. The father with two of his children, Fredrick Godwin and Sarah Antoinette, followed. The 1860 census shows the father and the two sons living in a hotel there while Sarah boarded with the family of M. W. Campbell, a coach maker. A third brother, Robert Jackson Gilbert, followed in the fall of 1860, while Sarah's mother moved to New York City to live with her daughter Josephine.

In late October 1860, the father and two brothers moved to Goldsboro while Sarah and her brother Robert moved to New Bern, North Carolina, and joined the family of J. L. Pennington, the publisher of the *Daily Press*. New Bern was a colonial town about twenty miles west of Kinston and was then a busy little seaport. It was here that Sarah met her husband-to-be, Rowan Slater, who was a music teacher and dance instructor. Rowan was about twice her age when they were married on June 12, 1861. He escaped enlistment by becoming a purchasing agent for the Confederate government. Sometime in the summer of 1863, Rowan and his bride moved near his family at Salisbury. Due to manpower shortages, Rowan Slater had to join the army and enlisted in Company A, Twentieth North Carolina Infantry on July 23, 1864. Meanwhile all three of Sarah's brothers joined the Confederate cause. The oldest, Eugene, thrived and became an officer in Company D, Thirteenth Battalion North Carolina Infantry and served honorably until captured at Farmville during Lee's retreat from Petersburg to Appomattox. Her other two brothers, Fredrick and Robert, joined the Second North Carolina Infantry.[15] One brother was killed and the other deserted. After Rowan left for the army, Sarah was all alone. Sometime in the late fall, she made her way to Richmond to seek a passport to join her mother in New York.

Sarah was recruited by Secretary of War James Seddon in January 1865 as she was applying for her passport. Seddon needed to get papers to Canada to prove the military status of five prisoners being held in a Canadian jail for their participation in the St. Albans bank robbery in October 1864. They were facing extradition back to the U.S. to face trial there for murder and bank robbery. Seddon saw potential in Sarah Slater as a courier. She was young, vital, good looking, and spoke fluent French. This would allow her to claim French citizenship and flee to the French embassy if she were caught. Seddon gave her money and dispatches for the Confederate agents to free the prisoners. She left Richmond on January 31, 1865.[16]

The next day another agent from Canada appeared in

Sarah Slater. (Public domain)

Richmond asking for papers. Seddon gave the agent, Rev. Stephen Cameron, a duplicate set of papers and forwarded him on as well.

On February 2, Sarah Slater, undoubtedly with a male escort, arrived at the Confederate signal camp near the mouth of Mattox Creek. There she met the Confederate secret agent Augustus Howell for the first time and was placed in his care.[17] Howell escorted her all the way to New York City, where they checked into the European Hotel. Sarah Slater arrived in Montreal on February 15 at 4:00 A.M. and registered at the St. Lawrence Hotel under the name of Mrs. N. Slater, New York. A William Polley from New York registered at the same time. The papers delivered by her and Cameron led to the release of the St. Albans prisoners shortly thereafter.

Slater was sent back to Richmond a day or two later with urgent dispatches and was met in New York City by none other than John Surratt.[18] They arrived back in Washington on February 22, where they appeared at the Surratt boarding house in Booth's rented carriage at about dusk. Augustus Howell was waiting and climbed aboard the coach without Slater even getting down, and the group departed for the Potomac River at Port Tobacco. From there George Atzerodt rowed them and another agent, James Fowle, across the Potomac to the signal camp commanded by Lieutenant Cawood.

The first week of March, Slater and Howell headed back to Canada with more dispatches. The contents of these dispatches are unknown but are suspected to have been orders transferring authority from Jacob Thompson to Gen. Edwin Lee, who had arrived there on January 24, 1865. However, that is just one possibility as Lee may have carried those papers himself.

Mrs. Slater next appeared at the Surratt boarding house one evening around March 10. Louis Weichmann watched as this attractive, mysterious veiled young lady stepped down from the carriage and entered the house. She held a private conversation with Mrs. Surratt. When Weichmann inquired about this young woman, Mrs. Surratt's response was to send him outside to fetch Slater's luggage. Then he had to surrender his room to her as well. When he returned from work the next day, she was gone. Now bursting with curiosity, he inquired again. John Surratt responded that she was Mrs. Slater from North Carolina and she was carrying dispatches for the agents in Canada.

Mrs. Slater's game plan was carefully thought out. She traveled in a widow's veil, concealing her features, and spoke little. Later witnesses could never adequately describe her and knew very little about her. She would soon begin her final, fateful trip to Richmond.

CHAPTER EIGHT

The Drama Begins

Three days after Sarah Slater left Mrs. Surratt's boarding house, John Surratt telegraphed Preston Parr in Baltimore to send Lewis Powell down to Washington.[1] Powell arrived sometime the next day. After attending a play at Ford's Theatre, the group met for a planning meeting in a private dining room at Gautier's, an upscale restaurant.[2] Booth had a surprise for them other than the oysters and champagne.[3] He laid out a plan to kidnap Lincoln during a play at Ford's Theatre, lower him to the stage after the gaslights had been extinguished, and hustle him out the back door to his waiting carriage, which they would commandeer from the street in front. Booth had wanted them to be familiar with the theatre before considering the plan.[4]

If anyone in the group was unafraid of or unimpressed with Booth, it was his old school chum Samuel Arnold. Arnold considered himself Booth's equal, acting career notwithstanding. With liquor to fortify him, Arnold lost no time in calling the plan ridiculous. He pointed out that Lincoln was a large man who would not allow himself to be kidnapped docilely. They did not have enough muscle for the job, and the theatre guests would not sit idly by while their president was attacked before their eyes. "You may be our leader, but you will not be my executioner," Arnold boldly stated. Several others sided with him, and Booth saw that he would have to back off from his cherished plan of creating history before a huge audience. Further, Arnold and O'Laughlen threatened to leave the group if they did not act soon. The war was going badly and as time went by, it grew more likely that the U.S.

government would discover the plan. As they talked, ate, and smoked into the wee hours, Booth promised to come up with a new plan and soon.

Two days later, on March 17, Booth hastily assembled the team in the early afternoon. The day had finally arrived. Booth and his gang would make history today. He informed them that Lincoln was expected at the Campbell Hospital for the play *Still Waters Run Deep,* which was to be performed for the wounded soldiers there. The Campbell Hospital was on the southern outskirts of town along a rural, sparsely populated road. It was also close to the Navy Yard Bridge crossing into southern Maryland. David Herold was dispatched south over the Navy Yard Bridge with the Spencer carbines, rope, various weapons, and a monkey wrench. Why a monkey wrench? It would be needed to remove the wheels from Lincoln's coach once it was rolled onto the fifteen-passenger boat hidden in Nanjemoy Creek. Armed to the teeth, the team headed down Seventh Street to a rural section near the bridge and waited.

For about two hours they waited. Booth knew when the play was scheduled to begin and that time had passed. Keeping the group in place, he rode to the hospital to determine what had delayed Lincoln. Booth found a friend, E. L. Davenport, at the hospital who told him that Lincoln had changed his plans at the last minute and would not be coming. A crestfallen Booth returned to his action team with the bad news. The irony here is that Lincoln went to Booth's own hotel to attend a ceremony congratulating the 140th Indiana Volunteers for capturing a rebel battle flag.[5]

Not knowing the reason behind Lincoln's change in plans, the gang was spooked. They suspected that their plot had been discovered. Far worse, they stood in peril of immediate arrest. According to Louis Weichmann's testimony at the conspiracy trial, John Surratt arrived home first. He appeared much excited and carried a pistol in his hand. When Weichmann inquired as to the reason behind his upset, the response was "My prospects are gone, my hopes are blasted." Ten minutes later, Lewis Powell arrived. Weichmann noticed a pistol in his waistband. Following him moments later, Booth himself joined them, also very excited as he marched around the room, flicking his riding whip back and forth. At a signal from Booth the three young men went upstairs to talk and left the house shortly thereafter.[6] Arnold and O'Laughlen did not appear at the boarding house. We can conclude that they headed immediately for Baltimore, wanting nothing more to do with Booth or his plans.

Booth stayed in Washington one more day to perform in his last play, *The Apostate,* a benefit performance for his friend John McCullough. The next morning, March 19, he departed by train for New York City.

Later that same day, a letter was sent to John Surratt from R. D. Watson in New York City:

> Mr. J. H. Surratt
>
> Dear Sir
> I would like to see you on important business, if you can spare the time to come to New York. Please telegraph me immediately on the reception of this, whether you can come on or not & oblige. Yours tr—, R. D. Watson
>
> Ps Address Care Demill & Co 178½ Water Street[7]

The letter was found in Surratt's room after the assassination and is an important clue in this book. The short letter tells us several things: The first is that 178½ Water Street was a known mail drop for Confederate secret agents. The second is that R. D. Watson was surely a member, if not the leader, of "the New York Crowd" referred to in the missing Atzerodt confession found in the late 1970s and which provides vital information in this book. Watson lived previously in southern Maryland next door to Thomas Jones, who was the ranking agent for the Confederate government in the state of Maryland and who would later assist Booth and Herold in their escape attempt. Both the Watsons and the Joneses lived high on a bluff overlooking the Potomac River. Watson's house afforded an unobstructed view of the Potomac River for miles both south and west, and it was his sister who would place a mannequin in her window as a signal that the river traffic was clear of Union patrols. Finally, we can glean that Demill & Co. was a major supplier of the Confederacy in the blockade-running operations.

Did Surratt heed Watson's request and go to New York? Some evidence suggests he did, while other clues suggest he did not. Investigator Lafayette Baker followed up on this letter with a trip to New York to talk to Watson. Watson lied to Baker about several things, but he did not say that Surratt failed to come. Watson represented himself to Baker as a cotton speculator from Kentucky who wanted to explore with Surratt the possibility of selling some cotton languishing in the South. The story is somewhat believable to historians in that there was a plan to exchange cotton for pork.[8]

Contradicting the theory that Surratt went to New York is a clue arising from a telegram Booth sent to Weichmann asking about an obscure address. Weichmann did not understand the message but claimed that he took the telegram to Surratt on the twenty-third and Surratt understood the vague language quickly and perfectly. It is unlikely but possible that Surratt could have been in both New York City and Washington on March 23 if Surratt took the early train from New York.

Whether or not Surratt ventured to New York, we know that during Booth's stay at the city's St. Nicholas Hotel, there was one of those meetings without minutes. There is only a whisper of it in history books. We don't know who was present or what they discussed, but we do know it was held between March 20 and 23. We know that Sarah Slater arrived in New York on March 22 or 23. We can speculate based on what we know happened later that Watson, Lewis Powell, maybe John Surratt, and perhaps Sarah Slater were there. We do know that Booth left that meeting determined to make another attempt at Lincoln's kidnapping.[9]

Watson's telegram summoned Surratt to the meeting either at the request of Booth or because he was needed to escort Sarah Slater to Washington to meet Augustus Howell. From there, Slater would continue to Richmond to deliver dispatches from Gen. Edwin Lee to Judah Benjamin. On March 22, Gen. Edwin Lee wrote in his diary, "Fixed up and sent off my letter to Mr. B, and helped . . . to get the messenger off. I pray she may go safely."[10]

Based on the confession of George Atzerodt, which has been largely forgotten by history, we now come to important questions. Was it during this meeting that R. D. Watson told Booth about the New York team's ability to infiltrate the basement of the White House and plant explosives below the Cabinet Room or even perhaps the East Room? Did Watson ask Sarah Slater to inform Judah Benjamin that they needed an explosive expert and gunpowder?

We can draw some conclusions at this point. Surratt probably did not escort Slater from New York. As Weichmann testified at the conspiracy trial, he approached John Surratt with Booth's confusing telegraph, so it is more likely than not that John Surratt was in Washington that day. Booth, therefore, was the more likely candidate for Slater's companion. This would mean that Slater carried the news of the New York Crowd's capabilities of penetrating the White House, not John Surratt. Booth himself likely passed this information on to Slater. We know from Gen. Edwin Lee's diary that she left Montreal either on March 22 or 23, and it is unlikely that she attended the meeting at the St. Nicholas Hotel unless it occurred after she arrived on the twenty-third. It is also possible that she met with R. D. Watson before her return trip south.

Regardless of who escorted Sarah Slater from New York City to Washington, Louis Weichmann looked out the window of the boarding house as he was eating breakfast on March 25 and saw Sarah Slater, Mary Surratt, and her son John sitting in a fancy carriage out front. The Surratts and Sarah Slater were on the way to Surrattsville to connect with Augustus Howell, who would escort Slater the rest of the way to Richmond.

When they arrived at the tavern, John introduced Slater as "Mrs. Brown" to the proprietor, John Lloyd. Lloyd had some bad news. Augustus Howell had been arrested at the tavern the night before by Union cavalry and was on his way to the Old Capitol Prison. The trio discussed the situation. We don't know the conversation but there were obvious topics to discuss. The Union cavalry was on to the Surratts' tavern, and Slater had vital dispatches for Richmond. She couldn't stay, and she couldn't go back. John Surratt would have to escort her the rest of the way to Richmond.[11]

Once it was decided that John Surratt should act as Slater's escort the rest of the way to Richmond, they recruited David Barry, a former Confederate soldier, to accompany them to Port Tobacco. Barry would return the carriage to Washington. Mrs. Surratt caught an afternoon stage back to Washington the same day.[12]

That same morning, March 25, Gen. Robert E. Lee made his last attack of the war. Grant had stretched Lee's army to the breaking point by sliding to his left and attacking and closing the Southern general's supply lines. Lee's plan was to pressure Grant so that he would recall the troops who continued to strike beyond Lee's right flank. Lee chose the young, talented, and intrepid John B. Gordon to conduct the attack. Gordon had distinguished himself at the Battle of the Wilderness the year before with his tactical vision and skill. Now he had Lee's full confidence. Gordon was the pride and the future of the South. He would later become the mayor of Atlanta.

The Union's Fort Stedman was chosen for the attack because of its close proximity to not only the Confederate lines but also two close forts in either direction. The attack commenced at 4:00 A.M. with initial success. The jaded Confederate troops overwhelmed the surprised Union troops, who spread each way to the adjacent forts as planned. Problems developed from there. The Union recovered and poured artillery fire into the three forts, two of which afforded little protection at all, causing serious Confederate losses. Lee called off the attack at 8:00 A.M. Now with full daylight the Confederate troops would have to run a gauntlet of withering fire to retreat back to their own lines, and more than two thousand troops elected to surrender.[13] The loss of four to five thousand soldiers reduced Lee's forces to approximately thirty-six thousand men.

The next day as John Surratt and Sarah Slater approached Richmond, Robert E. Lee sent a report of the attack to Jefferson Davis. He closed the report by saying, "I fear now it will be impossible to prevent a junction between Grant and Sherman nor do I deem it prudent that this army maintain its position until the latter shall approach too near."[14] In Lee's diplomatic language, this message warned Jefferson Davis that there was only a brief time before the Dimmock Line had to be evacuated. Jefferson Davis's reaction is not recorded, nor do we have any record of him alerting members of his cabinet, but any president would be remiss if he failed to do so.

Any plan to kidnap Lincoln and bring him to Richmond was no longer viable. Confederate leaders now had more important priorities. They had to plan for an evacuation. What locomotives and railcars were available or could be brought to Richmond in a short period of time? How many coaches were needed to carry passengers? How many boxcars for freight could be found and what was their capacity? What could be taken and what records must be destroyed? What about the treasury? How much railroad stock must be allocated for that? How many people could these trains carry? A priority list must be prepared. What route would they need to take? What supplies must be forwarded ahead and where could they be safely stored? What food and military supplies were on hand and how much needed to be forwarded to Lee on his retreat? Where could those supplied be safely stashed?

All these preparations couldn't have taken place on Sunday, April 2, when Davis received Lee's evacuation message in church. Those contingency preparations had to have been made in advance.[15] Judah Benjamin would have been made cognizant of these plans if for no other reason than to determine what confidential records of their clandestine operations must be evacuated with the government or destroyed. There were many things that the Confederates could not allow to fall into Union hands. Even so, the Confederates left a gold mine of information behind. They also failed to send food to General Lee at Amelia Court House as planned. That blunder cost Lee his twenty-four-hour head start on Grant and ultimately led to his surrender at Appomattox. But that was still days away and no one in Richmond could know exactly when that day would come. The fact that the trains were in place and the Treasury, as well as the cabinet and their families, could organize themselves in less than a day attests to the fact that a contingency plan was in place.

Benjamin attended to one more detail before he left Richmond: the $649,000 in gold sitting in the Ontario Bank in Montreal. This sum was verified by head teller Robert Campbell in testimony before the military commission charged with trying Booth's co-conspirators. When Surratt and Slater arrived on March 29, this money had to have been uppermost in the secretary of state's mind.

John Surratt checked into the Spotswood Hotel on March 29, reserving only one room. According to his Rockville, Maryland, lecture in 1870, he met with an old friend, Harry Brogden, a signal camp officer just below Cawood's camp; Judah Benjamin's secretary Lucius Quintus Washington; and later with Judah Benjamin himself. Benjamin gave Surratt two hundred dollars in gold to take dispatches to Jacob Thompson in Canada regarding the transfer of the money in the Ontario Bank.

Surratt's story to the lecture crowd five years later is full of lies and omissions. He did not mention Sarah Slater at all. She was still in hiding in 1870, and he told his audience that the Confederate government had no knowledge or complicity in the Lincoln abduction at all. When Lucius Quintus Washington was summoned to testify at John Surratt's trial, he tried to cover for the Confederate agent with a story full of lies yet sprinkled with some truth. He said that Surratt appeared "mutton headed" and was not completely trusted. He admitted that Surratt carried a dispatch to transfer the funds in Canada to England and France, but he claimed that Surratt did not know the content of the dispatches.[16] He did not mention Slater either.

Surratt's role in transferring the funds makes sense, but Slater also had to have met with Benjamin as she had dispatches for him from Gen. Edwin Lee. What makes sense is that Benjamin met with both Slater and Surratt. They had been working together on a kidnapping plot for months, and Surratt surely would have told Benjamin about the aborted kidnapping attempt two weeks earlier. Slater would have delivered her letter from Edwin Lee along with the message from "the New York Crowd" requesting a demolition expert to detonate a bomb to blow up the White House and Lincoln and his cabinet along with it.

At that point, Benjamin would have told Surratt that a kidnapping plan was no longer feasible. Benjamin would have then proposed that taking out Lincoln and as many cabinet members as possible was the best possible plan. The men Booth ultimately targeted held crucial offices. If Booth killed the president, the vice president, and the secretary of state or the Senate's president pro tempore, he would behead the Union government. The secretary of state, by law, would be the one to notify the states to send electors to Washington to elect a new president and vice president. The president pro tempore of the Senate would temporarily hold the office of president if both Abraham Lincoln and Andrew Johnson were assassinated. That was the law at the time, enacted in 1792.[17] Benjamin, the attorney, would have known the order of presidential succession, even if Booth did not. Prior to early April, there is no evidence that Booth had ever considered targeting anyone other than Lincoln. It was another meeting without minutes.

On the same day that Surratt and Slater met Benjamin, Gen. Gabriel Rains, who oversaw the Confederate Naval Demolitions Department, selected a demolition expert, Thomas F. Harney. Rains sent Harney and two other men to Col. John Mosby for insertion into Washington, D.C., but the men did not leave until April 1. That was the important business R. D. Watson referenced in his letter to John Surratt. The fact that all of these events lined up on the same day (March 29) ties this conspiracy into a very neat package. There is no way that it is a coincidence.[18] It is very strong circumstantial evidence. All you would need to make this clear and convincing evidence is a confession. Wait! That comes later.

Other historians have also determined a connection between Harney's movements and Surratt's visit with Benjamin. In the words of William A. Tidwell, former U.S. intelligence officer and author of *Come Retribution,* "the connection of the Thomas Harney enterprise and the visit of Surratt and Slater with Benjamin is obvious."[19] General Rains would not have made the decision to blow up a portion of the White House on his own. That decision would have been above his pay grade. That should have been a presidential decision. If the decision were usurped, it only would have been done so by Benjamin, who oversaw Secret Service operations. While Jefferson Davis approved the kidnapping plot after the

Dahlgren raid, no evidence exists that he ever wanted to kill Lincoln. Benjamin knew the Confederate president would never approve of either the White House plan or a plot for Booth to kill Lincoln. It makes sense that if Benjamin ever told Davis, he didn't make him aware until much later, when it was too late to stop or recall the couriers.

These same couriers carried the dispatches transferring the Canadian money, and had they been stopped they never would have arrived in Montreal. The funds in the Ontario Bank were probably Benjamin's golden parachute. The curious thing about the money is that once Jacob Thompson deposited the funds in a Liverpool bank, it is impossible to tell what happened to it. Benjamin could have used some of the money for personal expenses and redeemed Confederate bonds sold in Europe earlier in the war. This move would have salvaged some influential friends who had seen their investments in the Confederacy reduced to zero. The Union tried to recover it in a lawsuit the next year, but we don't know for sure what happened after that.[20] Benjamin lived very frugally for several years after he reached England and seemed to struggle financially until his English law career flourished.

On April 1, 1865, fifteen hundred dollars was withdrawn to pay Surratt and Thomas Harney for their part in the plan. That was the day they left Richmond. We know that two hundred dollars was paid to John Surratt for his courier service, but this amount could have been paid from gold already in Benjamin's possession. Harney, presumably, needed money to buy gunpowder once reaching Washington. How much was paid to the demolition expert and his two associates is unknown.[21]

Fortunately, a paper trail on this fifteen-hundred-dollar withdrawal on April 1 exists. Duke University has the disbursal warrant number 1504 showing the transfer of funds from the Treasury Department to Benjamin. A ledger in the possession of the Chicago Historical Society lists all the gold withdrawals for "secret service" purposes, authorized each time by Jefferson Davis himself. This list is published in the appendages of *April '65,* written by William Tidwell and published by the University of Kentucky Press in 1985.[22]

Interestingly, Benjamin's withdrawal is the only one missing from Jefferson Davis's list.

The question arises, did Jefferson Davis know about this withdrawal or did Benjamin work around him with the help of Secretary of the Treasury George A. Trenholm? When the money ended up at a banking enterprise in Liverpool, England, the name Trenholm was supplied as one of the owners. It is also possible that the weekend of the evacuation from Richmond was so hectic that the cabinet failed to follow all the regular procedures. However, Davis's authorization probably would have occurred a day or two prior to the transfer, which would have resulted in this withdrawal being listed in the ledger. There was no atmosphere of chaos then. The most likely scenario is that Davis never knew of the withdrawal.

Later, Booth targeted either three or four Northern leaders. In addition to Lincoln, Booth's list included Andrew Johnson and William Seward. Ulysses S. Grant was also a potential target. An assailant tried to enter his railroad car but was unable to penetrate the general's security. It's not certain that this was one of Booth's assistants, but it makes sense that the attack was part of Booth's operation. Why were those four men the chosen ones? The reasons behind the planned attacks on Lincoln, Seward, and Andrew Johnson are obvious. But Grant did not figure into the presidential succession, and Booth had never mentioned any grievances against him. So why would he have become a target?

If Benjamin was responsible for the assassination order to Booth, personal grievances that have never been considered before may have been a factor. Outwardly, Benjamin was a jovial, cultured, pleasant, and well-mannered person. Even though he cultivated gentile friends and appeared to be ashamed of his Jewish heritage, he never disavowed his Jewish religion. He harbored personal grudges and privately internalized anti-Semitic insults, which were prevalent at the time, and especially despised those insults from the "hated Yankee."

While Benjamin was a U.S. senator, he engaged in heated debates over the slavery issue on the Senate floor. His frequent opponent was none other than William Seward. These debates

Apr. 1, 1865

WARRANT.
TREASURY.

No. 3504

APPROPRIATION.

"Secret Service"

TREASURY DEPARTMENT.

To the Treasurer of the Confederate States, Greeting:

PAY to Hon. J. P. Benjamin, Secretary of State

or order, out of the appropriation named in the margin,

Fifteen Hundred Dollars

In Gold

And for which sum the said Hon. J. P. Benjamin is to be charged and held accountable. For so doing, this shall be your WARRANT.

GIVEN under my hand and the seal of the Treasury, this 1st day of April in the year one thousand eight hundred and sixty-five

Secretary of the Treasury.

$ 1500

COUNTERSIGNED, Apr. 1. 65.

RECORDED,

Register.

Comptroller.

RECEIVED payment of the above Warrant, draft

No. 7488 on Jas. N. Bender Jr. $ 1500

Paper trail of money Benjamin gave to John Surratt ($200.00) and Thomas Harney (amount unknown). (David M. Rubenstein Rare Book & Manuscript Library, Duke University) were reported in almost all Southern newspapers, which greatly enhanced Benjamin's exposure and reputation, but created a personal enemy out of Seward. If he believed, like many Southern leaders, that Lincoln sent Ulric Dahlgren on the raid to kill the Confederate cabinet members (which included him) then Lincoln would have become a personal enemy too. In 1864, Sen. Andrew Johnson made public comments in the New York papers denigrating Benjamin as that "doubly-dyed traitor." The venom dripped from Johnson's comments.[23] In July 1861, Johnson lashed out at Benjamin in a speech. He said, "Mr. Benjamin, of Louisiana, one that understands something about the idea of dividing garments: who belongs to that tribe that divided the garments of our Savior, and for this venture cast lots—went out of this body [the U.S. Senate] and was made Attorney General, to show his patriotism and disinterestedness."

We finally come to Ulysses S. Grant. Grant, responding to complaints from Sherman that Jews were buying up cotton in his region and in doing so were aiding the rebellion, issued the infamous General Order No. 11 on December 17, 1862, which expelled every Jew in the Tennessee Department within twenty-four hours of receipt of the order.[24] Sherman's complaint was unfounded in singling out the Jews. A great number of gentiles engaged in this profitable practice, including officers in the Union army. Nevertheless, Benjamin must have been outraged by this highly publicized order. Benjamin could have had the expulsion of the Jews on his mind if he included Grant in the alleged order to kill Union government leaders. According to modern-day Grant scholar Curt Fields, Grant regretted that order for the rest of his life.[25]

All Civil War buffs know that the Confederates had to evacuate Richmond just a few days later, on April 2, 1865. Davis and members of the cabinet said emotional goodbyes to the friends left behind in Richmond. All but one of the members of the cabinet were dejected and morose. You guessed it! Judah Benjamin was the exception.[26] Chaos erupted and much of the town burned to the ground that night. General Lee slipped across the Appomattox River, destroyed the bridges, and stole a march on Grant, who was in Petersburg. Lee gained a single day's head start.

The next day Slater and Surratt arrived in Washington about 4:00 P.M. and checked into the Metropolitan Hotel. John arrived at his mother's boarding house a few hours later, at 6:30 P.M. Mother and son apparently had another covert meeting. Did he pass on Benjamin's order for Booth to kill the top three members of the Union government? Did he leave with her a message in cipher? We'll never know. We only know that he did not stay that night at his mother's. After Howell's arrest, he couldn't risk getting caught with the dispatch, and he probably preferred the company of Mrs. Slater.[27]

Early the next morning, Slater and Surratt took the train for New York City. There, they missed Booth again. He had headed to Boston for reasons unknown. While Surratt traveled on to Canada, Slater may have stayed behind to find Booth or R. D. Watson and deliver Benjamin's message, or she could have accompanied Surratt on to Montreal. We do know by Gen. Edwin G. Lee's diary that Surratt (under the alias Charley Armstrong) arrived in Montreal and delivered the dispatch from Benjamin.

Booth arrived back in Washington on April 8. On April 10, Ms. Annie Ward received a letter from John Surratt. She took the letter that evening to Surratt's mother at the boarding house. Booth was there. He asked to see the letter and noted the address.[28] There is evidence that while in Montreal, Surratt received a letter from Booth on April 12. Surratt easily could have returned a letter to Booth, which would have arrived on April 14. But although there is a smoking gun, there is no real evidence that Surratt or Slater passed the message to Booth along with the information that the Confederates had sent Thomas Harney to Washington to blow up Lincoln and his cabinet.

On the other side of the fence, Lincoln toured the battlefield of Fort Stedman in the immediate aftermath of the attack, March 26. He was shaken and saddened by the carnage. He watched as mangled corpses were carried behind the lines for burial and stretchers were loaded with the wounded. The living groaned and screamed in agony as their litters bounced up and down on the way to hospitals where their wounds would be probed by unsanitary medical tools or their limbs would be amputated, leaving them crippled for life if they were lucky. Lincoln had seen the same after Fort Stevens the previous July. He was anxious to see the brutality end.

On March 27, the president was reviewing troops with the handsome Mrs. C. C. Ord sitting next to him, both astride horses, as Mary Lincoln, Julia Grant, and Lt. Col. Samuel Badeau, Grant's military secretary, rode up to the reviewing stand. Mrs. Lincoln launched into a tirade over the audacity of Mrs. Ord's sitting next to her husband. Mrs. Ord, noticing the arrival of Mrs. Lincoln's carriage, had pulled her horse out of line and ridden forward to pay her respects, only to receive the insults of her life from the first lady in front of a gathering crowd of staff officers. Mrs. Lincoln called her every word in the book from "slut" to "whore." When Mrs. Grant tried to come to the aid of her friend, Mrs. Lincoln turned on her too, saying, "I suppose you want to get to the White House yourself, don't you?" When Julia Grant tried to placate her by saying she had never dreamed of the position she had reached already, Mary exclaimed, "Oh, you better take it if you can get it, it's very nice." The rift between those two would have greater consequences just three weeks later.[29]

The next day, Lincoln had a summit meeting with Grant, Commodore Horace Porter, and General Sherman, summoned from North Carolina. They met on the presidential yacht *River Queen*. The first part of the meeting was a review of the military situation. Grant led by remarking that he had recalled Gen. Philip Sheridan from the Shenandoah Valley and stood ready to strike Lee's supply lines. If they were successful, the attack would leave Lee no choice but to surrender. If Lee managed to retreat and tried to join Gen. Joseph Johnston in North Carolina, George Meade and C. C. Ord would be hot on his heels. Sherman assured Lincoln that if Lee joined Johnston, he could hold them off if Grant could reinforce him right away. Grant and Sherman were both convinced that when the Southern army was cornered, they would come out and fight an Armageddon of a battle.

Lincoln paled, remembering the horrors of the Fort Stedman battlefield. He groaned, "My God, my God, can't you spare more effusions of blood? We have had so much of it." After a pregnant silence Grant and Sherman assured Lincoln that the choice was not theirs.[30]

Then Sherman asked the most important question of the conference: what was to be done with the rebel armies when defeated? Lincoln replied, "All I want is to defeat the opposing armies and to get the men composing the Confederate armies back to their farms and shops." Lincoln also declared that he was ready for the reorganization of civil affairs in the South as soon as the war was over. He authorized Sherman to reassure Governor Vance and the people of North Carolina that once the rebel armies laid down their arms and resumed their civil pursuits, they would at once be guaranteed all their rights as citizens of a common country.[31]

Therein lies the real tragedy of this story. The South was plotting to rid the country of the one and only Northern leader with any empathy and concern for Southern citizens as well as the political skills and fortitude to carry it out. Lincoln's greatness was recognized worldwide at the time of his death. People abroad did not know of Lincoln's awkwardness, homespun humor, or crudeness. He was judged by his eloquent speeches, profound logic, and simple empathy for the common man. General Grant said at the army review a few days after the president's death, "He was incontestably the greatest man I ever knew." Even one of the greatest writers of his time, Leo Tolstoy, said, "Washington was a typical American. Napoleon was a typical Frenchman, but Lincoln was a humanitarian as broad as the world. He was bigger than his country—bigger than all the presidents put together. We are still too near to his greatness, but after a few centuries more our posterity will find him considerably bigger than we do. His genius is still too strong and too powerful for the common understanding, just as the sun is too hot when its light beams directly upon us."[32]

CHAPTER NINE

The Alibi

At 10:30 A.M. on April 6, John Surratt checked in to Montreal's St. Lawrence Hotel and was issued two rooms, room 13 and room 50. Surratt either secured a room for Sarah Slater for the sake of appearances or he expected her to arrive shortly after him. It would have been wise for them to travel separately over the border with duplicate dispatches in case one was caught. Later, he cancelled the reservation for room 13.[1] When he released the room, it may have meant that Slater never arrived, choosing to stay in New York City a while longer to wait for Booth or R. D. Watson, or that she and Surratt stayed in one room together. In times past, Slater had always checked in to her own room, whether or not she was with a male companion. Gen. Edwin Lee notes in his diary, "Letter by Charley from Mr. Benjamin; my last received all safe."[2]

The next day, Surratt visited a tailor shop owned by John J. Reeves, a Confederate sympathizer, and ordered a Garibaldi jacket and a pair of pantaloons. Gen. Edwin Lee had reputedly ordered him to scout Elmira, New York, to see if freeing the Southern prisoners of war there was a possibility.[3] However, the bright red Garibaldi jacket would not have been the right choice of clothing in which to scout. That style of clothing was something to get noticed in.

While waiting for the clothing, Surratt wrote at least two letters from Montreal. One was to his mother. That letter disappeared despite the government's later thorough searches. It was probably burned, meaning that something incriminating, by code, was likely in the letter. The other

letter was sent to Ms. Annie Ward, the woman who sheltered
Lewis Powell. Surratt obviously wrote that letter with
the understanding that it would later be examined by the
government or a jury.[4] Its language was general and in it
Surratt seemed to give up completely on the Southern cause.
As related in the previous chapter, that letter was carried to
his mother's boarding house and shown to Mrs. Surratt and
others on the evening of April 10. By chance Booth was there,
and he asked to see the return address on the letter.

At his Rockville lecture in 1870, Surratt stated that he
received a letter from Booth on April 12.[5] After receiving this
letter, Surratt took the train to New York. Whether he took the
train to New York City or Elmira, New York, isn't clear. But it is
clear that he arrived in Elmira the next day, Thursday, April 13,
dressed in his fancy new jacket and checked into the Brainard
House as John Harrison. Five witnesses testified at his 1867
trial that they saw him the day before and the day after the
assassination. That conspicuous, eye-catching Garibaldi jacket
probably saved Surratt's life. Although many witnesses testified
that they saw Surratt in Washington on the day Lincoln was
assassinated, the testimony from those in Elmira, coupled with
Surratt's letter to Ms. Ward, obviously provided the reasonable
doubt as to his whereabouts on the fateful April 14.

John Surratt was young but not stupid. He must have had
reason to believe that an assassination would be attempted,
and he took pains to establish an alibi that placed him too far
away at the time to be complicit in any murders. As a resident
of Washington, he would have known the impact on the North
of losing not only Lincoln but also the entire cabinet. It would
not have taken a genius to know that Yankee retribution would
be swift and far reaching. If Booth succeeded in carrying out
the plan, Surratt knew he eventually would be linked to his
co-conspirator.

There has been speculation that Surratt may have had just
enough time to jump through hoops and reach Washington on
April 14, but this author views that as highly unlikely. Surratt
could not have known exactly when the assassination would
occur and may not have even known who would attempt

it. Booth himself didn't learn that Lincoln would attend the theatre until almost noon on April 14. In the view of this author, by preponderance of evidence, Surratt was in Elmira awaiting word that the assassination had been completed. He had no way of knowing that Booth would use his mother to carry messages for him that day or that Louis Weichmann would turn state's evidence against the co-conspirators.

I believe that if Surratt had been in Washington that day, Booth would have assigned him to murder Vice President Johnson or at the very least accompany George Atzerodt on the mission. Booth's biggest failure, as far as planning, was not properly casing Johnson's hotel suite at the Kirkwood Hotel. Many people have surmised that George Atzerodt was a poor excuse for a man and a coward, but I'm not so sure. It takes courage to row across a wide river with contraband of every sort and in all kinds of weather, knowing that if you are caught, you will probably hang. Atzerodt's courage may have failed when he realized that Vice President Johnson's suite was directly behind the check-in clerk's counter. Atzerodt would have had to kill two people, not one, and killing the first one would alert the second. Killing the desk clerk would also attract the attention of the staff and patrons at the busy hotel, including the drinkers at the bar.

Gen. Edwin Lee's diary states that Surratt was absent from Montreal from April 12 through April 17 and that "Charley Armstrong" provided sketches of the prisoner compound along with the needed intelligence to discourage any attempt to free the prisoners. This diary entry is somewhat suspect as this information could have been put in much later, maybe even just before Surratt's trial in 1867. Further, Jacob Thompson already had turned in a report back in December saying that it would be foolhardy to attempt the type of operation Surratt was ostensibly scouting. Michael Schein, author of *John Surratt: The Lincoln Assassin Who Got Away,* did a very good job covering this subject in chapter ten of his book. All of this was misdirection, but Surratt's efforts paid off two years later. With not only the federal government's top prosecution team but also Judge George P. Fisher against

John Surratt as he was dressed in Elmira, New York.
(Brady-Handy Collection, Library of Congress)

him, Surratt's precautions taken on the days of April 13-15 proved to be an insurmountable alibi.

But Surratt's actions tell us more. They tell us that he knew something would happen to the Union leaders and that he didn't want to be part of it. He was willing to participate in a war-saving kidnapping that would make him a hero but not kill off the entire Union leadership, which would make him a villain. His actions also tell us that it was apparent to him that even if the Union government were decapitated, it would not change the outcome of the war. As young as he was, it's clear that he carefully thought things through once Lee had surrendered and the capital had been evacuated.

In his book, Michael Schein suggests that Sarah Slater traveled with John Surratt over the Canadian border disguised as a man and they concluded a sizzling love affair during the summer months of 1865. Maybe she did and maybe she didn't and from my perspective, it doesn't matter. After any messages and dispatches were delivered, both ran fast and far and Slater virtually disappeared. She showed remarkable maturity and judgment both before and after the assassination by keeping a low profile and hiding under different married names.[6] She married several times after she divorced Rowan Slater in New York City the following year. Sarah Slater was one of the true spies who got away. She was arrested and held for a few days but released. Although the Union had Weichmann's testimony regarding her courier activities, he did not tie her directly to the conspiracy. She admitted nothing except a connection to a blockade runner.

Later, we will read about John Surratt's statements to others when he thought he was safe and talking to fellow Southerners. Sarah Slater never made that mistake. That may tell us something. Maybe she delivered a message to Booth in New York City. It is pure speculation but that may clear up the question of why Booth was committed to murder when he returned to Washington on April 8.

CHAPTER TEN

The Final Days

On Tuesday, April 11, Mary Surratt had Louis Weichmann drive her to the Surrattsville tavern to try to collect a debt owed by a local farmer, John Nothey. She was being pressured to satisfy a debt of her own and needed the money from Nothey to pay it. Along the road to Surrattsville, she passed her tenant, John Lloyd, heading in the other direction. According to Lloyd's testimony during the conspiracy trial, Mary Surratt led him out of hearing from the others and instructed him to get the "shootin' irons" out. They would be needed soon.[1] This story was backed up at the trial by Louis Weichmann.

Mary Surratt was referring to the two Spencer carbines that Booth had purchased in New York City back in November. Booth had first left his weapons with Samuel Arnold, but they were eventually brought to Washington, and John Surratt had taken them to the tavern. When the kidnapping attempt occurred on March 17, David Herold was sent south to retrieve them along with other supplies from the tavern. Herold had obviously returned them there for safekeeping. John Surratt hid them in the rafters in case the tavern was searched by Union forces. Mrs. Surratt's intent then was for John Lloyd to remove the weapons from the rafters so that they would be ready at a moment's notice.

Her conversation helps us to infer that Booth had passed this instruction on to Mary Surratt, making her a messenger for his action team. In the eyes of the law, this was a major point in proving her to be a co-conspirator, subject to the death penalty. It is highly unlikely that her son John knew in advance that Booth would involve her in this way. It stands to reason that if he would go to great lengths to distance himself from Booth on the plot to murder, he would have taken the same precautions for his own mother. If, on the other hand, he had left the message from Benjamin with her to give to Booth, then he would have implicated her himself. In all probability, John Surratt didn't give much thought to the consequences of his mother's passing on that message. The extent of her involvement would have been impossible to prove without testimony from Booth. If the message was in writing, it was burned; if it was verbal, no proof ever existed.

The evening before a crowd had gathered on the front lawn of the White House to hear a speech from President Lincoln. He spoke from the balcony of the executive mansion. The crowd was in good spirits as they were celebrating the surrender of Robert E. Lee's army. Lincoln had prepared his remarks to inform the public of some of his plans for postwar America. Booth and Powell were in the crowd listening. Near the end of the speech, Lincoln announced that he wanted to allow the most educated blacks as well as black Union soldiers to vote. Booth was infuriated by this. He ordered Powell to take out his pistol and shoot Lincoln on the spot. Powell looked around at all the people and wisely declined. As Booth and Powell walked away, Booth made a prophetic statement: "That is the last speech he will ever make."[2]

The same evening, many miles to the south in Greensboro, North Carolina, the Confederate government on wheels assembled in a railroad car for a council of war. On the run, they were dodging Union forces that were attacking and threatening the very railroad on which they were traveling, and they were receiving a chilly reception from the city itself. Greensboro had never been enthusiastic about secession and feared reprisals from Gen. George Stoneman's cavalry troops, reported to be headed in their direction. Jefferson Davis managed to secure board in half of a modest house owned by John T. Wood, Davis's first wife's nephew. The rest of the cabinet huddled in their train cars and did their best to make themselves comfortable, with the exception of the wealthy

George A. Trenholm. Trenholm was hosted by a banker angling to convince the Treasury secretary to exchange the banker's war bonds for some of that gold sitting in one of the boxcars.

Before leaving Danville, the cabinet had heard vague reports of Lee's surrender at Appomattox. There were no details on whether some part of the army had been surrendered or all of it. If some remained, they might be able to effect a junction with Joseph Johnston and perhaps win a victory. Gen. P. G. T. Beauregard, coming north from General Johnston, arrived before the travel-weary cabinet. After the cabinet arrived and settled in, Beauregard crossed the tracks to pay his respects to President Davis. Davis greeted him warmly, asking for news of Johnston's situation around Raleigh. Beauregard reported that Johnston had hurriedly evacuated Smithfield under pressure from Sherman and he was moving toward the state capital, which he did not intend to defend since Sherman outnumbered him three to one. Beauregard pointedly said the situation was hopeless. Davis was nonplussed, replying that Lee's surrender had not been confirmed yet. He hoped that some portion of his army might have escaped that could reinforce Johnston. The Confederate president dashed off a telegram to Johnston asking the general to come up and confer with him on his upcoming movements.

Johnston arrived the next morning, April 12, the fourth anniversary of the firing on Fort Sumter. He expected to give Davis a status report on his military capability to stop Sherman. Instead, he sat in amazement as Davis was more interested in giving him orders than informing himself of the situation. He ordered Johnston and Beauregard to begin rounding up deserters and conscripting more men to beef up the army. The two generals protested that these men who had previously demonstrated their reluctance to serve would be even more reluctant to do so now. Johnston then took the opportunity to ask permission to seek a truce that might lead to a conclusion of the conflict. Davis immediately rejected this move. He said a truce would have a demoralizing effect on the troops who had shown no disposition to surrender and that they should have no reason to suppose that the government contemplated violating its trust. The three men were at an impasse, agreeing to wait until John C. Breckinridge arrived from Virginia to report on the events of Lee's surrender.

During the afternoon, news poured in by telegraph. For President Davis, all of it was bad. James Wilson was riding unopposed into Montgomery, where Davis had been sworn in as president four years earlier. Montgomery, Alabama, had been the Confederacy's first capital. Edward Canby had entered Mobile that very morning, after it was abandoned by Dabney H. Maury, who retreated to avoid capture. Sherman was closing in on Raleigh, North Carolina, and would occupy it the next day. George Stoneman's raiders had bypassed Greensboro, striking at Salisbury, unaware that the Confederate government was virtually trapped at Greensboro. Stoneman had destroyed railroad bridges both north and south of Salisbury, which robbed the Confederate government on wheels its ability to ride the rails with speed, ease, and comfort. Fortunately, Davis had sent the Treasury cars on to Charlotte before Stoneman destroyed the bridges. Within a day of resuming his journey, Davis would have to resort to horseback and carriage before the swiftly closing Union cavalry forces.

Such bad news should have revealed to everyone in the traveling party that the end was here. Secretary of War John C. Breckinridge didn't arrive until after nightfall, so the war council did not reconvene until the morning of April 13. This time the entire cabinet was there except for the ill Trenholm. After Breckinridge reported that Lee had surrendered his entire army, the group agreed that the time to surrender was at hand. All except Jefferson Davis and Judah Benjamin.[3] Davis finally relented somewhat by dictating a letter to be signed by Joseph Johnston asking Sherman for a temporary suspension of active operations to allow the civilian authorities to enter into the needful arrangements to terminate the war. The meeting ended with Johnston returning to his retreating army and Davis making arrangements to continue his trip south.

Even knowing Jefferson Davis's intransigent personality, it is hard to understand him taking such an uncompromising position. At best, he was stalling for time. But what would that accomplish? Jefferson Davis was a West Point graduate. He had to know when any chance of victory was gone. But was there still a chance of victory? One that he could not afford to disclose? One clue here is who voted no with him: Judah Benjamin. Had Benjamin told him about the White House demolition plan and the Booth assassination plan? Once the train left Richmond, Benjamin would have had ten days to confer with Davis about the secret operation he had ordered and that there was a real possibility of the Union losing its entire leadership cadre. It was too late to recall the messengers. Whatever was going to happen was going to happen. All they had to do was wait. Benjamin easily could have withheld the information that he had transferred the money to Europe. It was a relatively small detail in light of current events and the amount of gold traveling with the train. It was small to everyone but Benjamin.

Back in Washington, Booth told a friend, Edward Person, that "he had the biggest thing on his hands that had ever turned up."[4] That doesn't sound like something Booth had concocted; it sounds more like an order that he was expected to carry out. If the assassination had been his idea, the statement would be more like "I've got on my hands the biggest thing that I've ever thought up." Booth had an ego that was larger than life. He would have never given the credit for something of this magnitude to someone else if it was in fact his own idea.

One thing is clear. By April 13, his task was unequivocal. There was no turning back. The plan was going forward. Now he had to wait for the right moment.

Celebrations had gone on all week with cannons booming during the day and fireworks continuing at night. Thursday night promised to bring the nightly illumination to a climactic end. Word had filtered through the government offices that Good Friday would be a holiday and any employee could take off to give God thanks for their hard-earned victory. No doubt Booth had gotten wind of this and expected Lincoln to spend his holiday at the theatre as he had countless times before. Theatres were his home ground, and Booth was forming a plan to attack the president there before a large crowd to feed his ego. He would then rely upon his knowledge of the terrain to help him escape.

That day, Booth visited Grover's Theatre and inquired of the owner, C. D. Hess, if Lincoln planned to attend his theatre the following evening. The owner thanked Booth for reminding him and said he would inquire of the president whether he would attend.[5] Booth next approached Ford's Theatre. Getting information from Ford's Theatre was never a problem. That was Booth's home away from home. He was friends with everyone there and could learn anything from them he desired. Then either Booth or Lewis Powell visited the home of Secretary of State William Seward and talked with a nurse, inquiring as to Seward's health after a carriage accident, all along casing the house. Seward, too, was in Booth's plans. With their preparations completed, the two men waited.

The city's grandest hotel, Willard's, received two distinguished guests that Thursday afternoon, General and Mrs. Ulysses S. Grant. Grant intended to pay a visit to President Lincoln the following day and make plans to reduce the army. When Mary Lincoln heard that they had arrived, she began planning a theatre party at Ford's for the general and his wife. Speculation buzzed throughout the capital. No doubt, Booth heard about this too. What he did not know was how Julia Grant felt about Mrs. Lincoln. Her tantrum at City Point three weeks prior would figure prominently in the events to follow.

Friday morning came quietly after Thursday evening's dazzling fireworks shows and serenades at the homes of government officials. Bright and cheerful bunting draped almost every window. As one wit said in a local newspaper, "Anyone caught sober on the streets would be arrested." Many of the government clerks slept in because of the holiday. By 10:00 A.M., though, the streets began coming to life.

The day started much earlier in the White House. Lincoln was at his desk by 7:00 handling his never-ending paperwork. After an hour, he joined his family for breakfast. His oldest son, Robert, was home from the war with tales to tell of the surrender of General Lee at Appomattox. Robert served on Grant's staff and was present at the surrender ceremony. After sharing details of the event, he showed his father a photograph of General Lee. Lincoln took his time in cleaning his glasses and studied Lee's face carefully. "It's a good face," he declared. "I'm glad the war is finally over."[6] After breakfast, Lincoln returned to his desk and agonized over pardon requests for young soldiers awaiting a firing squad for desertion, leaving their guard posts, or profiting from the existing bounty laws. Many had sold their services for three hundred dollars to fight in the place of other men. At this point, Lincoln did not want anyone else to die and acted accordingly.

At 11:00 A.M. the cabinet meeting began with everyone present except William Seward, who was recovering from his carriage accident. He was represented by his son. The guest of honor was Gen. Ulysses S. Grant, fresh from the Appomattox surrender. After he provided a full report, talk drifted to reconstruction details. Stanton had a plan to unite Virginia into one military district. Lincoln and others vetoed that idea, insisting on maintaining the integrity of the states.

Sometime during the meeting, Lincoln brought up a dream that he had had the night before. It was a recurring dream, he said. He was in some vessel moving rapidly toward an indistinct shore. He told the cabinet that every time he had experienced that dream, something great had happened. He'd had that dream before Sumter and before several battles, all of which had been Union victories, including Stones River. Grant replied that Stones River was certainly no victory. Lincoln nodded but said, "Regardless, he expected General Johnston to surrender to Sherman." The dream could mean no other.[7]

Lincoln did not tell them of another dream he had had three nights before. He dreamed that he had awoken to hear weeping downstairs and had gone down to discover what was the matter. He entered the East Room, where there were many people and a catafalque with a flag-draped coffin resting on the platform. There was a military guard there and Lincoln had asked the guard, "Who is dead? Who is dead in the White House?" "The President" came the answer. "He was assassinated."[8]

Lincoln was guarded that day by his friend William Crook. On more than one occasion, Lincoln warned Crook that people wanted to kill him. Lincoln seemed to have some mystical intuition of doom. Perhaps it was because of his dreams. Apparently, security bothered him more and more as the day wore on. He went to the War Department later that afternoon and asked Stanton to provide him the guard services of his assistant Thomas Eckert for the theatre that night. Stanton refused, saying that he could not spare Eckert that evening. He was working on an important project. The answer was a bald-faced lie. Two years later, Stanton would deny that the incident ever took place. But Crook and a telegraph operator who heard the conversation both swore that it did. Likely, this was Stanton's way of discouraging Lincoln from attending the theatre. We'll never know, but that was a skeleton rattling around Stanton's closet for the rest of his days. There would be one more.

Lincoln's need for more security that night rose when he learned that Grant would not attend the theatre with him and Mary. The reason for Grant's desire to leave Washington is clear. Julia wanted no part of Mary Todd Lincoln. About 4:00 P.M. the Grants headed to the train station to depart for Pennsylvania to visit their children. They passed a man sitting astride his horse talking to someone else. After they passed, the horseman galloped ahead of them and then wheeled his horse and walked slowly back, peering intently into the covered carriage. Julia later identified the horseman as John Wilkes Booth.[9]

It was a busy day for Booth once he learned that the Lincolns were attending Ford's Theatre. The plans were fast tracked. He met with Mary Surratt, sending her on an errand to take his field glasses to her Surrattsville tavern and carry another message to John Lloyd to have the Spencer rifles ready at a moment's notice. Mary Surratt told Lloyd that men would come for them later that night. Driving her down to her tavern was the government's future star witness,

Louis Weichmann. On the way home that evening, Mary Surratt and Weichmann stopped on a hill overlooking the city of Washington, which was still shooting off fireworks in celebration. Mary watched for a moment in silence and then uttered, "I am afraid that all this rejoicing will be turned into mourning and all this gladness to sorrow." Weichmann asked her what she meant. Her answer was that the people were too proud and licentious, and God would punish them.[10]

At the theatre, Booth cut a small board from a music stand and placed it behind the doorway of the hall leading to the boxes where Lincoln would sit. A niche was cut into the plaster so that the board could be wedged against the door, keeping it closed and preventing access to the hallway and the boxes from the dress circle (balcony). Legend has it that Booth also bored a hole that afternoon in the door looking into the box from the hallway, but in fact that hole was bored by John Ford's brother so that Lincoln's guard could peep through. It allowed him to see in without opening the door and disturbing the Lincolns.[11] Theatre employee Edman "Ned" Spangler would get the blame for it along with a prison sentence. The military commission who conducted the trial of the conspirators just assumed that he was responsible despite a lack of evidence.

Around four that afternoon, Booth ran into a friend, John Matthews, to whom he gave a letter to mail the next day to the editor of *The National Intelligencer*. He intended for the entire world to read it, but unfortunately, we will never know its contents. After the assassination, Matthews read the letter twice and destroyed it, afraid that possession of the letter would implicate him.[12]

Early that morning, Booth had moved George Atzerodt to the Kirkwood Hotel, where Andrew Johnson lived. Sometime in the late afternoon, Booth personally visited the lobby of the hotel, asking for the vice president. He left a note saying, "Don't wish to disturb you. Are you at home?" This move has confused historians for years. Why would Booth visit an intended victim? That's a difficult question to answer. They had met some years before, and Booth had no animosity towards him. Was he reconsidering? If not, and Booth was simply casing the hotel for Atzerodt, he did a very poor job. It is also possible that Booth left the card for Johnson's aide, William A. Browning, with whom Booth was likewise acquainted, and the hotel clerk put the card in Johnson's box instead of Browning's. Was Booth hoping to glean information about Andrew Johnson from Browning? We will never know for sure.

About 3:30 in the afternoon Booth met an unidentified woman in the alley behind Ford's Theatre. Two different free black women who lived in separate houses abutting the alley testified at the conspiracy trial to this meeting. Both women said that Booth pointed down the alley more than once, as if he was going through escape plans with this mystery woman.[13] Booth was also seen having breakfast at Willard's with two unidentified women about 10:00 that morning.

Between 4:00 and 4:15 P.M., Booth rented a fast steed for his getaway. He also visited stables holding the two horses that he owned and arranged to rent a fourth horse from stableman John Fletcher. Fletcher knew Booth, John Surratt, David Herold, and George Atzerodt. Each of them had rented horses from him before. When his horse was not returned on time that evening, it would be Fletcher who would go to the police and help them connect the names of the conspirators.[14]

At 7:00 P.M., Booth met Atzerodt, Herold, and Powell at the Herndon House to go over the plan one last time. The time to strike would be 10:15 P.M. Herold would guide Powell to Seward's house and hold the horses while Powell went inside with a package purported to be medicine and kill Seward. Atzerodt would stay in or near his room at the Kirkwood and kill Andrew Johnson, while the job of killing Lincoln was saved for Booth himself.[15] Shortly thereafter, they would cross the Navy Yard Bridge and meet several miles down the road on Soaper's Hill, ride to the Surrattsville tavern, pick up supplies and weapons, and then escape across the Potomac River to the friendly confines of Virginia before dawn.

It is obvious to this author that Powell and Herold already knew which jobs they would be assigned. Herold had to have known that Seward's doctor was F. S. Verdi for their subterfuge to work, and Powell had already cased the house the previous day.[16] Whether Atzerodt knew in advance that he was expected to kill Andrew Johnson is unclear. In his lost confession to Baltimore detective James McPhail, he claims that he did not, but that statement must be taken with a grain of salt. Atzerodt could have been lying and for good reason. It's the other details in that lost confession that lend credibility to Atzerodt's words.

The biggest question not discussed so far is at what point did Booth expand the plot to include Andrew Johnson and William Seward. It's easy to understand why, but it's difficult to believe that Booth was politically sophisticated enough to plan a complete breakdown in the Union government with just three murders. The constitutional law of succession at the time provided that if both the president and vice president were dead, the House of Representatives would choose a president while the president pro tempore of the Senate temporarily held the president's office. The procedure required the secretary of state to notify the states to send electors to Washington. The House could not elect a new president until they had chosen a secretary of state.[17] That first step could take weeks of wrangling and politicking and would leave the nation leaderless for quite a while. The old familiar Watergate question now arises. How did Booth know this and when did he know it? Booth wasn't a lawyer. He had not spoken of any grievances against either Seward or Johnson before. Yet he now had a plan that, if successful, would cripple the North.

When you look at his Confederate connections though, you find clues as to who may have provided this knowledge. It was either George Sanders, whom he met in October of 1864, or Judah Benjamin, who would have known the constitutional law and transmitted it to Booth through John Surratt or Sarah Slater that very month. Which one is more likely? Booth never mentioned a similar plan after meeting Sanders in Montreal in October, and we have no proof that they ever met again. Booth's source is more likely, in this author's view, to be Judah Benjamin, who provided the information when he met with Surratt and Slater. This conclusion is reached not from just this piece of logic but events and circumstances to follow.

Counting Ulysses and Julia Grant, a total of fourteen people turned down the Lincolns to attend the play that night. As the afternoon progressed, Lincoln seemed more and more reluctant to attend the play, but he did not want to disappoint Mrs. Lincoln or the public. He obviously had no faith in Crook's replacement for the evening, Washington police officer John Parker. Whether Lincoln ever knew of Parker's poor performance record is not recorded. Whether Parker was three hours late to report to duty that evening is unclear. What is certain is that Parker went ahead of the Lincolns to the theatre and was there to greet the carriage when it arrived about 8:20 P.M. Where Parker went after that is also not clear, but we know that he was not outside the box or in the hallway leading to the box. He was nowhere to be seen. Lincoln only had his unarmed carriage driver, Charles Forbes, sitting outside his box for protection. An assassin never had an easier path to an American president. With his fame, Booth might have been able to penetrate the box regardless of the number of guards, but after the shooting, escape would have been more difficult, if not impossible.

CHAPTER ELEVEN

The Great Tragedy

There were times in the war when momentous events were influenced by seemingly small details. One such small incident occurred on September 13, 1862. Union private B. W. Mitchell of the Twenty-Seventh Indiana Infantry picked up three cigars wrapped inside of a paper at Gen. D. H. Hill's bivouac area in Frederick, Maryland. A small detail.

At that time, the Confederate army was on a winning streak and could do no wrong. They had pushed George McClellan back from their own capital with the Seven Days Battles, crushed the hated Gen. John Pope at Second Manassas and sent him packing for the Indian Territories, crossed the Potomac River into enemy territory for the first time, and threatened Washington, D.C. from the north. A sizable victory now could win European recognition, perhaps seize the Union capital, and win the South's independence. If they ever had a chance to overcome the staggering logistical advantage of the North, this was the time. McClellan was back in command and there was no Union commander who was slower, more cautious, or more deliberate than he. Lee must have privately held him in utter contempt. Why else would he divide his army into not two, not three, not four, but five separate columns to invade the North and surround Harpers Ferry? There he planned to pick up a big prize that included twelve thousand men and a vast supply of war material and re-concentrate his forces before McClellan knew what hit him.

Most of the time the plan would have worked, but not this time. The paper found wrapped around Pvt. B. W. Mitchell's cigars was a copy of Special Order No. 191, which detailed Lee's entire battle plan. Union commander George B. McClellan might have been slow and cautious, but he did know enough to recognize that Lee had violated every strategic maxim in dividing his forces in this reckless manner. He moved with lightning speed, for him, and approached Lee on September 16 at Sharpsburg while the Southern forces were still divided. He squandered the entire day waiting for all of his own forces to arrive before attacking the next morning. By then, Lee had managed to recall Stonewall Jackson and managed a hard-fought battle that came to be known as Antietam. It wasn't exactly a victory for the Union, but when Lee retreated back into Virginia, Lincoln considered it enough of a success that he issued the Emancipation Proclamation, which was a major turning point in the war. All of this happened because a careless courier dropped a duplicate copy of an order, which Private Mitchell found wrapped around three cigars.[1]

Another small detail emerged the next year, following the battle of Gettysburg. On July 5, 1863, Gen. Robert E. Lee retreated from the costly battlefield with his army, now reduced to thirty-five thousand effectives, and followed a seventeen-mile-long wagon train of his wounded. Not only was his army whittled in half, but he was almost out of artillery ammunition and food. They traveled through the rain toward Williamsport where, supposedly, a pontoon bridge awaited. But a Union raiding party had destroyed the bridge and the usually tame Potomac River was a raging white-water monster that no one could ford. Lee was trapped north of the Potomac with a reduced army and almost no artillery ammunition with which to oppose a slow-approaching, angry, and victorious Union army determined to expel the invading foe.

George Meade was the new Union commander, just two weeks on the job, who complained to his wife that he hadn't even had time to wash his hands in days, let alone eat and get a good night's sleep. He confided to her that he had aged thirty years in just one week. Finally, on Sunday, July 12, as Lee was slowly getting his wounded across the still raging river and obtaining a little ammunition, Meade was on hand.

As he studied Lee's six-mile position, it was apparent that he had Lee trapped. A victory here could be the annihilation of Lee's army. The war would be virtually won! The experienced soldier readied the II, V, and VI Corps to attack as clouds gathered for more rain.

Then came another small detail. A Pennsylvania chaplain rode up and excitedly protested the violation of the Sabbath: "Couldn't the battle be fought tomorrow as well?" Meade, with remarkable patience, explained that he was like a carpenter building a box. He had completed four sides and a bottom. All that was needed now was to nail the lid shut. The chaplain was not impressed. He declared fervently, "As God's agent, I will show you that the Almighty will not permit you to desecrate his day. Look at the Heavens. See the threatening storm approaching?" On cue, several peals of thunder sounded and the heavens opened, showering the Union troops with a soaking rain. Meade was convinced and canceled the attack, deciding to wait until morning. He ended up waiting two days and allowed the fortunate Lee to escape in the night over the swollen rivers and live to fight another day. The chaplain's intervention is a minor detail now mostly forgotten, but Lee's army survived another twenty-one months as a result.[2]

Now two more minor details would change the course of history. Secretary of State William Seward, injured in a carriage accident and wearing steel neck braces that deflected Lewis Powell's knife thrusts, rolled off of his sickbed toward the wall to get away from his vicious and determined attacker. Meanwhile, Andrew Johnson's life was saved because Booth and Atzerodt had cased the wrong room. Those two small details prevented Booth from going three for three.

At approximately 10:15 P.M., David Herold and Lewis Powell arrived on horseback at the Seward home. Herold waited outside as Powell knocked on the door. Seward was convalescing from his accident, having suffered a broken jaw as well as other injuries. A manservant, William Bell, answered the door, and Powell showed him a brown paper package that he claimed was from Seward's physician, Dr. F. S. Verdi. Powell was to deliver it personally to Secretary Seward. The servant at the door told Powell that the secretary was already asleep and that he could leave the medicine with him. Powell raised his voice slightly and insisted that the medicine be administered at once. The old servant shook his head no and began to close the door. Powell used his strength to force the door and race up the stairs past the protesting servant.

The protests alerted Seward's son Frederick, who met Powell at the top of the stairs. Powell produced his pistol, aimed it at Frederick's head, and pulled the trigger. The gun misfired. Angered, Powell began pistol-whipping Frederick, cracking his skull twice and exposing his brain, ruining the pistol in the process.

Seward's daughter, Fanny, opened the door of her father's room, thus alerting Powell to the secretary's location. Powell charged into the room, knifing George Robinson, the nurse, and then falling over Secretary Seward on the bed as he repeatedly slashed Seward about the throat. Most of the blows were deflected by the metal braces protecting Seward's jaw. However, Seward suffered several deep knife wounds which would maim and scar him for life.[3] Another son, Augustus Seward, helped pull Powell off of his father and received seven knife wounds for his trouble. Seward did have the presence of mind to simply roll off the bed onto the floor as his family and Robinson, the wounded nurse, fought off

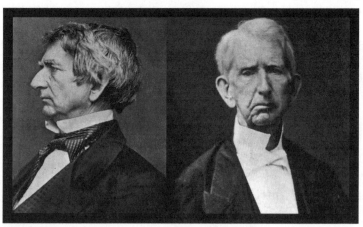

William Seward, before and after the assassination attempt. (National Archives)

the brute. The small act saved his life. Noticing that Seward had disappeared, Powell ran down the stairs screaming, "I'm mad" and plunged his knife into a messenger who had just arrived at the front door.

Powell burst outside to discover that his guide had abandoned him when the noise inside the house alerted passersby. In the melee, Powell had left behind his gun, knife, and slouch hat. He mounted his one-eyed horse and slowly walked away despite the screams of "Stop that man!" No doubt that was Mosby's training. Running away would attract attention to himself, but if he walked his horse, passersby would not know who the yells were aimed at. Good training notwithstanding, Powell was all alone in a strange city and unable to follow Herold and Booth to Soaper's Hill. He would hide in a tree for the next three days.[4]

George Atzerodt arrived at the Kirkwood Hotel and asked the desk clerk to direct him to Andrew Johnson's room. The clerk answered that it was right behind him and that Johnson had just arrived. Atzerodt headed to the hotel bar to think things over. That's as close to Johnson as he ever got. With all the lobby traffic, leaving a dead desk clerk would be a very bad idea. Atzerodt probably had no heart for murder in the first place and after a few drinks, he left the hotel. He threw his knife away on the street and found a flop house to stay overnight. He pawned his pistol the next morning, apparently afraid of being caught with it. Once sober, he escaped through the dragnet and left town, traveling north to find a relative.

Booth arrived at the rear entrance to Ford's Theatre around 9:30 P.M. He was dressed in black with thigh-high riding boots and carried a nine-inch Bowie knife and a .44-caliber derringer loaded with just one bullet.[5] It is amusing in a morbid way to contemplate what would have happened if Booth's pistol had misfired. Would he have tried to stab Lincoln to death despite the opposition of Lincoln's guest, Henry Rathbone? Could Rathbone have gotten the best of the assassin as he was trying to kill Lincoln? Would the escape have been affected? Booth left a navy Colt revolver in George Atzerodt's room at the Kirkwood Hotel. Why didn't he use that gun? Perhaps

Booth had the pistol professionally loaded. We'll never know.

Booth opened the back door and called for Ned Spangler. When Spangler arrived, Booth instructed Ned to hold his spirited horse's reins. But Spangler was busy working. It was his job to change and set the scenes used in the plays. As soon as Booth was out of sight, Spangler asked another theatre employee, Peanut John Burroughs, to hold the horse and Spangler got back to work. Since *Our American Cousin* was playing, the stage was in use and Booth descended steps to a crawl space beneath the stage that exited to an alley leading to Tenth Street at the front of Ford's Theatre. He walked next door to Taltavull's Saloon and ordered a drink, which he slowly nursed.[6]

Sometime after 10:00, he left the bar, entered the theatre, and climbed the stairs on the left side of the lobby to the dress circle (balcony). He strode quietly to the back wall and watched the play. Several theatre patrons noticed him. As the play progressed, he walked farther to his right until he stood near the hallway leading to the presidential boxes. Spying Lincoln's coachman, Charles Forbes, sitting in the chair nearest the hallway, Booth gave him his card, spoke a couple of words to him, and stepped inside the hallway and shut the door.[7] He then took the wood from the music stand and placed it in the niche in the plaster that he had carved earlier in the afternoon. The wood brace would prevent anyone from following him into the hallway. Kneeling down, he looked through the peephole into the presidential box and saw Lincoln sitting in a large rocker in the far left of the box with his wife, Mary, sitting next to him.

Booth waited a few moments until the stage only held one actor, Harry Hawke, who then issued the best laugh line of the play: "Don't know the manners of good society, eh? Well, I guess I know enough to turn you inside out, old gal—you sockdologizing old mantrap." As expected, the crowd roared, drowning out Booth as he stepped inside the box, pointed his derringer at Lincoln's head, who was looking down and to his left, and fired from four feet away. The bullet entered Lincoln's skull on the left side and traveled to the right, ending

Inside Ford's Theatre. (Library of Congress)

Outside Ford's Theatre. (Library of Congress)

just behind the president's right eye. Lincoln's head slumped down on his chest as he lost consciousness, never to regain it.

Maj. Henry Rathbone leaped from his sofa across the box and charged Booth. As he grappled with him, Booth slashed him with his knife, cutting him from elbow to shoulder, and pushed him back toward the sofa. With no further time to waste on Rathbone, he climbed the balustrade and leaped down eleven and a half feet to the stage.[8] Catching a spur on one of the draping flags, he landed awkwardly, breaking the small bone in his left leg about four inches above the ankle. Never one to waste the opportunity for a main-liner, he faced the audience, brandished his knife, and called out, "Sic semper tyrannis," Latin for "Thus always to tyrants" and the state motto of Virginia.

Turning to his right, he exited the stage and ran out the back door to his waiting horse. Seeing Peanut John instead of Spangler holding his horse, he struck Burroughs on the head with the butt of his knife, grabbed the reins, and swung onto his horse, just ahead of one theatre patron who had the presence of mind to follow and attempt to apprehend. Circling slightly to avoid the aroused citizen, Booth dug in his spurs and bolted down the alley into the darkness, leaving havoc behind.

Inside, screams arose from the box as men tried to open the door from the dress circle to the hallway. The wounded Rathbone finally unbarred the door from the inside, and army surgeon Charles Leale, wearing civilian clothes, rushed into the box to find Mary Lincoln sobbing and holding her husband's hand. Pushing her gently out of the way, Leale eased the unconscious Lincoln onto the floor and stripped him to the waist looking for wounds. He then checked for a pulse but found none. Lincoln was not breathing. Checking his head, Dr. Leale found the small hole in the back, clotted with blood. Using his little finger, Leale dislodged the clot and the wound began to bleed. With the release of pressure to the brain, Lincoln began to revive, breathing deeply with an ever-stronger pulse.[9] Another army surgeon, Charles Taft, arrived in the box and together they examined Lincoln from head to foot. A third doctor arrived and the men conferred. The wound appeared mortal. A decision was made not to return Lincoln to the White House over the rough cobblestone streets. But they needed to get him away from the theatre. Recruiting volunteers, they lifted Lincoln and carried him outside of the theatre, looking for a nearby house.

"Over here," someone yelled, and they headed for the Peterson House across the street as a squad of soldiers cleared the way through the crowd. Six men carried the president up the stairs and down a hallway to an empty bedroom and placed him diagonally across a bed too short for his six-foot, four-inch frame.

By this time Booth had made his way to the Navy Yard Bridge in the south-central part of the city. Using his own name and claiming that he was on his way home to Beantown, Maryland, he talked his way past Sgt. Silas Cobb, in charge of the squad guarding the bridge. This is the second time that we know of Booth using his real name instead of an alias when it might have served him better to assume another identity. The first time was on July 26 of the previous year, when he registered at the Parker House Hotel and likely met with Canadian Confederate agents. In providing his real name to Sergeant Cobb, he pointed the Union toward his escape route. By Saturday at noon Union troopers were within three miles of where he rested and convalesced at Dr. Mudd's house.

When Booth told Silas Cobb that he was going home to Charles County, perhaps that was the best he could offer under the stress of the moment. But I have a different view of the matter. Booth had to get across that bridge. He understood that he was well known, and an attempt to hide his identity would have aroused suspicion in any who recognized him. He couldn't chance Silas Cobb or one of his men holding him up and denying him permission to cross the bridge on that account. He was meeting his guide on this road, and his potential friends and allies were situated on the southern Maryland escape route. His only chance of a successful escape necessitated crossing that bridge. He would worry about pursuit later. The time between his shooting Lincoln and arriving at the bridge could have been no more than five minutes. The guards at the bridge would have had no way of knowing what had just transpired as orders to close the bridge would have taken at least an hour.

It is unlikely that Booth had not contemplated beforehand how he would get past the bridge's guards. Before he ever approached that bridge, he probably had decided not to misidentify himself. His remark that he was going home to Beantown was not uttered by chance either. Anyone in pursuit of him would have been misdirected and sent pursuers farther south than the boat hidden on Nanjemoy Creek.

Booth, probably still running on adrenaline, may not have realized that his leg was broken and at that time had no intention of going toward Dr. Mudd's Charles County home. He still could have planned to cross the Potomac that night with his co-conspirators, using someone, if not a member of his band, to ferry them across the river in Richard Smoot's boat hidden in Nanjemoy Creek. Only later, at Soaper's Hill, would it become apparent that Powell and Atzerodt would not be joining Booth and Herold. While he was waiting for them, Booth probably settled down some and experienced the pain from his broken leg. Only then would he have decided to visit Samuel Mudd and forever change the doctor's life.

Across town, as Secretary of War Edwin Stanton began to undress for bed, he was startled by his wife's screams from downstairs. Stanton called down the stairs, "Ellen, what's the matter?" The return cry intensified. "My God! Mr. Seward has been murdered!" Stanton's response was one of disbelief. He came down the stairs to see a messenger, who erroneously confirmed the news. Stanton ran outside to a carriage waiting nearby and directed the driver to Seward's home. There he met Secretary of the Navy Gideon Welles arriving at the same time. Welles revealed that he had heard that Lincoln had been shot as well. Both men ran upstairs to find Dr. Verdi treating Seward in his bed, which was saturated with blood. Once satisfied that Seward would survive, the two men headed for Ford's Theatre. Stanton's assistant, Thomas Eckert, followed the carriage as it fought its way through the crowded streets.[10] They arrived at the Peterson House shortly after 11:00. When Stanton saw

Lincoln's labored breathing, he knew the wound was mortal. He knew a death rattle when he heard one. "Damn the rebels!" he swore. "This is their work."[11]

Edwin Stanton stepped into the breach at the moment of crisis and took over nearly all government functions. Alongside Judge David Kellogg Cartter, he set up an investigation in one of the back rooms of the Peterson House and began interviewing witnesses with Union veteran and double amputee James Tanner taking down the testimony in shorthand. Tanner later would write to a friend that "within fifteen minutes, I heard enough testimony to hang John Wilkes Booth higher than Haman ever hanged."[12]

Stanton, though, was thinking like a commander in chief. He was more worried at the moment about what was to happen rather than what had already happened. He telegraphed notice of the assassination attempts to all military commanders in the field and police chiefs in the major cities. Through Thomas Eckert, he got a message to Grant on his train heading to Pennsylvania. By 4:00 A.M., Stanton had telegraphed his military commanders all over the country generally and in the areas surrounding the capital specifically to arrest all suspicious persons that could be connected to Booth.

There is no evidence that Stanton knew that night that Booth had escaped over the Navy Yard Bridge. He set a large dragnet in all directions. His first telegram was to the police chief in New York City, John Kennedy.[13] Stanton was thinking ahead and remembering November's attempted arson in New York City. He was taking steps to curb any further attempts by the rebels to create havoc.

Government officials would get early breaks in the case with the help of John Fletcher. Fletcher had rented David Herold a horse that afternoon with a warning to have him back at 9:00 P.M. About 11:00, Fletcher caught sight of Herold trotting his horse along Pennsylvania Avenue near Fourteenth Street. He shouted to Herold to return the horse, but Herold wheeled the horse away and took off down Fourteenth Street. Thoroughly convinced now that Herold intended to steal his horse, Fletcher ran back one block to his stable and saddled his own horse. Based on earlier information provided by Atzerodt, he headed for the Navy Yard Bridge.[14]

At the bridge, Silas Cobb verified that he had just missed Herold and another man who had crossed before him. Fletcher asked Cobb if he could pursue Herold. Cobb, following orders, would allow Fletcher to leave the city but he couldn't return until morning. Vexed, Fletcher turned around and headed to police headquarters to report his stolen horse. He reported to policeman Charles Stone. Stone replied that a horse had earlier been abandoned and was stabled at the Twenty-Second Army Corps Headquarters. As they walked toward the army headquarters, they were joined by Gen. Christopher Augur. At the headquarters, Fletcher saw a saddle he recognized. He couldn't remember the owner's name but knew he was a friend of Herold's, the same friend he believed Herold was joining across the bridge. Fletcher raced back to his stable to find the name and brought it back to Stone and Augur. The name was George Atzerodt.

By daybreak Metropolitan police officer John Lee was at the Kirkwood Hotel, guarding against an attack on Andrew Johnson. Lee asked the desk clerk and barkeep, Michael Henry, about any suspicious persons hanging around the hotel. They told him about a suspicious man who had checked in to room 126. Lee broke into the room and found a revolver and a coat. Inside a coat pocket, he found a bankbook with the name J. Wilkes Booth. When he checked the hotel register, Lee found the name George A. Atzerodt.

Now the police and General Augur could piece some things together. Herold was connected to Atzerodt and Atzerodt was connected to Booth. From Fletcher, they gleaned one more piece of information: all three were connected to John Surratt. Based at least in part on this information, General Augur dispatched a troop of the Thirteenth New York Cavalry across the Navy Yard Bridge under the command of David D. Dana. Dana arrived at the small village of Piscataway around 7:00 A.M. and learned from troops stationed there that no one had seen Booth and Herold during the night. Dana proceeded to Bryantown around noon and established his headquarters there. That was only about three miles from Booth, who was now resting at Dr. Samuel Mudd's house.[15]

Booth and Herold, after picking up their designated items at the Surrattsville tavern around midnight, arrived at Samuel Mudd's house about 4 A.M. It is unclear whether Booth or Herold told Mudd immediately about the assassinations, but what is undisputed is that Mudd set Booth's leg and rigged a set of crutches for him.

By daybreak War Department officers had entered and searched Booth's room at the National Hotel. There they found a letter from Samuel Arnold dated March 27, telling Booth to hold off on the enterprise until he had checked with R——d. In addition, they found a Confederate cipher which later proved to be keyed to a machine in Judah Benjamin's office in Richmond.[16] Other historians have not given much attention to this detail, but this book is all about Booth's connection to Benjamin. The presence of the key tells us that, in all probability, Benjamin sent a coded order to Booth via John Surratt and Sarah Slater. Surratt likely gave this coded order to his mother for safekeeping and delivery to Booth when he returned to town.

By the time the police found the cipher, the message was long destroyed, but the code device is a significant clue. John Surratt and Sarah Slater would not have brought the code device along with the message. That would have been folly. If caught, the Union would have in their possession not only the message but also the key to decipher it. It's probable that Booth had possession of this code device for quite a while, perhaps as far back as October. As you will read later in this book, Booth could have received the code device while he was in Montreal in October or perhaps even before that. The code overlay was 27 inches square and contained a series of letters. By overlaying the card on the cipher dispatch, the recipient could read the real message. We must ask ourselves, who would have had access to the overlays that could decode messages from Judah Benjamin's office?

Sometime during the night, with the help of John Fletcher, John Surratt was identified as one of the conspirators. About

2:30 A.M., Detectives James McDevitt and John Clarvoe led a raid on Mrs. Surratt's boarding house in Washington. While the detectives combed through the house, Mrs. Surratt's tenant Louis Weichmann sat in stunned horror after he discovered why they were there. John Wilkes Booth had assassinated President Lincoln and Secretary of State William Seward. And McDevitt and Clarvoe thought John Surratt was involved. Mrs. Surratt told them that John was in Canada and showed them a letter to prove it. After satisfying themselves with a search of the house, the detectives left. Weichmann, however, was sleepless for the rest of the night. By 7:30 A.M. he was at police headquarters telling everything he knew.[17]

All through the long, rainy night, Stanton, with the help of the military and the city police force, toiled to curtail further chaos from the rebels, discover who was involved, and restore order to the capital as Lincoln labored to breathe. The president's family and friends came and went, weeping as they left, knowing that the frantic efforts of the best doctors in town were in vain. Lincoln's pulse had dropped to fifty-four beats per minute and never rose higher. Gideon Welles sat at his bedside throughout the night as Dr. Charles Leale, Surgeon General Joseph K. Barnes, and other doctors tried mustard plasters, warm towels, and anything else they could think of to revive him.

Finally, around 7:00 A.M., Dr. Leale knew the final time was near. He held Lincoln's cold hand to let him know that someone was there for him. At 7:22 A.M., Abraham Lincoln breathed his last. Barnes placed his finger on the president's neck for a long moment, choked back his emotion, and announced, "He is gone." There was a lengthy silence followed by Stanton's prayer request to Lincoln's pastor, Dr. Phineas Gurley. Gurley prayed for the nation and for its wounds to heal and restore a reunited country. He asked that God receive the soul of Abraham Lincoln into his kingdom. When he finished, the men rose to their feet with a unanimous "Amen." Then Stanton uttered his famous words: "Now he belongs to the ages."[18]

CHAPTER TWELVE

The Pursuit of Justice

Responsibility for the investigation into the assassination ultimately fell to Joseph Holt, judge advocate general of the U.S. Army and head of the Bureau of Military Justice, referred to in this book as the "Bureau." Holt was born in 1807 and came from a fine old Kentucky family. While still in his forties, he made a fortune in law and retired early, buying a nice home on New Jersey Avenue in Washington, D.C. after traveling the world. His political background was with the Democratic Party, but when states began to secede, he switched allegiance to the Union. In the latter years of the Buchanan administration, he was appointed Secretary of War and served in the cabinet with Edwin Stanton. Although Southern in background, Holt turned on his former friends with vindictiveness and was unforgiving.[1] During the war years, Stanton relied upon Holt for prosecuting rebel sympathizers without mercy. With Holt as head of the investigation and ultimately chief prosecutor, Stanton had exactly the man he wanted for the job.

Stanton's foremost concern during the long night had been to staunch any rebel effort to create havoc and reverse the fortunes of war. He had heard vaguely of a plot to burn down the city of New York so his first steps that night were to safeguard the cities, protect the cabinet members, and maintain order throughout the North. Stanton's natural personality was to be slow but deliberate, and he was reluctant to name Booth as the primary suspect. Although Stanton had witnesses identifying Booth, some of the witnesses interviewed that night seemed uncertain as to whether Booth was the one who jumped onto the stage. Stanton's uncertainty, combined with his concern over preventing future attacks, allowed five hours to pass before Booth's name appeared in telegrams as the suspect. In fact, the local police were far ahead of him in the early investigation.

Taking over from the locals, Stanton ordered that the military spearhead the investigation. Naming the military to be head of the investigation was perfectly normal for Stanton since he controlled it. As a result all information started flowing through the Bureau. Stanton then ordered the arrest of anyone and everyone who aroused suspicion or had connections with Booth. More than five thousand people were arrested in this huge dragnet. Early evidence was massive, often conflicting, and challenging to sort through. Every employee of Ford's Theatre was arrested as well as every actor and actress in the play. Booth's brother, Edwin, and his brother-in-law, John Sleeper Clarke, were kept in the Old Capitol Prison for weeks. Michael O'Laughlen and Samuel Arnold were arrested on the same day in Baltimore and Fort Monroe, Virginia, respectively.[2] When the police couldn't find John Surratt, they raided the boarding house again on the Monday night following the assassination on testimony from Louis Weichmann. They arrested everyone there, including Lewis Powell, who had blundered onto the scene. They didn't know who they had in Powell at the time, but his and Mary Surratt's actions were suspicious.[3]

Weichmann was a very productive witness. In fact, he was a bonanza. He told them details of Booth's frequent visits to the house, the comings and goings of all the gang members, and described the lady in the veil, Sarah Slater. In addition, he told them of the meeting between Dr. Samuel Mudd, Booth, and John Surratt in Booth's hotel room. From Weichmann's perspective, Booth and Surratt had exposed him and everyone else in the house to danger with their plots and schemes. Now he turned the tables on them as well as his landlady. He told the police about the two trips he had taken the previous week to the Surrattsville tavern with Mary Surratt for some indiscernible purpose. He told them about Mary Surratt's prediction that these "licentious people" would soon change their celebrations into mourning. Weichmann tied up the damning evidence for the Bureau in a nice package with a pretty bow. By the following Thursday, the government had all the conspirators they believed to be involved except John Surratt, Booth, and Herold. They even had George Atzerodt, captured at his cousin's farm in Germantown, Maryland. The less-than-bright Atzerodt had slipped through the roadblocks around Washington but had attracted attention by talking too much about the assassination.[4] Fortunately for historians, Atzerodt would talk a lot more.

The Thirteenth New York Cavalry under Lt. David Dana were closer to Booth and Herold on Saturday than they would have ever dreamed. Dr. Mudd's early statements about Booth and Herold keeping the assassination from him could be true. Dr. Mudd was an ally. He had helped Booth with the kidnapping plot. He had brought Thomas Harbin and John Surratt into the fold. He had traveled with Booth down the back roads in the area. Booth, with a broken leg, had to have a doctor and there was no one that he could trust more than Dr. Mudd. When the plan changed to murder, Booth never had any intention of enlisting the aid of a married man with a home and family. Booth's action team consisted of single men who could cut and run. But Booth was desperate. Now he couldn't run, at least not very well. Revealing to Mudd what he had done would run him the risk of being thrown out of the house.

Dr. Samuel Mudd may have had a rude awakening when he arrived in Bryantown by mid-afternoon and discovered the Thirteenth New York Cavalry in the town searching for Booth and Herold.[5] The electrifying news that Booth had killed Lincoln would have sent chills down his spine. Everyone in the neighborhood knew Booth had visited him at least once. The cavalry would get wind of this sooner or later, probably sooner. Mudd had a neighbor, George Gardner, who lived just a few yards away. Gardner had sold Booth the one-eyed horse and knew what Booth looked like. His household could see just about everything going on at the Mudd farm. Mudd had slaves, a white servant named Best, who had helped fashion crutches for Booth earlier in the day, and four small children. None of these people could be trusted to keep quiet about anything they saw, especially if put under pressure. Dozens had seen Mudd with Booth at church. Mudd was undeniably tied to the assassin.

Mudd probably considered three options as he returned home from Bryantown. The first was to hope that the cavalry didn't arrive that day and search his home. After dark Mudd could send Booth and Herold on their way and hope no one saw them leave. He could say nothing at all to the troops and deny that Booth had come there at all. His second option was to turn Booth in to the authorities and risk what the actor would say to his captors about his prior relationship with Dr. Mudd. However, the captors soon would know all about Booth's previous visits from his neighbors anyway, and Mudd knew that if he turned Booth in, Booth would have no further loyalty to him. His role in introducing Booth to Thomas Harbin and John Surratt placed him in a position of high risk. Mudd obviously chose a third option: using his Hippocratic oath as a defense and pretending that he didn't know the men or their deeds. He could wait long enough to make sure the fugitives were well on their way and then lead the cavalry in the wrong direction. Mudd could not afford for Booth to get caught and talk. He had a family and a home. He could not cut and run.

So, did Dr. Mudd lie about harboring a fugitive? Did he hide the fact that he helped Booth with his kidnapping plot? Of course he did. Any man wanting to escape the gallows would have done the same. His guilt under the law was the same as that of Samuel Arnold and Michael O'Laughlen, perhaps more.

Once decided, Mudd began dropping hints and laying the groundwork for delay and eventual partial disclosure. On the way home, Mudd met with two friends, Francis Farrell and John F. Hardy. He gave them the news about Lincoln and that the chief suspect was a man named Booth. Farrell asked if the man was the same Booth who had been around the neighborhood the previous fall. Mudd said he didn't know if it was the same man, as he knew of three or four other Booths, but if it was the same man then Mudd acknowledged knowing him.[6]

Traveling on to his home, he confronted Booth and Herold and told them they had to leave at once. He must have told Booth about the soldiers in Bryantown because the men circled to the east of the town to avoid them. Mudd said nothing else about his visitors until he talked to his brother George at church the next morning. That gave Booth and Herold some valuable time to make their escape.

Following Mudd's vague directions the two fugitives struggled in the dark until they ran across a free black farmer named Oswell Swann.[7] They paid him twelve dollars to lead them through the Zekiah Swamp and guide them to Rich Hill, the home of respected secession leader Samuel Cox.[8]

Samuel Cox. (Courtesy Surratt House Museum/ MNCPPC)

They arrived at the Cox home a few minutes after midnight. Cox probably expected them. He didn't let them into the house until he thought Swann was out of sight, but Swann looked back and saw them ushered in. The men talked until daylight, with Cox giving them food and allowing them to rest. After daybreak, he told them he could not risk keeping them in the house and had his overseer, Franklin Roby, take them to a pine thicket at the edge of his property.

Cox then sent his son to fetch his foster brother, Thomas Jones, to the house.[9] Thomas Jones had a house on the bluffs overlooking the Potomac where he farmed his land and fished the river. Cox directed Jones to provide the two men the help they needed and get them across the river. Jones was the signal and mail system's ranking Confederate officer in southern Maryland. No one was more loyal to the Confederacy. He brought the two men food and newspapers for five days, all while monitoring the Union troops so he could decide when to risk sending Booth and Herold across the Potomac River.

Thomas Jones had invested his fortune in Confederate war bonds. In 1865 the bonds were worthless, and Jones was dead broke. Yet one night as he harbored the fugitives, he visited a barroom in the Browner's Hotel in Port Tobacco to glean information about the Union troopers. A bounty hunter named William Williams sidled up to him and bought him a drink. Casual conversation soon led to the manhunt. The bounty hunter explained that he could arrange to put one hundred thousand dollars into the man's hand that led him to Booth. One hundred thousand dollars was an enormous sum in those days, yet Jones was not tempted to betray Booth. His only remark was "That's a lot of money. Should be enough to do it."[10] Jones waited five days until the troops cleared out of Port Tobacco before bringing the two tired, bedraggled fugitives near his home. For the five days that they hid in the woods, Jones had kept his slave and good friend, Henry Woodland, out in his boat fishing, thus preventing it from being confiscated by the Union troops.

By now, Booth was miserable and discouraged. Nothing had

Thomas A. Jones. (Public domain)

gone as planned. The newspapers were painting him as a fiend and a low-life killer. No one thought of him as a hero. His friend John Matthews had not mailed his letter to the newspaper so he had not been able to state his side of the story. His leg was killing him. He had been days without shelter and a hot meal. Either Herold or Samuel Cox's overseer had shot the horses. They were afraid that the animals would make noise when the busy and vigilant troopers raced by on the road outside their thicket. His plan had not worked. Seward and Johnson were still alive, and the Federal government appeared to be working just fine. Huge rewards were offered for his capture. Now it would be difficult to trust anyone.

But finally, things were looking up. He would be able to escape to the friendly confines of Virginia. Booth paid a small sum of eighteen dollars to Jones for his boat. That's all Jones would accept.[11] Jones furnished Booth and Herold with a candle and a compass, along with the compass reading to a Mrs. Quesenberry's house. Booth was almost tearful in gratitude as they parted: "God bless you, dear friend, for all you have done for me." Jones pushed off the boat and they were off to Virginia.

Two days earlier, Lieutenant Dana had acted on the information from Dr. Samuel Mudd's brother, George, about two strangers who had come to the doctor's home. At this point, no Union pursuers knew that Booth had injured his leg so George Mudd's information didn't exactly excite anybody at cavalry headquarters. It wasn't until forty hours after Booth had left the Mudd farm that a team of detectives headed by Lt. Alexander Lovett paid a visit to the Mudds. Dr. Mudd was out in the fields when the detectives arrived so the men talked to Mrs. Mudd first.[12] The visit was somewhat casual. Mudd's wife told the interrogators that two men had arrived early Saturday morning, one with a broken leg. One was about eighteen and the other over thirty. The older man was wearing whiskers and Mrs. Mudd thought perhaps they were false whiskers. While they were at the Mudds' home, the older man had shaved his moustache off and then left toward the Zekiah Swamp after asking directions to Parson Wilmer's house, which was west of the Mudd farm and opposite to the direction they actually took. Parson Wilmer was also one of the few Union men in the area. The detectives asked Dr. Mudd to give a written statement, and then they left.

The doctor's statement was full of lies, omissions, and discrepancies. Mudd never mentioned the false whiskers that his wife had told them about before he had arrived from the fields. The detectives waited for him to volunteer this information, but he never did. This raised their suspicions, and on Friday, April 21, they returned with more questions and an intent to take him into custody. When the detectives arrested Mudd, they announced that they were going to search the house. At this point Mudd instructed his wife to go upstairs and retrieve the boot that the older man had left under the bed. The boot was presented to a rather startled Lieutenant Lovett, who looked inside the boot and saw the name "J. Wilkes" inscribed on the inner top edge.[13] When Lovett showed Mudd the name inside, Mudd admitted that he had deduced that his patient was John Wilkes Booth. However, he didn't specify when he had made that deduction.

Now that Mudd was in custody, he knew that he was in trouble. He compounded the problem on the way to Bryantown. He told Lovett that he knew Booth and that Booth had been to his home the previous fall. Mudd knew that the detectives would learn that sooner or later. He must have figured that it was better to volunteer the information. When he got into town, he was turned over to Col. H. H. Wells, who was now the officer in charge. This led to a second written statement that was inconsistent with the first and again full of omissions.

Truth be told, Dr. Mudd was a liar. What's more, he was a very bad liar. He had not rehearsed a story with his wife, nor had he thought through the details very well. He must have hoped that the false whisker story would satisfy the cavalry. Why he didn't bury the boot in the field some night is beyond this author's comprehension. Mudd's lies and inconsistent stories have led to much debate by historians over the years, but in the end, it doesn't matter. Louis Weichmann's testimony would have brought detectives to Mudd's door anyway.

Earlier in the week, both Samuel Arnold and George Atzerodt sang like canaries. Both thought they were innocent—Arnold, because he had left Booth before a murder was contemplated and Atzerodt, because he had refused to kill Andrew Johnson. Both men wrote detailed statements implicating all the alleged conspirators except Edman Spangler. Each statement was made independently of the other and had almost no contradictions.[14]

But the best witness was Louis Weichmann, who was loosely in the custody of Almarin C. Richards, the head of the Metropolitan Police Department. By Thursday, April 19, Richards had sent Weichmann and another boarder, John Holohan, to Canada under the loose custody of Detective James McDevitt. They were looking for John Surratt. Weichmann was certain that he was in Montreal. He was right.

On April 18, Surratt checked in to the St. Lawrence Hotel with Miss H. C. Slater.[15] Gen. Edwin Lee's diary shows that on April 19, "Charley Armstrong," his alias for Surratt, was paid forty dollars for expenses and one hundred dollars for services. Lee also probably told him that he was too hot and needed to make himself scarce. Surratt immediately checked out of his room and told the desk clerk that he was headed to Quebec City. He then hid out in General Lee's suite.[16]

In the late evening of April 19, the detectives and Weichmann arrived at the St. Lawrence Hotel and just missed Surratt. Surratt saw them as he was returning to the hotel and ducked out, taking a carriage elsewhere with friends. While Weichmann and the detectives searched for Surratt, he played cat-and-mouse with them, sending them on wild goose chases until he was able to leave town and hide out in Saint-Liboire under the protection of Father Charles Boucher. John Surratt would prove to be very clever and elusive, perhaps with the help of the Confederate agents and the Catholic Church.[17]

Some others would never be caught or prosecuted. Some were Confederate military under parole such as Thomas Nelson Conrad, Thomas Harbin,[18] and Col. John Mosby. Harbin went to England and found asylum for five years before returning and working as a clerk at the National Hotel for many years. The government never had a handle on him because George Atzerodt mispronounced his name. In the 1880s he would tell his story through war correspondent George Alfred Townsend.

Thomas Nelson Conrad, although paroled, was arrested for complicity on July 9. He made a daring escape and hid in the Shenandoah Mountains for a year. He would write two short books about his spying and his role in the plot to kidnap Lincoln and bring him to Boyd's Hole.

Another spy who scouted Lincoln was Benjamin Franklin Stringfellow, who hid in Canada for more than a year despite the distress of his fiancée, who was waiting for him in Alexandria, Virginia.

Samuel Cox and Thomas Jones were arrested but never charged due to lack of evidence. Samuel Cox was threatened with torture unless he talked, but he remained silent. Jones, like Harbin, would tell his story through George Alfred Townsend.

Thomas Jones had the ability to behave mentally incompetent whenever he was under arrest. He had been arrested before and his strategy was consistent. He could act like he had an I.Q. below seventy. He would put off questions as if he was incapable of understanding anything that was being asked. He never let his guard down, and the Union prison authorities eventually gave up. The truth was that Jones could be a better actor than Booth when he wanted to be.

When Booth and Herold pushed off for Virginia on Thursday night, they were directed to the mouth of Machodoc Creek, two miles south of their embarkation point near where Mrs. Elizabeth Quesenberry lived. About the time they left, the Union gunboat USS *Juniper* anchored near the mouth of the creek as a heavy fog settled in. To make matters worse, the USS *Heliotrope* passed the *Juniper* about 11:45 P.M., going north. In the heavy fog, Booth's little fourteen-foot boat nearly hit the *Juniper*.[19] A diary entry by Booth hints that the other boat was a problem too. Fearing discovery, they pulled in their oars and drifted away with the tide and wind, which carried them north. The boat carried them back to the southern Maryland shore on Nanjemoy Creek. Herold recognized where they were, and they hid the boat and contacted the Hughes family near Indiantown. The Hughes family fed them and allowed them to hide near their house. They remained there for two days.[20]

On Saturday evening they tried again, ignoring the easier direct route across the river to Chotank Creek, where Conrad had kept his lookout point before he surrendered. But Booth was looking for Harbin, whom he knew, and tried again for Mrs. Quesenberry's home, where he knew he could be connected to Harbin. Once again, the wind gave them trouble, but they made it to Gambo Creek, about a mile north of Machodoc Creek, early the next morning.[21] They had reached Virginia at last.

Booth stayed in the boat while Herold headed for Mrs.

Quesenberry's. Herold made up a story about a brother who had a broken leg and was stranded on Gambo Creek. Mrs. Quesenberry promised to send food but offered no other help. After Herold left, she sent for Thomas Harbin and Joseph Baden.[22] Harbin took the food and found Booth and Herold. Harbin found Booth two horses at a nearby farm owned by William Bryant and, as requested by Booth, sent them along to Dr. Richard H. Stuart. Bryant's son went along with them to retrieve the horses.

They arrived at Cleydael, the summer home of Dr. Richard Stuart, about 8:00 P.M. Accounts differ, but Stuart had a house full of people and shuffled some food out to the two fugitives in the yard. Booth pleaded for medical attention, which Stuart declined, but he did tell them that they could find transportation to the Rappahannock River on a wagon owned by a free black man named William Lucas. Booth, Herold, and Bryant headed there.

Lucas lived with his wife and six children in a little cabin that could best be described as a hovel. By the time Booth arrived, he was in a surly mood. He sent a note back to Dr. Stuart by Bryant complaining of the treatment he had received at Cleydael and included $2.50 for the food that Stuart gave them. He claimed he felt obliged to pay for it because of the spirit in which it was offered.[23] That note probably saved Stuart from prison when he later produced it to his interrogators.

When William Lucas expressed his reluctance to leave for Fort Conway on the Rappahannock River ferry until morning, Booth threatened him with his knife and threw the family out in the yard so he could stay inside that night. It had been many nights since he had slept with a roof over his head. The Lucas family huddled in fright as the arrogant white man with the crippled leg slept inside their cabin.

When daylight appeared on April 24, Booth quarreled with Lucas again.[24] Herold stepped in and negotiated a wagon ride to the Port Conway ferry for twenty dollars. Lucas's son would drive the wagon. By 7:00 A.M. they were on their way. When they arrived at the tiny village of Port Conway, they went to the home of William and Bettie Rollins. Rollins owned a small fishing boat, and Herold negotiated for transportation across the river and several miles beyond. Rollins wasn't enthusiastic and told them he needed to tend to his fishing nets first.

As Booth and Herold waited, three men on horseback came slowly riding toward them. Herold struck up a conversation with a Confederate private named Willie Jett.[25] He told Jett his name was Boyd and identified Booth as his brother James W. Boyd, who was suffering from a war wound. Jett may have been dubious. He knew just about everyone in the northern neck of Virginia as well as the soldiers in Mosby's command. Herold may have discerned this because he admitted who they were.

The identities of the two strangers perked up the ears of the senior man in the group, Lt. Mortimer Ruggles. Mortimer was the son of Gen. Daniel Ruggles, an officer in the Confederate Secret Service and a hero in the battle of Shiloh. Many historians believe Ruggles, Jett, and Absalom Bainbridge, the final member of the trio, were on the lookout for Booth and had been instructed either to aid in his escape or to kill him, if necessary, to keep him from revealing to his captors Confederate complicity in the kidnapping plot. This author would want a lot more proof than what has previously been offered to reach that conclusion. It's true that Ruggles was a courier for Thomas Nelson Conrad, and he was connected to the Secret Service. The Signal Corps and intelligence personnel had certainly been alerted to watch for Booth too. When William Rollins returned from his fishing nets, the three soldiers told him that his help was unnecessary and signaled across the river for the ferryman, James Thornton.

After the crossing, Ruggles had to decide what to do with Booth. After several ideas were rejected, Willie Jett finally offered an acceptable solution. He would take Booth to the farm of Richard Garrett, about three miles up the road from Port Royal, the village on the south side of the Rappahannock. Garrett readily agreed to take in the wounded soldier posing as James W. Boyd for a day or two. Herold and the other three rode on. Willie Jett wanted to see his girlfriend Izora Gouldman, the daughter of Henry Gouldman, who operated the Star Hotel in Bowling Green. On the way, the four men couldn't pass up the opportunity to visit the Trap, a local house of delight, for some gentlemanly recreation.[26] Arriving in Bowling Green, Ruggles and Jett checked in to the Star Hotel, while Bainbridge and Herold spent the night at the Widow Clarke's home.

Things appeared to be looking up for Booth. On the morning of April 24, Booth's trail was getting cold. Cavalry had scoured the southern Maryland countryside, and gunboats heavily patrolled the Potomac River to prevent a crossing. Police threats and huge reward money had borne no fruit.

On the evening of April 18, Maj. James R. O'Beirne, a Washington provost marshal, along with a team of detectives took the steam tug *William Fisher* down the Potomac. The next morning they started searching houses on the riverbank below Port Tobacco. They were hoping to catch Booth as he tried to cross. Acting on a tip, they called at the home of Richard Clagett. There the group learned that Clagett's son had seen men rowing across the river early Sunday morning, April 16. What the young Clagett had seen was Thomas Harbin and Joseph Baden being rowed across by James Owens.[27] A fruitless search along the river took two more days, and on the morning of April 24, O'Beirne was in Port Tobacco.

There the provost marshal ran into General Grant's telegraph specialist, Samuel Beckwith, who was with two detectives from Col. Lafayette Baker's staff. O'Beirne told him about the men who had rowed across the river. Beckwith immediately sent a telegram to Thomas Eckert in the War Department. Eckert showed the telegram to Col. Lafayette Baker, who happened to be in the office. Baker concluded that the men had to be Booth and Herold. The timing was right. The fugitives had last been seen the night before at Samuel Cox's home. They could have gone straight to the river and crossed. If the search of King George County had been fruitless, then the fugitives had moved on. But where? Baker spread out a map of Virginia and pondered. It made no sense for Booth and Herold to go south to Richmond. The Federals were there. They must have gone west at some point, maybe after crossing the Rappahannock River.

So, Baker requested a troop of cavalry from Stanton and reinforced them with two of his detectives, Everton Conger and Luther Baker, who accompanied the Sixteenth New York Cavalry under the command of Lt. Edward Doherty. Thus O'Beirne was excluded from the reward money for Booth's capture and Lafayette Baker's nephew was included. With O'Beirne already in the field, it would have made more sense to send him to Virginia than to send a new group from the capital. But the reward money had to be a factor. Lafayette Baker himself received the largest share of the reward.

The new cavalry company traveled forty miles down the river aboard the 186-ton *John S. Ide* and disembarked near Belle Plains, Virginia, about 10:00 P.M. Their search would start toward Fredericksburg and then swing southeast. The search party took the only road around a swamp that ended at the Rappahannock about twelve miles west of Port Conway. Throughout the night they rousted farmers and physicians looking for the fugitives.[28] They then headed east along the river and by noon the next day, after several adventures, arrived at Port Conway.

In the tiny village, the patrol came across fisherman William Rollins and Dick Wilson, who was assisting Rollins with his fishing nets. Wilson told Lieutenant Doherty that two men answering the description of Booth and Herold had been there the day before. William Rollins confirmed this information and identified Booth from a photograph. He also named one of the soldiers accompanying them as Willie Jett. His wife, Bettie, being a woman who kept up with relationships, told them they could probably find Jett at his girlfriend's place in Bowling Green. Galvanized, the troop took Rollins into courtesy custody and began to cross the river by ferry, six at a time. It took three hours to cross, all under the eyes of Confederate scouts on the other side of the river. Meanwhile, Conger decided to head for Bowling Green and find Willie Jett, who could lead them to Booth. Shortly

Lt. Edward Doherty. (National Archives)

after six, the troop had reassembled and were galloping down the road in the direction of Garrett's farm.

By now Ruggles had brought Herold back to the Garrett farm, and it is likely that he was one of the Southern scouts watching the Federal cavalry cross the river. As the horsemen slowly ferried their number to the opposite bank, someone, probably Ruggles, rode ahead and warned Booth and Herold that Union troopers were headed their way. Booth and Herold made for the nearby woods and watched the Union troopers racing by.

Their behavior raised the suspicions of Richard Garrett. Why would this J. W. Boyd, the name Booth had assumed around Garrett, be afraid of Union troopers? When asked, Booth told him that he had had a run-in with some Union soldiers and wanted to avoid trouble. Garrett didn't buy it. He had heard about the assassination only the day before and now he was really worried about these two men. He told them they would have to leave his house. Booth begged and pleaded. How could Garrett turn away a wounded soldier in pain? Garrett relented a little, allowing them to stay for one more night. Booth offered to buy Garrett's two horses, but Garrett declined. Those were the only two he owned. He told Booth he would try to get them a wagon from a neighbor the next morning.

Garrett now had a new concern. He feared Booth intended to steal his horses. He told the two men that they couldn't stay in his house but could sleep in the old tobacco shed. It wasn't a barn, really, just a small building used to cure tobacco. After dinner Booth and Herold went to the shed to sleep. Garrett had his son lock the door to the shed to prevent the men from getting out and stealing his horses.[29] He gave both sons orders to watch them during the night.

As Booth slept, the cavalry troop rode into the night, stressing their horses, knowing that they were close to their prize. First, they stopped at the Trap, getting information about three of the four men who were there the previous afternoon. Three had been back again that day, but Jett had not been with them. Convinced that Jett was in Bowling Green, the troop surged forward. They were dead on their feet but anxious to get their hands on Booth. Arriving in Bowling Green around midnight, they surrounded the Star Hotel. Baker pounded on the front door. No one answered. Conger and Doherty went to the back and found a black man at the back door. He let them in and they met the proprietor's wife, Julia Gouldman, who escorted them to a front parlor. Then she opened the front door to admit the others. She told them that her husband was away and the only ones there were her children and Willie Jett. When she revealed his location, Conger ran upstairs, found the sleeping Jett, and woke him with a revolver pressed against his head. Conger took him downstairs, and Jett told them where Booth and Herold were hiding. The troop had passed them on the road. Conger took Jett into courtesy custody for appearances and the group raced back toward Port Royal.[30]

They arrived at the Garrett farm about 2 A.M. Leaving their

courtesy prisoners, Rollins and Jett, at the gate, the troopers dismounted from their weary horses and quietly surrounded the house. The silence was disturbed only by barking dogs. Detective Baker pounded on the door. After a while, Garrett opened the door a crack and peered out. Baker grabbed him and dragged him outside. When Garrett was slow to answer their questions, the troopers threatened him with hanging. One of them threw a rope over a tree limb in the front yard. At this point Garrett's son, Jack, came running from his guard post in the corn crib and shouted for them not to hurt his father. He would tell them what they wanted to know. The men they were seeking were in the tobacco barn.[31]

The troopers quickly surrounded the shed. Baker repeatedly pounded at the door. A voice from inside asked who they were. "Never mind who we are. We know who you are, and you better come out quick." The response was silence. Baker turned to Jack Garrett and demanded that he go in and bring out the men or their weapons. Despite his protests, Baker pushed Jack Garrett through the now unlocked door. That attempt led to nothing. Jack Garrett came running back out, screaming that they were going to kill him. The leaders conferred and decided to take immediate action. Baker told the men inside that they had ten minutes to surrender or they would fire the barn.

"Captain, that's kind of rough," Booth responded. "I am nothing but a cripple. I have but one leg, and you ought to give me a chance for a fair fight. If you will withdraw your men thirty rods, I will come out and shoot it out. I'll fight you single handed, but I won't surrender."

Baker replied that it wasn't his intent to fight him but capture him.

Booth was determined. "Captain, I consider you a brave and honorable man. I have had half a dozen opportunities to shoot you, but I didn't do it."

Baker put down a candle that he was holding and granted Booth five more minutes before he fired the shed.

Herold had had enough and was ready to surrender. Booth cursed him for a coward while Herold pleaded with him to surrender. Booth told him, "Surrender if you want, but I will fight and die like a man." Then he shouted to Baker, "Captain, there is a man in here who wants to surrender mighty bad."

Baker ordered for Herold to pass out his weapons first. Booth protested, "Captain, the arms are mine and I intend to keep them. I declare before my maker that this man is innocent of any crime whatever."

Conger nodded yes to Baker. There would be one less man to fight. Baker agreed and ordered Herold to come out. When Herold extended his arms through the door, someone grabbed him and tied him to a tree, Herold whimpering and crying all the way.

Baker gave Booth one last chance. "You have two minutes before we burn the shed."

Booth knew his time was up. "All right, my brave boys. You may prepare a stretcher for me. Throw open your door, draw up your men in a line and let's have a fair fight. It will be one more stain on the old banner."[32]

Conger went to the back of the shed. He fashioned a torch of hay, lit it, and tossed it into the shed through a gap in some of the planks. There were many kinds of combustible materials inside, and the fire was an inferno in a very short time. Several men rushed to the edge of the shed to watch in fascination as Booth got up from a seat on the hay to make a feeble attempt to extinguish the fire. He quickly turned and headed for the door, dropping his crutches along the way. After a couple of steps, he raised his carbine and approached the door with a halting limp and a jump. He held a pistol in his other hand. He seemed ready to fight the whole Union army. Suddenly, a shot rang out and Booth threw up his hands and fell to the floor.

Baker ran to Booth, who was lying motionless on the floor. The bullet had entered below the right ear and exited out the other side of his neck after severing the spinal cord. Baker and Conger dragged Booth from the burning shed.[33] The heat was becoming intense. Conger and Baker held a short conference about whether Booth had shot himself, with Baker insisting that he had not. Two troopers were then ordered to carry

Booth to the front porch of Garrett's home. The troops were questioned about who had fired the shot, and Sgt. Boston Corbett admitted that he had, saying that when Booth raised his carbine, Corbett thought he was going to shoot one of the troopers.[34] He later told Conger that God told him to do it.

Boston Corbett was a strange duck. He was the original "Mad Hatter." He was born in England in 1832 as Thomas P. Corbett. At age seven, his family immigrated to the United States and settled in Troy, New York. In Troy he learned the trade of hat finishing and speedily became a journeyman. While he was very young, he married but lost his wife in childbirth. He drifted to Albany, New York City, Richmond, and finally Boston. Depressed over the loss of his wife, he took to drink and his life spiraled downhill. On the streets of Boston one night he stopped to listen to a sidewalk revival and was instantly saved. He worked on hats during the day and preached on the streets by night. He joined the Methodist Episcopal church and decided that since Christ's disciples had been given new names, he would also take on a new one. He chose the name Boston. In July 1858, he was preaching to a group of prostitutes and decided that he should never be tempted by the sins of the flesh. He ran home and castrated himself. Bleeding profusely, he was admitted to Massachusetts General Hospital, where he was treated for self-castration until his release on August 18.[35] He spent the next three years working on hats in various cities and using his earnings to publish religious pamphlets, which he gave away on the streets. His drifting took him back to Richmond, where he preached in the streets about the evils of slavery. He was speedily chased out of town.

When the Civil War broke out, he was among the first to enlist. On April 12, 1861, he joined the Twelfth New York Militia, commanded by Col. Daniel Butterfield, who would later become a staff member for Joseph Hooker. One day, Butterfield broke out a string of profanities about the awkwardness of his troops. Corbett stepped forward and asked politely, "Colonel, don't you know that you are breaking God's laws?" Butterfield was furious and ordered him put in the guardhouse for insubordination. Unfazed, Corbett began singing hymns with a loud fervor. The out-of-tune hymns drowned out everything in the camp.[36] Flustered, Butterfield sent him a message stating that if Corbett would apologize, he would be released. Corbett refused, saying that it was Butterfield who had done wrong. He wouldn't apologize until Butterfield apologized to God. Butterfield relented and released Corbett, who later said that he had a great time in the guardhouse with his God. He prayed morning and evening until his fellow soldiers called him the "Glory to God" man.[37]

Corbett was a tiger in battle, even if he was a pain to his superiors at other times. He was captured in 1863 by Colonel Mosby, who spared him from being killed because of his bravery. He was sent to the terrible prison at Andersonville. He was in his element there, providing religious comfort to the wounded and dying. After living out in the elements for three months, he escaped only to be recaptured. A short time later he was exchanged; the rebels had all they wanted of the Mad Hatter. Thoroughly emaciated, he convalesced for several months, but he was back at the regimental headquarters of the Sixteenth New York Cavalry when Lee surrendered. He was promoted to sergeant. The troop was stationed at Vienna, Virginia, and helped search for Booth for several days before being ordered to join two detectives for a trip to Virginia to look for the assassin there. Two nights later the company had Booth surrounded in the tobacco shed. Corbett was assigned a position near a large gap in the boards in the shed. When it looked to Corbett like Booth was going to start shooting, he fired one shot, striking Booth down.

Once back in Washington, Corbett was an instant hero, being interviewed several times a day by news reporters. His popularity was so strong that Stanton did not dare discipline him for violating orders to take Booth alive. Corbett received a private's share in the reward as his only punishment. The amount was $1,653.85. The officers received much more after a great deal of posturing and arguing before a congressional committee. But Corbett didn't care about the money. He preferred being a hero. When he mustered out, he began a

Boston Corbett. (Brady-Handy Collection, Library of Congress)

lecture circuit, with his notoriety and pocketbook increasing.

For a few years he served as a minister, staying no more than a few months at each place before the congregation blessed him and sent him on his way. The year 1877 found him as the doorman to the Kansas legislature. On the morning of February 15, someone made fun of the opening prayer for the day's session, and Corbett went berserk. He quietly closed and locked the front doors. He pulled two revolvers and started shooting at the legislative members. They hid behind water coolers and tried to climb walls to the balcony as they desperately avoided the flying bullets. Somehow Corbett managed to miss everybody.[38] He was remanded to the state asylum for the insane. A year and a half later he escaped, disappearing into history.

Corbett, with the officers and troops, gathered on the porch and watched Booth as he labored to breathe. He was paralyzed from the neck down. His diaphragm enabled him to breathe intermittently. He was able to talk a little. He wanted to know how he was betrayed. He wanted his mother to know that he died for his country. He asked to be put out of his misery. Conger sent two troopers to Port Royal for a doctor. He arrived a little after sunrise. After he examined Booth, he proclaimed that his condition was hopeless. Booth, with his head in the lap of Garrett's sister-in-law Lucinda Holloway, asked for his hands to be raised so he could see them. "Useless," he said. "Useless." Within a few minutes he breathed his last.

Before the body was sewn into two blankets, Conger went through his pockets carefully and extracted several items: a little memo book used as a diary; a stickpin with the inscription "Dan Bryant to J.W.B."; a bill of exchange from the Ontario Bank for "61+" pounds; five small photographs of women, including his fiancée Lucy Hale; a small boxed compass given by Thomas Jones; a small file with cork on the end; a small pipe; and a spur. Also secured were his weapons: his Spencer carbine picked up at Surrattsville, two revolvers, and Booth's large knife, marked "Rio Grande Camp Knife."[39]

Here a question begs to be asked that no else has posed. No greenbacks are mentioned in the list of Booth's possessions. What happened to his money? We know Booth spent around fifty dollars during the course of his escape. Did he leave town headed for Texas or Mexico with just fifty dollars in cash? Not likely. What was Booth going to buy Garrett's horses with? The answer looks pretty plain. The Sixteenth New York Cavalry commandeered his greenbacks. Each man received his share or we would have heard about it. Under the watchful eyes of the cavalry, it's not likely that the Garrett family got it, and Booth wouldn't have bothered to discard it in the burning tobacco shed. He had other things on his mind. Oh, those small details.

Conger ordered Corbett to saddle up, and they left ahead of the rest of the group. They hurried to Port Royal, where Conger left Corbett and made his way to Belle Plains. There he hailed the steamer *Keyport* and raced to Washington with the news.

While everyone in the federal government celebrated, no one knew that they had captured all the conspirators that they were ever going to get. John Surratt would come over a year later. They would eventually have Jefferson Davis and Clement Clay with no proof. But they did snare most of the small fry: David Herold, Mary Surratt, Lewis Powell, George Atzerodt, Dr. Samuel Mudd, Samuel Arnold, Michael O'Laughlen, and for some obscure reason Edman Spangler.

CHAPTER THIRTEEN

The Trial of the Century

There were several issues and circumstances facing the federal government as they tried Booth's co-conspirators. In addition to personal enmities between the defense attorneys and the government's men involved in the case, there were undertones of unionists versus secessionists, military versus civilians, Republicans versus Democrats, and even Catholics versus Protestants. But the most prominent feature of this trial was the tight control exerted by both Secretary of War Edwin Stanton and Judge Advocate General Joseph Holt. The two had worked together for several years and had both served in James Buchanan's cabinet following the resignation of his Southern cabinet members during the last year of his administration. Stanton and Holt had similar personalities as well as philosophies on preserving the Union. Both were devoted to duty as they saw it and were extremely emotional about punishing the South for its transgressions. Both were willing to go to extremes to ensure victory, and neither had hobbies or any other interests outside of work. Both could and did imprison thousands of alleged dissenters during the war without trial for months on end. Once the trial started, Stanton left the details to Holt. Stanton's time was consumed with ending the rebellion and establishing Reconstruction governments in the South.

The first issue to resolve was whether to try the defendants by military tribunal or civil court. Stanton recognized that there were many Southern-leaning citizens in Washington, D.C., and a trial by jury in a Southern town would be risky,

Prosecutor Joseph Holt. (Public domain)

to say the least. In addition, Holt wanted to hold secret trials.[1] This un-American legal move brought objections from everywhere. In this matter, Andrew Johnson, who was now president, and Stanton, who was really in charge, both sought the legal opinion of Attorney General James Speed. However, there is no doubt that Stanton influenced Speed. Speed was intimidated by Stanton, who had a better legal pedigree as well as a domineering personality.[2]

On May 1, after some maneuvering, Speed came out with his opinion. He stated that the defendants weren't really civilians but "enemy belligerents" who killed Abraham Lincoln in his capacity as commander in chief, and therefore the plot maintained military status. Further, the conspirators did not act for personal gain, but in furtherance of the Confederate government's goal to create turmoil in the Union chain of command.

With this opinion in hand, Andrew Johnson issued an order

Attorney General James Speed. (Brady-Handy Photograph Collection, Library of Congress)

Military prosecutors. *Left to right:* John Bingham, Joseph Holt, and Henry Burnett. (Liljenquist Family Collection, Library of Congress)

to the assistant adjutant general to select nine competent military officers to serve as a commission for the trial. Assistant Adjutant General W. A. Nichols announced on May 6 the names of those selected to serve on the commission: Maj. Gen David Hunter, Maj. Gen. Lewis Wallace, Bvt. Maj. Gen. August Kautz, Brig. Gen. Albion P. Howe, Brig. Gen. Robert S. Foster, Bvt. Brig. Gen. Cyrus B. Comstock, Brig. Gen. T. M. Harris, Bvt. Col. Horace Porter, and Brig. Gen. Fredrick H. Collier. Later, orders relieved Collier from duty and substituted Lt. Col. David R. Clendenin.[3]

The group finally convened on May 8, 1865, for its first day of duty. The charges were read to the court officers and delivered to each defendant in their cell. The charges against each of the defendants were the same in many respects, alleging conspiracy with John Surratt, John Wilkes Booth, Jefferson Davis, and the Canadian Confederate agents to commit murder on Lincoln, Grant, Seward, and Johnson. In addition, the charges included treason.

The next day the court read the charges to each defendant in person. Holt presented the members of the prosecution: John A. Bingham and Col. H. L. Burnett. Following these introductions, the defendants were led into the courtroom in chains, manacles, and hoods. They could hardly walk with the restrictions. It was a shocking sight to the members of the commission to see prisoners treated in this fashion.[4] It was a sight unparalleled in American jurisprudence.

Several members of the commission held the same reservations about trying civilians via military tribunal that had been expressed by the newspapers, members of the cabinet, the general public, and, later, the defense attorneys.[5] Some of them bristled as Holt read them the rules of the trial. Cyrus Comstock and Horace Porter objected strenuously to secret hearings as well as to the commission's jurisdiction over the defendants. They also objected to limiting defense attorneys to five minutes to present arguments. Holt, however, seemed to hold no qualms in being as repressive as possible, and the rules were as harsh as the physical restrictions on the defendants.

The next morning when the commission reconvened, the two complaining junior members found that they had been relieved of their duties. The two officers were replaced by Bvt. Brig. Gen. James Ekin and Bvt. Col. C. H. Tompkins. Holt and Stanton had worked during the night to ensure that they only had commissioners who would fall in line with the program.[6] They stacked the deck with hardliners. One commissioner, Robert Sanford Foster, had no business on the panel. He had handled the investigation of Mary Surratt.[7] That should have been a conflict of interest even in those days. Another commissioner, T. M Harris, was a witness at Ford's Theatre that night. An argument could be made that Booth was dead and therefore not a defendant, but Edman Spangler, a Ford's Theatre employee, was standing trial for his life.[8]

May 10 was a short day as each defendant pled not guilty and since there were no defense attorneys yet, the commission adjourned. The rest of the day was spent organizing the security force for the courtroom, each commissioner and prosecutor, and the areas surrounding the building and grounds. It involved hundreds of soldiers.

Military tribunal commissioners and judges. *Standing, left to right:* Harris, Wallace, Kautz, and Burnett. *Seated, left to right:* Clendenin, Tomkins, Howe, Ekin, Hunter, Foster, Bingham, and Holt. (Library of Congress)

Before adjournment the previous day, the defendants had been asked if they wanted counsel. All eight answered yes. And all eight would have trouble obtaining an attorney. Most attorneys wouldn't touch the case. They had no wish to jeopardize their careers for a hopeless cause. Finally, a legal team was assembled. Thomas Ewing, Jr. represented four of the eight defendants: Dr. Samuel Mudd, Edman Spangler, Michael O'Laughlen, and Samuel Arnold. Frederick Stone represented David Herold and assisted in representing Dr. Mudd. He also served a minor role in Mary Surratt's defense. William E. Doster represented George Atzerodt and was later convinced to represent Lewis Powell. The distinguished Reverdy Johnson originally represented Mary Surratt but quickly delegated her defense to two of his inexperienced underlings, John W. Clampitt and Frederick Aiken. Walter Cox served as co-counsel for Michael O'Laughlen.[9]

Reverdy Johnson was the most prestigious of all the defense attorneys. A member of the bar since 1816, he had had a distinguished career. He had served as deputy attorney general in Maryland, a state senator from 1821 to 1829, a U.S. senator from 1845 to 1849, and attorney general from 1849 to 1850.[10] He came from a Whig and Democratic Party background.[11] Reverdy Johnson was a study in contrasts and divided loyalties that reflected the attitude of Marylanders during the Civil War. Although loyal to the Union, he remained loyal to friends and supporters who were not. As a Democrat, he wasn't fond of martial law or military tribunals and spoke out publicly against them. Somehow, he became close friends with President Lincoln and was one of his pallbearers.

In 1864, Maryland had held a constitutional convention. Among the issues to be resolved was the status of slavery. The convention promulgated rules that required each Marylander who voted on the convention's actions to take a loyalty oath. Reverdy Johnson saw the patent unfairness of this. Maryland slaveholders had to disavow their Confederate leanings to vote against losing their slaves. He openly counseled his Maryland constituents to take the oath whether they meant it or not. This inflamed the Republican hardliners at the time, and it was not forgotten in this courtroom. In addition, Reverdy had clashed with Chief Justice David Hunter and Gen. Lew Wallace over their strong abolitionist positions. When he looked over the table at the judges who would decide his client's fate, he found no friends, only enemies.

T. M. Harris brought up the loyalty oath question from the year before and demanded that Reverdy Johnson take a loyalty oath to the court. This started a battle royale between the judicial officers and Johnson, who rightfully declared that they had no authority to determine the moral character of any attorney before them. Johnson declared that he was licensed to try cases before the Supreme Court and sat in Congress, which authorized and funded military tribunals. In his arguments, he avowed that his moral convictions precluded him from representing anyone whom he thought was not innocent and that moral conviction extended even to his client, Mary Surratt.

Historians differ as to what happened after that. After unsuccessfully challenging the jurisdiction of the court, Reverdy Johnson sat quietly until, later in the day, the state called Louis Weichmann to the witness stand. Weichmann brought forth damning testimony about Mary Surratt and the activities at her boarding house. Her two trips to the Surratt tavern the week of the assassination were of particular interest, especially since Booth paid for the trips and was with her just before she boarded the carriage for the Good Friday trip. Upon cross examination, Reverdy Johnson questioned Weichmann closely about Mrs. Surratt's activities on critical days. After that, he virtually disappeared from the courtroom.[12]

Some say that Johnson did not want to hurt his client with his continued appearance since he was at odds with so many of the commissioners. Others say he was convinced of her guilt and, as promised, did not actively represent her in court. All agree, though, that he helped his two inexperienced associates from behind the scenes.

The other attorney at odds with the court was Thomas Ewing, Jr., who was originally hired by Mrs. Sarah Mudd to defend her husband. He ended up representing Spangler,

Arnold, and O'Laughlen as well. The son of a respected jurist, the younger Ewing was a Union war hero, rising to the rank of brigadier general before resigning to run unsuccessfully for the U.S. Senate. In addition, he was Gen. William Tecumseh Sherman's brother-in-law. At that time Sherman was in a running feud with Stanton over the surrender terms the general had given to Joseph Johnston's army in North Carolina. During the trial, Ewing clashed constantly with the prosecutors and the judges over procedure, jurisdiction, and his hard-hitting cross examinations. But when all was said and done, none of his clients suffered the death penalty.[13] At times, he was aided by his distinguished father, attorney Orville Browning.

Frederick Stone represented both Dr. Mudd and David Herold. He was from Port Tobacco and a descendant of Thomas Stone, a signer of the Declaration of Independence. He had been a lawyer for over twenty years but had only a modest reputation in Washington, D.C. Stone's representation of Mudd was hampered by the doctor's distrust of everyone, even his own attorneys.[14]

William E. Doster was hired by George Atzerodt, and the prosecution prevailed on him to represent Lewis Powell, too, since no one else would touch him due to the overwhelming evidence against him. Doster agreed to represent Powell until someone else could be found, but that never happened.[15] Doster tried feebly to present a defense of insanity for Powell, but his own psychiatrist wouldn't back him up. Then he tried to get his charges reduced to assault and battery with intent to kill, but that didn't work either. There was still the problem of conspiracy, which carried the death penalty. Doster never had a chance with either of his clients.

Frederick A. Aiken likewise would prove unsuccessful in the cause of his client, Mary Surratt, whose defense he had inherited from Reverdy Johnson. A graduate of Harvard Law School, Aiken was from Boston. He became the secretary of the National Democratic Committee and then, during the war, served on Gen. Winfield Hancock's staff until he was wounded. As a Democrat, he opposed the accumulation of power by the Lincoln administration, especially Seward and Stanton.[16]

Aiken's partner in this effort was John Wesley Clampitt, who graduated from Columbia (now George Washington University) in 1864. He served in the Washington Light Infantry and was active in Democratic politics. Thus, he became connected to Reverdy Johnson.

The inexperience and youth of Aiken and Clampitt probably were not major factors in Mrs. Surratt's receiving the death penalty. The two young men could not overcome the damning testimony of both Weichmann and Mrs. Surratt's tenant, John Lloyd. Together, the two witnesses proved that she was a messenger and delivery person for John Wilkes Booth during the week of the murder.[17] The problem they faced was no different than a case today wherein a getaway driver in a bank robbery is considered just as guilty as a trigger man who shoots a guard to death. The treason laws, then and now, state that anyone who participates in a conspiracy at any point is just as guilty as all the others involved in the conspiracy, even if the scope and purpose of the conspiracy change. Unless a conspirator comes forward and notifies the proper authorities so that they can stop the illegal act, that conspirator is guilty. Those two witnesses and others proved that Mary Surratt knew not only what was transpiring but also that she was involved throughout the process. Booth consulted her often, and she knew the details of all the suspicious visitors who moved through her boarding house, including Sarah Slater and the fact that Slater could run to the French embassy anytime she got in trouble.

A fact unknown for another forty years aids historians in determining Mrs. Surratt's guilt. Richard Smoot, the man who sold the boat to John Surratt and Thomas Harbin, came to Mary Surratt's boarding house to press for his remaining money. Mary assured him that the boat's use was imminent and asked him to be patient. Still not satisfied, Smoot returned to the boarding house on Friday night, just forty-five minutes before the assassination, to demand the release of the money. Mary Surratt became agitated and told him that the boat would be used that very night and that he should leave the city immediately. Smoot took her advice because she emphasized that he could be in danger if he remained in Washington. He walked across the bridge to Alexandria, a distance of eight miles. Smoot later had a man named George Bateman smash the boat into little pieces. In 1904, he wrote and published a short memoir, but the publishing company burned before the work could be distributed. The memoir was again published in 1908.[18]

In the early stages of the trial, Holt made every effort to keep the trial and all of its aspects secret from the public. This created ire amongst the commissioners, members of the press, and the public as well. Holt lamely claimed that public knowledge would hamper the government's efforts to arrest other conspirators. After about three days of testimony, Holt caved and allowed newspaper reporters into the proceeding. After that, visitor passes were granted on a limited basis.[19]

The prosecution's attempt to link the murder plot to Confederate leaders was a fiasco. Their case hinged on three witnesses: Sandford Conover, Dr. James B. Merritt, and Richard Montgomery. Conover was the chief witness, but their stories were similar for the most part. All three were supposedly from Canada. They claimed to have seen Booth with Confederate agents George Sanders and Jacob Thompson on particular dates. Merritt claimed that Jefferson Davis had authorized the murder in writing.

Within days of their testimony, their credibility was destroyed. Articles appeared in several newspapers stating that Jacob Thompson was nowhere near the city where Conover and the other two witnesses claimed to have seen him with Booth.[20] Sanders was quoted in the papers as saying that all three were known to the Confederate agents, and they never would have been trusted with such information, the content of which wasn't true anyway. The Canadian government searched Conover's room and discovered that he operated under many aliases. The one he used in Canada was James Watson Wallace. This information was passed along to the U.S. government as well as to the newspapers.

Military tribunal in progress. (Surratt House Museum/MNCPPC)

Merritt claimed that he went over the border in Minnesota and turned over his knowledge of Booth's interactions to a justice of the peace named Squire Davidson. Davidson denied this claim. Conover was recalled late in the trial and admitted that some of the information that he gave the court was false. His real name was Charles Dunham. Even the name he had given them was a lie.

On May 14, Stanton wrote Gen. Henry Halleck that if Jefferson Davis were to be tried, it would happen in Virginia.[21] As the trial progressed, conditions deteriorated. The heat became almost unbearable. Water had to be made available to all, and frequent relief of the guards was necessary. For almost everyone, the pace was grueling. The sessions lasted from 10:00 A.M. until 6:00 P.M. After court recessed for the day, newspaper reporters had to get their stories in, and three sets of court reporters had to transcribe the minutes from shorthand so that they could be read the following morning. The strain on the prisoners was noticeable, especially Mary Surratt, who, when she didn't have her head buried in her hands, was heard moaning in low tones throughout the day.

All the other prisoners were manacled hand and foot with a guard posted between them to prevent communication. The defense attorneys had to do their research, hunt down witnesses, and consult between themselves after hours. The prosecution was in the same boat, as many more Confederate records were forwarded to Washington by Franz Lieber, who was charged with gathering, indexing, and transporting the records to the War Department. Only the commissioners could have leisure time after 6:00 P.M.

During the trial, the defendants reacted in several different ways. Mrs. Surratt was ill and constantly read a prayer book, quite often ignoring the proceedings. Most of the time she rested her head in her hands with her arms supported by the railing. Dr. Mudd spent a lot of time keeping up appearances and reading religious books. O'Laughlen paced his cell at night with his hooded head hung low, obviously dejected after learning that his friend Samuel Arnold had implicated him in the plot with his confession. He appeared to be expecting death. Lewis Powell, or Payne, as he was known at the trial, remained erect and defiant. He would fix a stare at almost anyone in the room from time to time. He seemed unruffled and unconcerned, his huge size dominating the room. The only time he showed emotion was remorse when he learned that Seward was still alive. Having been confined in solitary, he always assumed he had done his job and killed the secretary of state. Now he seemed disappointed that he would die for a job that he, a soldier, did not complete. Herold giggled a lot and acted like a child. Arnold was usually quiet and pleasant, causing no trouble in court or in his cell. Spangler was talkative and somewhat light hearted.[22]

The prosecution moved forward with little finesse, calling whatever witnesses they had available in no particular order. But even so, within a few days they had easily provided the proof needed to convict. They called forth Weichmann, John Lloyd, and the witnesses at the Seward household. They used Arnold's confession, wherein he named many of the conspirators, and called to the stand the detectives who arrested Mary Surratt. Their testimony connected her to

Lewis Payne (Powell). They brought forth the soldiers who had arrested Herold and been present at Booth's death, and they questioned the soldiers who investigated and arrested Dr. Samuel Mudd. Assistant Secretary of War Charles Dana and Thomas Eckert testified to the cipher machine found in Judah Benjamin's office and linked the cipher to messages found in Booth's trunk that dated back to October 13, 1864.[23]

The message read:

> We again urge the necessity of our gaining immediate advantages. Strain every nerve for victory. We now look upon the re-election of Lincoln in November as almost certain, and we need to whip his hirelings to prevent it. Besides, with Lincoln re-elected and his armies victorious we need not hope even for recognition, much less the help mentioned in our last. Holcombe will explain this. Those figures of the Yankee are correct to a unit. Your friend shall be immediately put to work as you direct.

This communication reveals much more than just its contents. Booth was probably the leader of the Washington, D.C. action team from that date and Benjamin was communicating with him in that capacity. Also, Benjamin is telling him and/or the Canadian agents to strike as quickly as possible on the kidnapping attempt. We don't know when or how this message reached Booth. He could have received the message through Canadian agents such as George Sanders, George Kane, or Patrick Martin. Further, the letter could have been brought to Canada by James Holcombe himself because the message indicates that Holcombe could explain the letter further. It is unlikely that Booth received the message before he left for Montreal, and it's not possible that it could have been waiting for him upon his arrival in Canada. But it could have reached him before he left on October 28. How he received messages before he met Harbin and Surratt remains a mystery.

In the letter, Benjamin requests that Booth and/or the Canadian agents attempt the kidnapping as quickly as possible. The message could have incited urgency amongst the Canadian agents. Booth received the message from Benjamin before he met with Patrick Martin, and it could have prompted the letters of introduction to Dr. Queen and Dr. Mudd.

One of the biggest mysteries of this trial is that in spite of the government's desire to implicate the Confederate government in the murder and despite their knowledge of Benjamin's leadership role in the Secret Service, they chose not to pursue him. The prosecution included some of the Canadian agents in its opening statement, but they did not mention Judah Benjamin. His cipher machine connection to Booth seemed to go unnoticed.

On May 20, a teller from the Ontario Bank in Montreal named Robert Campbell testified that the Confederate bank account there had $649,000 in it and was closed by Jacob Thompson on April 11, 1865. Further, he knew Booth and said that Booth had an open account there with a balance of $400.[24]

John Surratt and possibly Sarah Slater arrived in Montreal on April 6.[25] According to Surratt's 1870 Rockville lecture, the dispatches from Benjamin ordered the transfer of the money to Europe. The timelines are perfect in the testimony of the bank clerk who handled the transfer, Robert Campbell, and Surratt at his lecture. There is a ring of truth to this. We know that both Jacob Thompson and Judah Benjamin ended up in London. Campbell's testimony adds strength to the theory that Benjamin was headed to this golden parachute in London. Jacob Thompson was finished with his tasks in Canada and had been relieved by Gen. Edwin Lee several months before. He was excess baggage in Canada. It makes sense that the job of transporting a bank draft for such a large amount would fall to him. He would have required a few days to make travel arrangements and pack for a trip from which he would not return. Thompson booked passage for Liverpool out of Portland, Maine, where he arrived on the night of the assassination.

The provost marshal in Portland telegraphed the U.S. War Department that morning that Jacob Thompson was expected to arrive there that evening. He was standing by for instructions about what he was supposed to do. Assistant Secretary of War Charles Dana brought the telegram to Lincoln for orders. Lincoln asked Dana what Stanton wanted to do. Dana replied that Stanton wanted to arrest him. Lincoln shook his head no. He told Dana, "I rather guess not. When you have an elephant in hand, and he wants to run away, you better let him run." Thus, Lincoln himself decided to let one of the primary conspirators escape, along with $650,000 in his pocket for Benjamin, who had ordered his own murder. Oh, those small details![26]

In trials, there are rules of procedure, burdens of proof on the prosecution, and established sequences of events. After opening statements, the prosecution proceeds with presenting its evidence. Each of the prosecution witnesses can be cross examined in turn. The state lays a foundation to admit exhibits through their witnesses. The defense can object, if it wishes, as to the physical exhibits or personal testimony presented. When the state is finished with its witnesses and exhibits, it rests. Then the defense takes its turn in the same manner, with the prosecution objecting when it sees fit to do so. When the defense is through, it rests. The prosecution can then call rebuttal witnesses, and the defense can object when it wishes to do so. Then the defense can call counter rebuttal witnesses. Sometimes this sequence of rebuttal witnesses can go back and forth for a while, at the court's discretion or by local rules of court. When both the defense and the prosecution are finished, the prosecution has its first final argument. Then the defense gets its final argument. New evidence cannot be brought up during final arguments. It is a summation only of admitted evidence before both sides have rested. After the defense finishes its final argument, the prosecution gets a final rebuttal summation because the state has the burden of proof and the verdict of a jury must be unanimous. If the defendant(s) is found guilty, then a penalty phase occurs. The prosecution goes first and in this phase can bring up prior convictions and establish the reputation of the defendant(s). The prosecution is not allowed this in the guilt phase. The defense then calls witnesses to show the court reasons for mercy and/or probation. In some states, victims and/or their families can confront the perpetrator. Then the case goes to jury.

That didn't happen in this trial. No standard sequence of

events or procedures was followed, and the resulting historical record can be impossibly confusing to the reader. There are three official accounts of the trial, recorded by three different court reporters, and their versions are each slightly different. There are many details and versions of events to reconcile. Between three hundred fifty and four hundred witnesses were called, some from long distances. Therefore, witnesses on both sides testified when they arrived in court. The defendants were not allowed to testify, and the burden of proof appears to have been different. Instead of the state having the burden of proof beyond reasonable doubt, it seems that the defendants had some burden of proving themselves innocent. In addition to the defendants, there were unindicted co-conspirators that the court considered. The prosecution officers were called judges and the judges (or jury) were called commissioners. The prosecution officers sat with the commissioners (jury) during deliberations. This is unheard of in modern courts. Because of these circumstances, this book will take much of the evidence out of sequence and focus on each defendant in turn, discussing the evidence against them. A complete exploration of the trial could comprise a book of its own.

Edman Spangler: Spangler was an employee at Ford's Theatre and a friend of Booth's. No evidence was presented that placed him at any meetings or events with anyone other than Booth. His meetings with Booth occurred either at the theatre itself or at the stables behind the theatre where Booth kept his horses and buggy. The evidence showed that Spangler did some carpentry work at the stable to accommodate a buggy owned by Booth for a short while. The detectives also found an eighty-foot length of rope in his room, which the prosecution speculated was intended to be tied between trees so that pursuing horsemen would be thrown from their horses in the dark. The defense countered that ropes of this kind were standard tools in theatre stage setting.

A witness testified that Spangler was near the back door shortly after the shooting. He claimed that Spangler slapped a witness and told him not to reveal which direction Booth took in his escape. An assumption was made that it was Spangler who bored the small hole in the door leading into the presidential box. That assumption figured largely in the trial and would prove to be his downfall. Many years later, a descendant of the Ford family disclosed that it was Harry Ford who actually bored the hole through which Lincoln's security guard could monitor the Lincolns without disturbing them during the play. That was the case in chief against Spangler. In a civil court, a case this weak probably wouldn't even go beyond indictment. The defendant would be no-billed. Nevertheless, Spangler was given a six-year sentence.

Samuel Arnold: Arnold was a boyhood friend of Booth's who was brought into the kidnapping plot in August of 1864 along with Michael O'Laughlen (sometimes spelled O'Laughlin). Arnold confessed immediately after his arrest on April 17, 1865. He had carried weapons to Washington, D.C., met with Booth several times, and was present on March 17, during the attempt to kidnap Lincoln. The detectives also found a letter Arnold had written to Booth dated March 27 wherein he cautioned Booth to see how Richmond would accept Booth's scheme. He walked away from Booth and his plots immediately after the aborted kidnapping attempt on March 17. Arnold was miles away from Washington, D.C. at the time of the assassination. Arnold's legal problem, which he shared with O'Laughlen, was the theory of vicarious liability. Under the law, each conspirator was responsible for every act of the conspiracy unless he timely turned in all of the other conspirators. As to the charge of treason, any act to hinder the government during a national emergency was potentially punishable by death. Arnold was given a life sentence.

Michael O'Laughlen: O'Laughlen's case was almost identical to Arnold's except that the evidence showed that he came to Washington with some friends the night before the murder for the illumination (celebration). One witness placed him at Secretary of War Edwin Stanton's home that evening, but O'Laughlen did not attempt any wrongdoing and left the premises when requested to do so. O'Laughlen's witnesses were the men who accompanied him on the drunken spree to Washington, and they successfully destroyed the state's case for complicity in the assassination plan. Vicarious liability, however, earned him a life sentence. When the four surviving defendants were shipped to the disease-infested Dry Tortugas, one could easily conclude the War Department intended the life sentence to be a slower death sentence. In O'Laughlen's case, it was.

Dr. Samuel Mudd: Dr. Mudd's case is far more complex than the other conspirators. There are a lot of details. First, Mudd was one of two contacts provided by Patrick Martin when Booth was in Montreal in October 1864. Shortly thereafter, Mudd traveled the area extensively with Booth, and Booth was his overnight guest more than once. The prosecution's star witness, Louis Weichmann, testified that Mudd introduced Booth to John Surratt in Weichmann's presence on or about January 15, 1865. Actually, the date was December 23, 1864, but that wasn't established until after the trial. The evidence proved that Mudd set Booth' s broken left leg in the early morning hours of April 15, 1865, just hours after Booth fired the fatal shot. The evidence also showed that Mudd concealed that fact from the soldiers in the area for two days, denied that he knew Booth, and sent the soldiers in the wrong direction in their attempt to capture Booth and David Herold.

Mudd was blessed with a good attorney but cursed with his own mistrust of everyone, including his attorney. It was proved that he lied repeatedly; therefore, he gained no sympathy from the commission. Evidence uncovered over the years has revealed that Mudd introduced Booth to Thomas Harbin just before he introduced Booth to Surratt. Harbin was a Secret Service agent for the Confederacy in the northern Virginia area. There is no doubt that Harbin suggested to Booth that he include John Surratt, Jr. in the kidnapping plot. Many years after the trial, it came to light that Harbin and Surratt purchased the fifteen-passenger boat from Richard Smoot, which they hid in Nanjemoy Creek on the Maryland shore of the Potomac River.

Dr. Mudd escaped the death penalty by only one vote. He received a life sentence and was lucky to get it.

George Atzerodt: Atzerodt was a victim of vicarious liability.

He had neither the nerve nor the skill or the instincts to commit murder. His problem was that he remained in the plot to the very night of Lincoln's assassination. Atzerodt was implicated by many witnesses, including Weichmann and Mrs. Surratt's daughter Anna, as a frequent visitor to the Surratt boarding house. He ran countless errands for Booth, and he was to ferry a kidnapped Lincoln across the Potomac River on that fifteen-passenger boat, although this was not in evidence at the time. He was recruited into the group by John Surratt. According to one of his four confessions, he didn't know the plot had changed from kidnapping to murder until four hours before he was supposed to take part. He declared that he never had any intention of murdering Vice President Andrew Johnson, the task Booth had assigned him. Atzerodt probably never understood why he was given the death penalty. Vicarious liability was a concept far above his pay grade. Fortunately for historians, his forgotten confession to Detective McPhail of Baltimore was a major key to unlocking the mystery disclosed in this book. In that confession, he showed knowledge of participants that only Booth could have shared with him. Atzerodt wasn't smart enough to even dream of some of those people.

Lewis Powell, aka Lewis Payne: His was the easiest case for the court to determine. The witnesses at the Seward household were clear about identifying him as the assailant who had tried to kill the secretary of state and had succeeded in maiming several other members of the family and household in the process. There was never any doubt as to the outcome of his case, and Powell knew it all along. In Powell's mind, he was a soldier in civilian clothing who was caught doing his job, and the penalty of getting caught was death. He never complained about his sentence and remained true to his Confederacy to the very end. He knew far more than he ever revealed, carrying the names of co-conspirators to his grave. During the trial, he remained stolid, silent, and defiant. He was so silent that no one on the prosecution team even knew his real name. Powell's only hope of escaping the death penalty was a finding of insanity, which his reluctant attorney valiantly attempted. He was hampered by a lack of doctors specializing in mental health, and the doctors who did examine him were reluctant to go so far as to diagnose him with insanity.

Evidence discovered over the years suggests that Col. John Mosby assigned Powell to John Surratt for the kidnapping plot, and he remained loyal to Booth ever after, considering him to be his leader and commander. He was a formidable asset to Booth. He was a huge brute of a young man, especially for that time, and fierce as well. A question for historians in the years to come is whether Booth intended to abandon Powell during the escape from Washington so that he would take the fall for the conspirators. There is no evidence either way, but this author believes that Booth did not intend that. David Herold deserted him at the Seward home because he lost his nerve. Had Herold remained, Powell would have had a guide and would have been able to find his way to Booth on Soaper's Hill. Booth could have used the extra hand, and a strong hand it would have been. Booth's plan probably included the fifteen-passenger boat, which could have carried the entire team to Virginia. That detail has never been pursued and probably never will.

David Herold: David Herold was an immature boy of twenty-three with the mental faculties of an eleven year old. He was easily led and showed his immaturity on a daily basis during the court proceedings by giggling and acting crazy. His case was simple as well. He was involved in the conspiracy on the last day by both guiding Powell to the Seward home and coming up with the plan for delivering medicine to Seward with instructions to administer the medicine personally. Then he aided and abetted Booth in his escape, which called for the death penalty. Case closed! For those conspiracy enthusiasts who insist that Booth wasn't the man in the burning shed at the Garrett farm, if that were so, Herold would certainly have commented on it. In addition, he was an active participant in the aborted attempt to capture Lincoln on March 17. Booth gave him the job of going ahead of the team to retrieve the guns, rope, and monkey wrench. Herold was instructed to move those items to the general area where the boat was hidden.

Mary Surratt: Mrs. Surratt's case was simple and clear cut but remains the most controversial to this day. The two principle witnesses against her were Louis Weichmann and her tavern tenant, John Lloyd. The two men testified independently of each other, but their testimony was remarkably consistent. A lot of evidence was presented both for and against her, but these two were the cornerstone witnesses regarding her two trips to her Surrattsville tavern, when she delivered messages and field glasses for Booth during the week of the assassination. There were bitter and emotional disputes over the credibility of both witnesses—Weichmann was accused of lying to cover up his own complicity, and Lloyd was a heavy drinker—but their testimony came out clear and consistent. Furthermore, their stories never wavered, even under withering cross examination.

According to the information provided by Weichmann and Lloyd, Mrs. Surratt's first trip was on Tuesday, April 11, ostensibly to collect a debt from a John Nothey. She needed the money to pay off a debt on the tavern. On that day, Weichmann drove her down to Surrattsville in a rented buggy paid for by Booth. On the way, they passed John Lloyd traveling in the other direction. Lloyd testified that Mrs. Surratt told him to get those "shootin' irons" ready; they would be needed soon. This conversation was semi-private, with Weichmann unable to hear what was said.

The second trip also was undertaken to collect the debt from Mr. Nothey. On Friday, April 14, she gave Weichmann ten dollars and told him to rent another horse and buggy. She needed to see Mr. Nothey again. When Weichmann returned with the buggy, he saw Mrs. Surratt deep in conversation with John Wilkes Booth. Booth left and Weichmann and Mrs. Surratt headed to Surrattsville. Mrs. Surratt had some article wrapped in paper that she told Weichmann was china. It turned out to be Booth's field glasses. When they reached her tavern, John Lloyd was absent. Instead of continuing another five miles to the Nothey home, Mrs. Surratt stayed at her tavern and waited for Lloyd to return, opting to write a letter to John Nothey instead. When Lloyd arrived, Mrs. Surratt went out in the yard to talk to him privately. Lloyd testified that she gave him the package and told him to get the guns, two bottles of whiskey, and the field glasses ready and give them to the men who would call for them that night.

The defense claimed that Lloyd was drunk that day. There is no doubt that he was drinking but he must have remained functional. He was able to repair her carriage before she returned to Washington, which would have required a measure of sobriety.

When Mrs. Surratt and Weichmann reached a hill close to Washington, they stopped to watch a fireworks show in progress. The North was still celebrating their victory. According to Weichmann, Mrs. Surratt commented that all this gladness would soon turn to sorrow. Weichmann asked why, and she replied that the North were a proud and licentious people; that God would punish them. That statement was prophetic and was not lost on the court.[27]

Weichmann also testified that Mrs. Surratt sheltered Confederate agents and spies on a routine basis and had knowledge of Sarah Slater's role as a dispatch courier for the Confederate government. She reportedly said that if Slater were ever caught, she could run to the French embassy and seek asylum there. On March 25, Weichmann saw Mrs. Surratt, her son John, and Slater leave in a fancy carriage. Neither Weichmann nor the court knew that Mrs. Surratt had accompanied them to the Surrattsville tavern to deliver Slater to the Confederate agent Augustus Howell. However, Howell had been arrested at the tavern the night before. Although he did not realize it, Weichmann was also witness to Mrs. Surratt's reaction to Booth's failed kidnapping attempt. He came home from work on March 17 to find Mrs. Surratt crying. She said that John had gone away and was in a lot of danger. In January, the deeply involved Mrs. Surratt had intervened with John's new employer to get him a leave of absence so that he could take part in the Confederate conspiracy.

When all the evidence was in, it showed that Mary Surratt knew everything. She was an information conduit for all the conspirators. The court and the prosecution focused on her boarding house as a shelter for the conspirators, but her participation goes much deeper than that.

Although she received the death penalty, five of the nine

commissioners signed a plea for clemency for Pres. Andrew Johnson's consideration. The five were Hunter, Kautz, Foster, Ekin, and Tompkins.[28] This document would cause a furor of controversy for decades. Because of her gender, few believed that she would be hanged. The U.S. Government had never given the death penalty to a woman. According to Theodore Roscoe in his 1959 book *Web of Conspiracy,* the first vote on the Mary Surratt sentence only had four commissioners in favor of hanging: Wallace, Harris, Howe, and Clendenin. But Joseph Holt argued long and hard for the ultimate sentence. He asked and received permission to consult with Stanton before a final decision was made. Stanton made a deceptive offer of compromise. If the commission voted to hang, an offer for clemency could then be forwarded to President Johnson. The offer was accepted, and the clemency plea was drafted and signed by Hunter, Foster, Kautz, Ekin, and Tompkins.[29] Controversy continues to this day as to whether Andrew Johnson ever saw the plea, but one thing is certain: Stanton never asked the president for clemency for Mary Surratt.

That is the tragedy of a military tribunal trying this case. Prosecutors should never be allowed to be involved in the deliberations. The words of Surratt's attorney, Reverdy Johnson, still ring true: "Maliciously, unlawfully, and traitorously, and in aid of the existing rebellion against the United States of America . . . combining, confederating, and conspiring, together with . . . Jefferson Davis . . . and others unknown, to kill and murder, within the Military Department of Washington . . . Abraham Lincoln . . . and lying in wait with intent . . . to kill . . . Andrew Johnson . . . and . . . Ulysses Grant . . .", the charges and specifications boil down to treason. Treason, by law, can only be brought in a civil court and therefore any findings, rulings, and sentences brought by a military tribunal are therefore invalid. Later actions by Pres. Andrew Johnson tell us that argument troubled him to his dying day.

Although the rules of a military tribunal were harsh, the commission's logic is easy to follow. The commissioners gave the death penalty to the conspirators who were present and working with Booth on the day of the assassination. They gave prison sentences to those who weren't. Judging by his sentence, Spangler obviously was not considered a conspirator. It seems to be a pragmatic approach, but an argument can be made that two sentences were unjustifiably harsh.

The first such sentence was Spangler's. No one ever identified him as a conspirator. His only wrongdoing was to slap a witness and tell him not to reveal which way Booth had gone. However, the prevailing sentiment of the commission was that Booth got out of the theatre fast, and Spangler must have helped him. No one proved that Spangler bored the hole in the door leading into the presidential box. No one testified that Spangler did any work in the presidential box that would help Booth in any way.

The second questionable sentence was George Atzerodt's death penalty. Even though he was guilty under the vicarious liability theory, the commissioners could have ruled that Atzerodt had not cooperated with Booth on the murder plot. However, Atzerodt's own actions show his intent to carry out his mission. He checked himself into the Kirkwood Hotel early in the day so his confession to Detectives McPhail and Smith, wherein he claimed that he didn't know about his assignment to kill Andrew Johnson until 6:00 P.M. that evening, doesn't add up. The biggest problem Atzerodt faced in killing the vice president was Johnson's inaccessibility. Atzerodt couldn't kill Johnson without killing the hotel clerk first, and that would have drawn attention from the nearby hotel bar patrons. The truth was that Booth had given him an impossible job.

The commission knew their verdicts would be analyzed for decades. But they read the newspapers and also knew that they were being judged by a vengeful public. The North's blood was up. To the Northerners, Lincoln's murder was senseless, and few Southerners supported it, as it had accomplished nothing for the South. News of the sentences received few complaints from the Southern newspapers and general approval from the Northern newspapers. Recriminations would come later, after the blood cooled. Pitiful appeals fell on the deaf ears of President Johnson. There were no reviews or appeals other than a presidential review, and Andrew Johnson picked this critical time to get sick and be unavailable to reconsider the sentences.

CHAPTER FOURTEEN

The Final Hours

The commission reached its verdicts on June 29 and 30. Because Pres. Andrew Johnson was ill, he did not request the court's findings until July 5. During this interlude, the court's verdicts and the resulting sentences were withheld from the prisoners and the public. However, word leaked on July 3.[1] Likely only speculation or second-hand information, the rumor gave no indication of the sentences, just the news that all eight defendants were found guilty.[2]

On July 5, Joseph Holt took the findings to the president, and they closeted themselves with orders not to be disturbed. They reviewed the evidence for hours. Mary Surratt's plea for clemency was attached upside down to the last page of the voluminous sheaf of papers.[3] Whether Holt ever showed the clemency plea to Johnson has been bitterly disputed and led to strife between the two that was never resolved. Months later, when a political backlash occurred over the hanging of Mrs. Surratt, Johnson swore that Holt had never mentioned the clemency plea or shown him the document. There were no witnesses to the meeting, so it was one man's word against the other. For his part, Holt swore that he showed the plea to Johnson, and they discussed at length the issue of hanging a woman, with Johnson remarking that Mrs. Surratt kept the nest where the egg was hatched and that if she wasn't given the supreme penalty, conspirators in the future would use women for their schemes to avoid the maximum penalty. According to Holt, Johnson claimed that hanging Mary Surratt was actually an act of mercy for womankind. It would save many women in the future if they knew that the supreme penalty would be carried out whenever treason was committed, regardless of gender.[4]

The dispute ruined the reputations and legacies of both men. Each man had a quantity of enemies who delighted in disparaging their foes, but Andrew Johnson had many more issues than just the clemency plea. He narrowly missed impeachment, was denied his party's nomination, and left Washington in disgrace. After Johnson won a seat in the U.S. Senate in 1872, he lashed out against Holt and Stanton (now dead) for using trickery and chicanery to deceive him on the clemency plea. Joseph Holt went to Johnson's aide and secretary, Gen. R. D. Mussey, for confirmation that he had shown the plea to President Johnson. Mussey had talked to Johnson immediately after his meeting with Holt about what had transpired. Mussey wrote back:

Mary Surratt. (Surratt House Museum/MNCPPC)

I asked what the decision was. He told me of the approval of the findings and sentence of the court. I am very confident, though not absolutely assured, that it was at this interview Mr. Johnson told me that the Court had recommended Mrs. Surratt mercy on the ground of her sex (and age, I believe). But I am certain he did so inform me about that time; and that he said he thought the grounds insufficient, and that he had refused to interfere; that if she was guilty at all, her sex did not make her less guilty, that he told me there had not been women enough hanged in the war.[5]

Andrew Johnson died of a stroke seven years later, but Holt lived for another seventeen years. He soon retired to his front porch, where he watched the world go by and turned into a bitter recluse.

In carefully reviewing the testimony, the preponderance of credible evidence falls to Joseph Holt. Failure to disclose a plea of this magnitude to the president of the United States would be fraught with political risk for the judge advocate general. Getting fired would be the least of his problems. This plea was a political hot potato even before she was hanged, and everyone knew it. Andrew Johnson's personal secretary backs Holt's story. While both men showed moral deficiencies and were overzealous, Johnson made many lifelong enemies, suggesting dishonest dealings may have been his modus operandi.

Late in the afternoon on July 5, Holt rushed over to the War Department to give Stanton the news. The president had approved the sentences, and the hangings would occur between 10:00 A.M. and 2:00 P.M. on July 7, less than two days hence.[6] It took the rest of the day to draft the necessary orders to Gen. Winfield Hancock, who delivered the death warrants the next morning to Gen. John Hartranft, the chief officer of the prison. He began notifying the condemned prisoners about noon on July 6, one day before their executions.[7] In U.S. history, no group of condemned defendants has received worse treatment, other than the alleged witches of Salem. Lewis Powell received the news stoically enough. He had expected the sentence.[8] The reactions of the three other condemned conspirators were much different. The news came like a thunderbolt, and they had only twenty-four hours to prepare to meet their maker as well as settle their earthly affairs. The authorities told the remaining four prisoners nothing, leaving them to wonder what was awaiting them. Was this just the first round of hangings? Arnold thought so.

The condemned were moved to the north side of the ground floor to smaller cells within hearing of the frantic building of the gallows. The racket added to their discomfort and fears. Last minute visitations with family and ministers went on at a frantic pace throughout the afternoon and evening. Only Lewis Powell received no visitors. He had left instructions that he would see his lady friend from Baltimore if she came, but he would not send for her.[9]

That afternoon Anna Surratt and a former Pennsylvania senator named Thomas Florence, accompanied by an angry priest named Jacob A. Walter, came to the White House to seek an interview with President Johnson. Father Walter had been in a dispute with the War Department all day and had been told to keep his opinions to himself if he wanted a pass to provide comfort to Mrs. Surratt. The three ascended the steps to the second-floor room next to President Johnson's office. Sen. Preston King and the president's private secretary met them. Father Walter demanded repeatedly to see the president,[10] but they were turned away and told to see Holt. The group got the same response from Holt. Later in the evening, Father Walter returned with Mrs. Surratt's attorney, Frederick Aiken, to ask for just a few days' reprieve to allow Mrs. Surratt more time to prepare for death. The president was adamant. He would see no one.[11] The duo was met at the door by Senator King. He refused them entrance and pointed to a guard with a glistening bayonet as he closed the door. King would commit suicide six months later.

David Herold's sisters also tried to see President Johnson, but they were met with the same lack of success. The next morning, an unexpected ally—one whom Johnson could not refuse—did get through to the president. While Anna Surratt waited helplessly in an anteroom, a fine carriage pulled up in front of the White House and an elegantly dressed, beautiful young lady descended. She walked into the White House like she owned the place. It was the young widow of Stephen Douglas, Adele Cutts Douglas. Mrs. Douglas, very familiar

Anna Surratt. (Public domain)

with Johnson, pushed her way past the bayoneted guards and burst into Johnson's office. She had been recruited by fellow Catholics to intercede on behalf of Mrs. Surratt.

Mrs. Douglas came from a fine family, distantly related to Dolly Madison, and was the niece of the famous Confederate spy Rose Greenhow. Johnson was astonished at her confident resolve but was also intimidated by her status and royal demeanor. He listened politely as she dutifully presented her arguments, both emotional and legal. She offered nothing new, but a young, pretty face could get just about anything from this president. When she finished, he patiently explained that she had been misinformed by her recruiters and outlined his reasons why Mrs. Surratt had to die. Unabashed, Mrs. Douglas thanked him for his time and left in as dashing a manner as she had arrived.

Downstairs, she told Anna she had done everything that she could, but there appeared to be no hope. Anna and her ally, John Brophy, gave her a note from General Hartranft. In it, the general communicated that Lewis Powell had told him that while he was guilty, and would accept justice, Mrs.

Surratt was innocent and hanging her would be a miscarriage of justice. The indomitable Mrs. Douglas turned around, brushed past the guards once again, and showed the president the note. But Andrew Johnson remained firm.[12]

The sun peeped over the eastern horizon on July 7, 1865, promising another windless, sweltering day. Long shadows crossed the unfinished gallows at the prison. The hangman, Christian Rath, entered the yard with a length of rope and a sack of shot. He headed for the tallest tree as soldiers and morbid thrill seekers watched in silence. Rath had to test the ¾-inch rope he had purchased for the hangings. As everyone looked on, he climbed up on a limb and tied one end of the rope to the sack of shot. He tied the other end to the limb and walked out to the edge, where he could watch the bag of shot fall. He dropped the sack. The shot reached the end of the rope and jerked. The limb Rath was standing on snapped under the pressure, sending him to the ground, where he landed on his head. He sat up and rubbed the knot on his head amid the loud guffaws of the spectators and soldiers. As he scowled, some rolled on the ground, holding their splitting sides, howling with glee.[13]

Public humiliation was only one of Rath's problems. The prison employees refused to dig the prisoners' graves as a protest against the government hanging a woman. Rath hurried to the prison office to see Lt. Col. W. H. McCall about the problem. McCall assembled the regiment and told the men he needed volunteers to man the spades, tie the arms and legs of the prisoners, and handle the support beams. He promised every man a drink of whiskey when it was done. Every man in the regiment stepped forward, and soon there was enough digging and hammering to finish the gallows. Rath's day was getting better.

However, the news for the defendants was getting worse. Holt never bothered to tell the defendants' attorneys of the court's decision. That was an unjust oversight as bad as giving the defendants the news only one day before their executions. Mrs. Surratt's attorneys, Aiken and Clampitt, learned of the sentence from an excited newsboy about 5:00 on July 6.[14] They hurried to the White House to ask for three days' time but were turned back by Preston King. They drove to the prison to pick up Anna and went to see Joseph Holt. On her bended knees, Anna tearfully begged Holt for just three more days for her mother. Holt agreed to meet them at the White House. There, Holt met them as he came out of the president's office. He told them that Johnson was immovable and had no reason to delay the execution.

Returning to their legal office, the two attorneys sent for Reverdy Johnson. He advised them to seek a writ of habeas corpus to place Mrs. Surratt in the custody of the Supreme Court. The two worked into the night, finishing the application for the writ about 2:00 A.M. They woke Judge Alexander Wylie, a justice of the Supreme Court of the District of Columbia. Judge Wylie signed the writ, saying at that time, "I am about to perform an act which before tomorrow's sun may consign me to the Old Capitol Prison." The writ was addressed to Gen. Winfield Hancock and Pres. Andrew Johnson.[15] By 4:00 A.M. they had the writ in the hands of a U.S. marshal, who delivered it to General Hancock at 8:30 A.M. He took it to the White House. President Johnson then held a meeting with Stanton, Seward, Secretary of the Navy Gideon Welles, Secretary of the Interior James Harlan, and others. At 10:00 A.M., President Johnson told Hancock that he was suspending the writ and to proceed with the executions. At 11:30 A.M., General Hancock appeared before Justice Wylie and sadly informed him of the president's decision.[16] All legal hopes were gone.

The evening before the executions, Stanton had Thomas Eckert fetch Baptist minister A. D. Gillette to provide emotional succor to the defendants on their last night on earth. All of the doomed accepted his aid except Mary Surratt, who had her own priests with her. Gillette's first visit was to Lewis Payne, as he was known. This time the young man was willing to talk. He confided that his father was a Baptist minister in Florida named Powell and that his two brothers had been killed in the war. He had six sisters. He was born in southern Georgia, but the family had moved to Live Oak Station, an area near modern-day Ocala, Florida.[17]

No one had visited George Atzerodt since the trial began except his brother-in-law and Detective McPhail. Now his mother arrived with great sorrow, bringing tears to the eyes of the hardened guards who had seen such grief countless times. After she left, another woman arrived dressed in deep mourning. She carried a prayer book and seemed deeply concerned. The mysterious lady left after midnight, weighed down with grief. No doubt it was his secret love, Mrs.Wheeler.[18]

Anna Surratt was given permission to spend the last night with her mother. Mary Surratt's priests were there most of the night as well. Several times Mrs. Surratt lost her composure in front of her distressed daughter. She slept very little, if at all. She required constant attention and suffered with cramps and other pains all night.

After daylight, carpenters continued work on the gallows and tested the trap doors. The noise was disquieting to the prisoners.[19] The hangman, Christian Rath, busied himself testing everything and tying strong ropes. It was becoming oppressively hot with no breeze to diminish the heat. After General Hancock appeared at the Supreme Court about the habeas corpus writ, he returned to the prison, finding Anna Surratt's path to the prison blocked by the huge gathering crowd. Anna was on her way back from the White House. In the crowd was the now famous photographer Alexander Gardiner, who had set up his cameras in a building directly across from the gallows to photograph the event, and we have those photos for posterity. After directing a troop of cavalry to clear the way for her, Hancock followed Anna into the prison grounds. It was nearing noon and Hancock knew that Mary Surratt had run out of options. Neither Hancock nor General Hartranft wanted to see her hang, so Hancock set up a relay of well-mounted troopers from the prison to the White House in the hope that President Johnson would relent and grant a commutation or a temporary reprieve.[20]

After an hour, Hancock knew that he could wait no longer. Orders were orders. He gave the order to commence. At 1:02 P.M. the condemned were led out of the prison building. Mary Surratt was first, escorted by Fathers Wiget and Walter. She could hardly stand, let alone walk. Soldiers supported her under her arms and walked her along slowly. Atzerodt came next, followed by David Herold. Powell was last, accompanied by

Reverend Gillette.[21] After the four were seated in chairs on the scaffold, General Hartranft read them the order of execution. When he was finished, Gillette made a statement on behalf of Powell, thanking Hartranft and his men for their kind treatment. The prisoners were then prodded to their feet and had their legs and hands bound with white linen. The nooses were adjusted so that the knots were placed on the side of the head to ensure that the prisoners' necks would be broken to provide a quick and humane death rather than slowly strangling.

At twenty-one minutes past one o'clock, Christian Rath clapped his hands three times and four soldiers swung the pair of bludgeons against the support pillars. The trap doors fell, and the condemned fell six feet to their deaths. The end came quickly for all but Powell. His size and strength worked against him. It took six minutes for him to strangle to death.[22] After a few minutes, the bodies were cut down, placed in wooden coffins, and buried in graves that had been dug by the side of the gallows. For most of Booth's connections, it was over. But his closest associate was still alive and at large, Mary Surratt's son, John.

Four hung conspirators. (National Archives)

CHAPTER FIFTEEN

After the Executions

Gen. Levi A. Dodd visited Samuel Arnold's cell and informed him that four of his co-defendants had just been hanged. Arnold and his remaining defendants still had not been informed of their own fate. The men exercised under the shadow of the scaffold, near the fresh graves, for the next ten days. On July 17, the four were assembled, manacled, and led to a steamboat on the Potomac after being formally notified of their sentences.[1] The boat steamed down the river while the prisoners speculated about their destination. No one had told them that. At Fort Monroe, they were transferred to a warship, the *Florida.* Originally the four were to be imprisoned in the penitentiary in Albany, New York, but Edwin Stanton decided to keep the prisoners in military custody. They were now on their way to the Fort Jefferson prison in the Dry Tortugas.[2]

On board the *Florida,* the rules were relaxed, and they were allowed on the deck more and more as the heat intensified. They were also allowed to talk to the ship's crew. On the trip south, Dr. Samuel Mudd confessed to Capt. George Dutton, the officer in charge of the military escort, that Louis Weichmann's testimony about the meeting in Washington during which Mudd had introduced Booth to Surratt had been true.[3] Mudd also revealed that he knew who Booth was when he treated him after the assassination. He had made a similar statement to a *New York Tribune* reporter after the hangings, but it received little attention at the time. Mudd's admission was also overheard by Gen. Levi Dodd and a crew member, William F. Keeler. When the ship returned to Washington,

Captain Dutton filed an affidavit with the War Department, which was released to the press. In his new prison, Mudd denied the admission. Another controversy commenced, but by this time, Mudd's lack of credibility had been established.

Fort Jefferson could house two thousand military prisoners. Its walls were forty-five feet high and it sat on an underwater foundation fourteen feet in width. The warden kept the premises meticulously clean, and the prison's inmates and staff were healthy. Upon arrival, Dr. Mudd was assigned to the hospital and for a short time was reasonably content. His letters to his wife and family were upbeat. Then conditions soured for the white supremacist Mudd.

The 161st New York Infantry was replaced by the 82nd U.S. Colored Troops. Whether these soldiers treated him any differently than their predecessors is unknown, but he was incensed about being lorded over by a set of "ignorant, prejudiced, and irresponsible set of the 'unbleached humanity.'"[4] Three weeks after this letter of complaint to his wife, he attempted to escape. Having hospital privileges, he donned clean clothes and walked up the plank of a visiting supply ship, *Thomas A. Scott.* An accomplice, Henry Kelly, hid him under some loose planks below decks. A routine roll call was taken before the ship left the prison and Mudd's absence was discovered. A search of the ship soon turned up the doctor, who promptly threw his accomplice under the bus. Kelly was arrested and placed in the fort before the ship departed.[5] Mudd temporarily lost his work privileges in the infirmary, but he was not severely punished. He was assigned to scrubbing bricks. He was then transferred to the carpentry shop, where he made some small pieces of furniture that remain in the Mudd home today.

While his co-conspirators were serving their sentences, the other fugitive from justice was boarding a ship for Europe. John Surratt had been hiding in the tiny village of Saint-Liboire at the lodgings of Fr. Charles Boucher. It's unclear if that was within the confines of a church facility or a private residence. He had hidden there for almost three months as the trial of his mother and the other defendants progressed.[6]

According to John Surratt, he never felt that his mother's life was in danger. Circumstances do not bear this out. Newspapers, even the Canadian ones, carried every detail of the trial. By mid-May he would have known of the specific charges against his mother and the potential legal consequences of her actions. Many have chastised him for not coming to rescue her, but this author doesn't believe that he ever had that option. John Surratt certainly believed, with good cause, that if he returned, the court would have added one more noose to the gallows. His mother wouldn't have benefitted at all. With her involvement as a messenger and courier on the day of the assassination, she was doomed. We will never know if and when her son realized that.

Surratt was discovered in Father Boucher's home by a servant girl in late July,[7] at which point the priest told Surratt that he could no longer stay with him. With the hanging of his mother fresh on his mind, Surratt traveled with a young Canadian named Bouthillier to Murray Bay, about four hundred kilometers from Montreal, and was joined there by Gen. Edwin Lee and several other parties, including possibly Sarah Slater.[8] The whole group vacationed there August 11 to 14. Maybe Surratt and Slater had a love affair, as the author suggests in *John Surratt: The Lincoln Assassin Who Got Away.* If they did, it was a relationship that never had a chance. Slater was too careful to get caught in Surratt's limelight. While working as a spy, she took every precaution to avoid showing her face and said practically nothing in the presence of strangers.[9]

Hiding behind the Bishop's Palace in Montreal, Canada, John Surratt read about the recruiting efforts of the Papal Zouaves. The army of the Pope was at war with the secular government forces of the Garibaldi movement.[10] A Canadian priest, Fr. Andre Lapierre, obtained approval from the church and arranged, along with Gen. Edwin Lee, passage to Europe so that Surratt could join the papal forces. This solved everybody's problems. The church and the extinct Confederacy could rid itself of an embarrassing problem, while Surratt could melt into a distant army and disappear from the Union's radar.

In early September, Father Lapierre approached Dr. Lewis McMillan, a surgeon working with the Montreal Ocean Steamship Company. The priest told him of a friend who planned to travel by ship to Quebec on September 15 and who would appreciate the doctor's assistance.[11] With the doctor's help, Surratt, using the name McCarty, booked travel on the steamer *Peruvian,* bound for Liverpool. To make his way to Quebec City, from which he would depart, Surratt changed his appearance with dyed hair and glasses.

Surratt was not the only conspirator making his way overseas. After an arduous trip, Judah Benjamin arrived in England. He had left the presidential party in Abbeville, South Carolina, in a flimsy cart drawn by a pair of worn-down horses and, paralleling Jefferson Davis's route, traveled south through Georgia, using the name of M. M. Bonfals.[12] He never planned to go to Mexico, and $649,000 and a new legal career awaited him in England. As he neared the Florida border, he changed his disguise to that of a poor farmer on horseback looking for land to buy and farm. This permitted him to move faster. The roads were crowded with soldiers returning home, and he had to stop often while in the cart to answer all types of inquiries. On horseback, he didn't have to stop and talk unless he wanted to. He began to travel at night, avoiding towns and villages when he could. He kept gold hidden in his drab clothing. He made his way to relatives and gave them some of the gold before hurrying on his way to the Gamble Plantation in Ellenton, Florida.[13]

The Gamble Plantation was owned by the Confederate government and used to grow crops for the army. The house sat back about five hundred yards from the Manatee River, which flowed into the Gulf of Mexico about ten miles away. If any Union soldiers docked at the plantation, he could see them from his second-story window and have plenty of time to make for the woods.[14]

He stayed at the plantation for three days while he made arrangements for a boat to Bimini, in the Bahamas. Plantation overseer Archibald McNeil took him across the Manatee River to the home of Fred Tresca, who had vast knowledge of the

Floridian waterways. He stayed there two weeks while Tresca made arrangements for Benjamin to continue south. Tresca, Benjamin, and a pilot named H. A. McLeod secured a sailing yawl. They headed south from Sarasota, dodging Yankee patrol boats and thunderstorms with waterspouts on a treacherous two-week journey to Bimini. From there, Benjamin took a small sponge-carrying vessel bound for Cuba. The vessel exploded during the journey when the sponges got wet and expanded. Benjamin and three black seamen made it back to Bimini, where he chartered Tresca's vessel to Nassau. Benjamin gave Tresca a fifteen-hundred-dollar parting gift. From there, he went to Havana, where he booked passage to England. His problems weren't over yet. The ship caught fire, but the crew put it out. He finally made it to Southampton on August 30, 1865.

Benjamin would achieve remarkable success in England. His most valuable traits were determination, a work ethic that would exhaust younger men, and fluency in both English and French. He was also well versed in mercantile issues under the old Napoleonic Code. His experience and talent far exceeded most of his peers, allowing him to overcome a legal caste system that rewarded referrals from solicitor to barrister based upon family and friendships that, in many cases, went back generations. Surpassing the success of the work he had written while an attorney in Louisiana, he published a legal treatise on sales between France, the British Isles, and the United States. The book was so necessary that every judge and attorney in the three countries required a copy. His referrals skyrocketed. He gained fame in the appellate courts with his unique presentation style of first lecturing the judges on the existing law then showing them how those laws benefitted his client. He was a formidable foe in an appeal case. Solicitors who cared for their client's welfare chose Benjamin over their brothers in law simply because of his talent and industry. By the mid-1870s, Benjamin was earning eighty thousand dollars a year, a veritable fortune in those days. His royalties from his book nearly equaled his legal fees.

Benjamin retired to Paris in 1882 for health reasons. He was invited back from Paris the next year for an honorarium by his peers, the first banquet of that kind ever held in England. Every judge, solicitor, and barrister who was anyone attended the banquet. Those who toasted him spoke of him as being the most admired barrister in the British Isles. He accomplished all this in fifteen years as an outsider to the British legal system.[15]

Other conspirators had their own adventuresome escapes. Confederate agent Thomas Nelson Conrad was arrested soon after the assassination and imprisoned under the friendly and accommodating jailer Col. William Wood. When no evidence surfaced connecting Conrad to the plot, at the suggestion of Colonel Wood, he received a pass from Lafayette Baker so that he could visit Virginia. Nelson was put aboard a steamer used to transport witnesses from Virginia to the conspiracy trial. For two months, Conrad was undisturbed, but about midnight on July 9, he was re-arrested and jailed in Fredericksburg, pending transportation to Richmond. Conrad had no doubt that he would be hanged as a spy, so at Ashland, he leaped from the moving train while his guards slept and ran for his life. By the time the train could stop, Conrad was long gone. He met a friend, by pre-arrangement, on the Rappahannock River with his horse. With his friend, Mountjoy, Conrad headed for the Shenandoah Mountains, where he would hide for the next year.[16]

On May 10, Jefferson Davis was caught near Irwinville, Georgia, dashing for the woods. He was wearing a woman's shawl, a detail that kept cartoonists in the North busy for weeks.[17] Davis was transported by horseback, then rail, and finally aboard the steamer *William P. Clyde*. He ended up at Fort Monroe, where he was kept for two years awaiting a trial that the Union prosecution could never quite put together. The witnesses linking him to the murder plot were known perjurers, and statute required that Davis's trial for treason be held in Virginia. The North knew that no jury in Virginia would convict Davis. So he sat in prison while the Union government pondered what to do. Finally, in 1867, a hundred-thousand-dollar bail was set and made. Davis was finally out of jail but remained under indictment. While traveling in Europe in 1869, he heard the good news that the indictment had been quashed. Davis was finally free.

On September 15, Surratt and the two priests, Boucher and Lapierre, slipped aboard the steamer *Montreal,* bound for Quebec City. Surratt was introduced to Dr. McMillan onboard the boat as it steamed down the St. Lawrence River. The next day, Surratt and McMillan boarded the *Peruvian* for the trip to Liverpool. Assuming that McMillan was a kindred spirit, as the trip progressed Surratt told McMillan almost every detail of his adventures as a Confederate courier and spy. He embellished occasionally, as when he insinuated that he was an equal partner with Booth and the kidnapping plot was "their own." Surratt refrained from involving himself with the assassination plot though. Two years later, when McMillan would testify against him at his trial, he could not claim that Surratt had gone that far. One thing is certain: Surratt was not nearly as smart as his partner, Sarah Slater, who never told anyone, as far as we know, about her role in the plot. Surratt seemed bound and determined to brag to somebody. Surratt also told McMillan that he hoped to return home someday, not from love of country but to "serve Andrew Johnson as Lincoln had been served." Surratt apparently knew enough about Johnson's refusal to see his sister to know that Johnson was responsible for the hanging of his mother, and he was thirsting for revenge.[18]

Surratt got off the ship at the first landfall, Londonderry, just in case someone from the federal government was waiting for him in Liverpool. Later that day, Surratt's friend and assumed confidant McMillan landed in Liverpool and provided intelligence of Surratt's presence in England to U.S. Vice-Consul Henry Wilding. When Surratt arrived in Liverpool the next day, his supposed friend helped him find sanctuary at the oratory of the Roman Catholic Church of the Holy Cross. McMillan then reported his exact whereabouts back to Wilding. Wilding notified the ambassador to England, a Mr. Adams, who cabled the information on to Washington. The shocking instructions came back: "It is thought advisable that no action be taken in regard to the arrest of the supposed

John Surratt at present."[19] What was Washington thinking? The only thing that makes sense is that the administration was catching flak for the hanging of Mary Surratt and/or criticism for trying the conspirators by military tribunal.

Dr. McMillan came back to Canada on the *Peruvian*'s return trip and filed an affidavit with the Canadian U.S. consul, John Potter, who also cabled Washington asking for orders to apprehend Surratt. In fact, he sent several cables with little response other than that Washington would take the matter under advisement. Then on November 24, Washington rescinded the reward for John Surratt.[20]

The government no longer sought the number one fugitive in the land, even when he was in its grasp. Johnson was clearly paying the price for his callous disregard of the distraught Anna Surratt's pleas. Even though they couldn't be sure of the nature of John Surratt's role in the plot, Seward by this time knew that his assailant had not been Surratt. *Ex Parte Milligan* had not been established yet, but Johnson, Stanton, and Holt must have known that if Surratt were apprehended, this time there would be a civil trial, with unpredictable results. That was a trial that they could not afford to lose.

Surratt traveled to London on September 30. There is no evidence that he met Judah Benjamin there. At the time, Benjamin most likely would have been in Liverpool, the Confederate money stashed safely nearby. Jacob Thompson had placed that big bank draft with Frazier, Trenholm & Co. in Liverpool. We know that those funds totaled $649,000, less any expenses deducted during travel. We don't know what cut Jacob Thompson received. But we know that the account was in the name of Judah Benjamin-Secret Service.[21] With a stroke of a pen, Benjamin could have transferred some of that money to a different bank in London and omitted the words "Secret Service."

Sen. James Bayard of Delaware was an old friend with whom Benjamin had corresponded for decades. Bayard offered Benjamin financial assistance, but Benjamin declined, saying that he had managed to get possession of a hundred bales of cotton, which had brought him the bonanza of twenty thousand dollars.[22]

Benjamin never would have told such a friend about his real income. He was careful. He went to Lincoln's Inn, a British law school in Liverpool, and studied law there for a few months, having used his connections to get the three-year study requirement for admission to the English bar waived. We must wonder how much that cost. Then he set up practice in London.

Surratt received more money from Canada to continue his trip. After traveling to Paris, he dropped out of sight, but he arrived in central Italy dead broke. The Catholic church rode to the rescue again and furnished him with fifty francs to get him the rest of the way to Rome.

While Surratt was traveling through Europe, the case of *Ex Parte Milligan* was progressing to the Supreme Court. Lambin Milligan was an attorney in Indiana and a member of the Knights of the Golden Circle, the leading group of Copperheads. He, along with some half a dozen others, were arrested in 1864 and charged with giving aid and comfort to the Confederates, inciting insurrections, disloyal practices, violations of the laws of war, establishing a secret organization that would free Southern prisoners of war, planning to seize weapons in a U.S. arsenal, and joining and arming Confederate prisoners of war to invade Indiana, Illinois, and Kentucky and make war on the United States. In October 1864, a military tribunal tried him and sentenced Milligan to death by hanging.

On May 10, during the trial of the conspirators, a writ of habeas corpus was filed in the Indiana federal court system by Milligan's attorney. Milligan's execution date was postponed until June 2 by Pres. Andrew Johnson. On May 30, Johnson commuted Milligan's death penalty to life imprisonment. Where did this leniency come from? The issue raised in Milligan's federal case was the jurisdiction of a military tribunal to try civilians when the civil courts were open and in session—the same issue protested by the conspirators' attorneys. The case was reviewed by two justices and (by design) they were unable to agree on the issue and passed the case on to the Supreme Court.

Even while the Milligan trial progressed, its existence would have come to the notice of Joseph Holt, the head of the Bureau of Military Justice, who would have advised Stanton and Andrew Johnson of its potential impact. With peace in sight, pressure was building to avoid trying civilians in military courts. Later in the fall, this case would have been an additional factor as Johnson faced the problem of John Surratt. It appears that Mary Surratt had become Andrew Johnson's worst nightmare. Everything he did from this point forward points to his avoidance of all things Surratt. He was catching hell for his conscious indifference to the pleadings of her daughter, Anna. Perhaps he was even having private misgivings about his actions toward her. The public perceived that the government had overdone vengeance by hanging a woman, and Johnson would not be allowed to forget it.

Ex Parte Milligan was argued in March 1866 by a battery of heavy hitters on both sides.[23] The merits of Milligan's case were not considered, only the right to try civilians in a military court when civil courts were functioning. On April 3, 1866, the U.S. Supreme Court handed down its decision. Military courts could not try civilians while civil courts were functioning if the alleged acts did not occur in a war zone.[24] This decision cast a long shadow over the military tribunal that tried the Lincoln conspirators, as it would over the trial of John Surratt the following year.

John Surratt enlisted into the Papal Zouaves on December 11, 1865, under the alias of Giovanni Watson. The Papal Zouaves were an international mercenary force comprised of Catholic men from around the world. The Zouaves were opposed by the "Red Shirt" brigades of the Garibaldi army, which sought to unite the various kingdoms of Italy into one national government. The Zouave army numbered about 4,600 men wearing uniforms of gray trimmed in red. When a man entered the Papal Zouaves, he was required to cast off all his personal possessions, which discouraged desertion. Surratt as Watson would have had no problem shedding his possessions, which included a big wanted poster. He could now put that life behind him. After he finished basic training, he was assigned to Company C in the Third Regiment and stationed in Sezze, about forty miles southeast of Rome.

Surratt had been placed in the dragoons, the mounted infantry.[25] Surratt's days were filled with training, guard duty, keeping equipment clean, and practice with his weapons. Life was routine, and America's dangers were dimming.

Sometime in late March or early April, 1866, the Papal Zouaves acquired another recruit, Henri Beaumont de Sainte Marie. Sainte Marie wasn't interested in preserving the Vatican. Interested only in money, he was a bounty hunter who had been tracking Surratt across Europe and into the Zouaves. He had met Surratt three years earlier in Little Texas, Maryland, and had come face to face with Surratt and Weichmann sometime in early April 1863. The two renewed their acquaintance in the papal guards. Sainte Marie told him that he knew that he was John Surratt. Surratt begged Sainte Marie not to expose him. Fat chance of that.

At Surratt's trial, Henri Sainte Marie was considered a questionable witness, and his credibility was challenged. But in his affidavits to Rufus King, the U.S. consul to Rome, he provided information that he could not have made up. As time passed, Surratt had gone back to his bragging ways and disclosed to Sainte Marie several interesting facts that the bounty hunter could not have made up on the witness stand. On April 23, 1867, Rufus King cabled Secretary of State William H. Seward to tell him that Surratt had acknowledged to Sainte Marie his participation in the plot against Mr. Lincoln's life and declared that Jefferson Davis had incited it or was privy to it.[26] This information finally pushed the Union into slow, deliberate action. There were several cables sent back and forth, and finally Washington ordered Rufus King to request a written statement from Sainte Marie. The statement was obtained on June 21, 1866, and forwarded to Washington two days later. It read:

> Speaking of the murder, [Surratt] said they had acted under the orders of men not yet known, some of whom are still in New York, and others in London. I have also asked him if he knew Jefferson Davis. He said no, but that he had acted under the instructions of persons under his immediate orders. Being asked if Jefferson Davis had anything to do with the assassination, he said "I am not

going to tell you." My impression is that he brought the order from Richmond, as he was in the habit of going there weekly. He must have bribed others to do it [i.e., carry out the assassination], for when the event took place he told me he was in New York, prepared to fly as soon as the deed was done. He says he does not regret what had taken place. . . . This is the exact truth of what I know of Surratt. More, I could not learn, being afraid to awaken his suspicions.[27]

This is the final bombshell in this book. If Sainte Marie were lying, as Sandford Conover had during the conspirators' trial, he would have told Washington what they wanted to hear, according to author Michael Schein in his book *John Surratt: The Lincoln Assassin Who Got Away*. Mr. Schein is correct in this conclusion. The only two Confederates under Jefferson Davis's immediate orders who were in London were Judah Benjamin and Jacob Thompson. Sainte Marie could not have made that up. That is information only Surratt could have known. That is why Sainte Marie should be believed. It's the best confession from a presidential assassin participant that history will ever get. Further, it is consistent with everything else we know. The clues in sequence will be discussed at the end of this book.

CHAPTER SIXTEEN

Off the Hook

Members of the federal government were still cautious and skeptical as they considered Henri Sainte Marie's statement. Finally, Secretary Seward sent a cable to Rufus King asking the Vatican for four things: (1) a picture of Surratt; (2) an assurance from Cardinal Giacomo Antonelli that in the absence of an extradition treaty, the Vatican would surrender Surratt upon the request of the American government; (3) keep both Surratt and Sainte Marie in the Zouaves until the American government had time to communicate concerning them; and (4) pay Sainte Marie $250 in gold for the information that he had given them.[1] Maybe they hoped the money would pacify Sainte Marie.

Without waiting further, Cardinal Antonelli ordered the arrest of Watson (Surratt), whose unit had moved farther away from Rome into some mountains near the monastery of Trisulti, near the top of Mount Rotonario. The arrest warrant was issued to Surratt's regimental commander, Lt. Col. M. Allet. Allet passed the order on to Surratt's company commander, Captain De Lambilly, who sent a sergeant and six men to arrest the American. Through a misdirected letter to Sainte Marie, Surratt was warned about his impending arrest. Thus apprised, he obtained leave and traveled twelve miles to Veroli. He eluded the arrest party, but he was too slow in obtaining civilian clothes and was arrested by a corporal in his own command and locked in a stone prison in Veroli.

At 4:00 A.M. he was awakened and told to prepare himself for immediate transport to Rome. Surratt rose quietly and sullenly put on his uniform before he was marched out into the darkness between a guard of six men. At the far end of the courtyard was a parapet with a steep drop of about a hundred feet onto broken rocks. Sticking out about fifteen feet below the parapet was a ledge of rock covered with human waste from the three outhouses directly above it. Surratt had obviously observed this in the previous three days. He casually asked to go to the privy before the trip, and his request was granted. Without further warning, he leaped over the parapet and disappeared into the darkness. He had a relatively soft landing in the filth below the privies and made his miraculous escape.[2]

As many as fifty Zouaves gave chase to Surratt as he headed down the mountain toward the Garibaldi enemies in the valley. Surratt was a popular soldier in his regiment and the pursuit could have been less than zealous on the part of his fellow soldiers. Eight days later, the regimental commander finally notified Rufus King that Surratt had escaped and was probably in the vicinity of Sora, which was enemy territory to the Zouaves.

Surratt had injured his shoulder and lower back in the fall but found a stream in the valley where he could take a cleansing swim before traveling farther. He then found a hospital in the town of Sora, about fifteen miles down the valley, where his wounds were treated. He told his Garibaldi captors that he was a Zouave deserter. From there, Surratt made his way to Naples, where he sought refuge in the local jail so that he could get food and shelter. He was dirty and bedraggled. The police probably were happy to accommodate him so they could keep an eye on a suspicious person. But he was not a prisoner. After three days, claiming his name was Walters, he sought asylum with the British consul. A British traveler paid for his passage to Alexandria, Egypt, on the ship *Tripoli*.

By 2:00 P.M. the day after the ship had set sail, Mr. Swan, the American consul in Naples, discovered that Surratt was aboard the *Tripoli*. He passed this information on to Rufus King. King cabled Charles Hale, the American consul in Alexandria, with instructions to arrest Surratt there. A myriad of communication problems between Naples and Alexandria slowed the transmission of instructions to Egypt, but Surratt's luck finally ran out in Alexandria. He was quarantined on the ship as a result of the *Tripoli's* brief stop for coal in Malta, where a cholera epidemic had broken out. As he sat helplessly on the boat, the telegram from Italy reached the American consulate. On November 27, Charles Hale boarded the ship and arrested Surratt without incident.[3]

Sometime in late November or early December, the USS *Swatara* received orders to proceed to Rome to pick up a prisoner. The ship was commanded by Capt. William N. Jeffers.[4] When he arrived in Rome, Jeffers was told that the prisoner had escaped but had been recaptured in Alexandria. Before departing from the port at Civitavecchia, Jeffers took on board Henri Sainte Marie. Sainte Marie seemed to be considered a "snitch" and was not given the best of treatment while on board. When the ship reached Egypt, Surratt, on orders, was held in solitary confinement, could talk to no one, and was kept under the strictest guard. The U.S. was taking no more chances with the elusive Surratt.

The ship was in no hurry and spent the Christmas holidays in Alexandria before continuing on to Villefranche-sur-Mer, on the French Riviera, where Admiral Louis Goldsborough inspected the prisoner and gave Jeffers his final orders. Sainte Marie, incensed by his poor and disrespectful treatment, disembarked the *Swatara* and took another ship headed for the U.S. Due to bad weather, Jeffers' ship took two weeks to get from France to Washington, arriving on February 17, 1867. Sainte Marie had beaten the *Swatara* to Washington, and there was concern that the ship transferring the federal prisoner had been lost at sea. But after almost two years, Surratt was back in the United States.

The country to which Surratt returned was different, at least legally. Surratt would face no military tribunal but a twelve-man jury in a civil court, courtesy of the *Ex Parte Milligan* Supreme Court ruling. The bloodlust of the North had dissipated, and the country had moved on. Not that the country was disinterested; it wasn't. The Surratts made good copy, and dime novels were cranking out the story of Surratt's leap into legend.

Surratt was also returning to a federal government in turmoil. The feud between Andrew Johnson and the Radical

Republicans in Congress was heating up. Trouble was also brewing between the triangle of Johnson, Stanton, and Lafayette Baker. Baker had caught Johnson passing out pardons to Southern leaders like candy bars on Halloween. The wily Southerners were using attractive, sassy young women as pardon brokers, and Johnson couldn't refuse a pretty face. Baker didn't catch the president taking money from these young ladies, but he came really close.[5] Using marked bills, he snared one broker and confronted President Johnson about it, starting a feud that he couldn't stop and bringing his boss, Edwin Stanton, into the quarrel. Baker ultimately lost his job over his arrest of the young pardon broker. The breach was never healed, and he didn't return to Washington until it was time to testify in Congress against Johnson. By the time the government got around to preparing the case against Surratt, the executive branch was in disarray.

As the government prepared the case against John Surratt, prosecutors had no way of knowing how meticulously he had set up his alibi. Their strategy was to charge him with the murder of Abraham Lincoln. In addition to Sainte Marie's statements, they had witnesses who claimed to have seen Surratt in Washington on the night of the murder. They could have convicted Surratt of conspiracy standing on their head, but they opted for a conviction of murder. The trial was going to be a train wreck.

The trial began on June 10, 1867, in the District of Columbia Criminal Court on D Street, between Fourth and Fifth Streets, with Judge George P. Fisher presiding. Fisher was mostly a prosecutor's judge, a Union colonel who commanded the Third Delaware Regiment, which counted Henri Beaumont de Sainte Marie a private. Lincoln had appointed Fisher judge. In modern times, that would be grounds for recusal. The government called eighty-five witnesses in its case in chief. The defense countered by calling ninety-seven witnesses of its own, and the government, with its case in tatters, called ninety-six rebuttal witnesses. Then the defense called twenty-three counter rebuttal witnesses.[6]

The government, in its opening statement, promised to prove that Surratt was with Booth in front of Ford's Theatre aiding and abetting the murder and that he was the brains behind both Lincoln's assassination and Seward's attack. Under the laws of any crime, it is not necessary for a defendant to be present, as the prosecution later would claim, to be found guilty. But the government made his presence the central issue in the case.[7]

The government started with the story of Booth's role in the assassination. These facts were undisputed. Then came the testimony of Sgt. Joseph Dye, who placed Surratt in front of the theatre, calling out the time. Several other witnesses put Surratt in Washington on the day of April 14. The government rehashed the roles of Surratt's mother and George Atzerodt and bored the jury with testimony from witnesses who claimed to have seen Surratt with other members of the plot on that day. The prosecution then put Weichmann on the stand, where he stayed for three days. He retold the story that he had given during the conspiracy trial and was slapped around by the defense because he provided the wrong date for the Booth-Surratt meeting set up by Dr. Samuel Mudd. Encompassing sixty-seven pages of transcript, Weichmann's testimony was a lot of smoke and not much fire, with the most damaging testimony against the mother and not the son.[8]

On July 2, Henri Sainte Marie came to the stand amid a furor of possible witness intimidation moves. For about a week, defense attorney Joseph H. Bradley, Jr. had been referring to the witness room as the penitentiary. Although warned by the judge, he continued his aggressive remarks that those who sat "in the penitentiary" would soon be sitting in another one. The clash became so bitter between the prosecution and defense that the prosecution was put "off kilter" and hardly asked Sainte Marie any questions at all,[9] even though the government had spent a thousand dollars in expenses and ultimately ten thousand dollars in reward money for their star witness. Sainte Marie had the most damaging testimony of all, yet the government got so flustered by Bradley that it forgot to pin down Surratt with his own confession to Sainte Marie. Once again, the Surratt luck held, and Bradley pulled off the greatest strategically successful defensive ploy of all.

The government never challenged Congress's decision, a

month after the trial, to pay Sainte Marie the ten thousand dollars in reward money, even though his testimony did not lead to a conviction. From that, we can deduce that the defense got inside the prosecution's head at exactly the right time. To use a poker term, Bradley owned the prosecution from that day forward. Henri Sainte Marie is considered a questionable witness mostly because of this bounty. The fact that he was a bounty hunter shouldn't be a huge factor considering the facts. Had he recanted his testimony, that would have been different, but that doesn't seem to be the case. The information that he provided Rufus King in Italy stands unchallenged to this day. The prosecution's failure to bring out this critical testimony is the greatest question of this trial and probably the reason for the resulting hung jury. As a caveat though, even had the prosecution used Sainte Marie effectively, the government may not have been able to overcome the eight Southern men on the jury anyway.

Another possibility for the government's clumsy use of Sainte Marie is that the prosecution was afraid his testimony would damage the reputation of Louis Weichmann. Sainte Marie had written a letter to Joseph Holt on May 20, 1865, accusing Weichmann of Southern sentiments.[10] He clearly didn't like Weichmann and said so in the letter. However, the defense did not have a copy of the letter sent to Holt two years before. The prosecution may have had second thoughts about presenting conflicting witnesses to a jury, but it's difficult to understand why Sainte Marie's startling revelations about alleged orders from "people in London and New York" to kill Lincoln would not become the main testimony in the case and steer Sainte Marie's testimony away from Weichmann. Perhaps Surratt was aware of Sainte Marie's intense dislike for Weichmann and that scared the prosecution. It remains a puzzle. In closing, one thing is clear: Sainte Marie stood ready to testify. There is no logical reason to disbelieve his affidavit to Rufus King in Italy. As Michael Schein stated in his book *John Surratt: The Lincoln Assassin Who Got Away*, "Whatever the reason, powerful evidence against Surratt and the Confederate high command was suppressed."

Although the government's case was a little weak, it did

prove three things before it rested: (1) John Surratt secured a hotel room for Lewis Paine (Powell); (2) he delivered the two carbines to John Lloyd at the tavern for safekeeping; and (3) he recruited George Atzerodt and secured a getaway boat, which he had hidden in Nanjemoy Creek. All of these things made him an accomplice. That was more than enough, under ordinary circumstances, to hang him.

But they overdid the indictment, which consisted of four parts. The first part of the indictment had Surratt, not John Wilkes Booth, pulling the trigger on Abraham Lincoln. The second and third alleged that he was present to aid and abet the crime of murder. The fourth suggested his participation in a conspiracy to murder. The indictment nowhere alleges a conspiracy to kidnap.

The defense hit the ground running on the faulty indictment. They claimed that this was no indictment for conspiracy but an indictment to murder. They tiptoed around the conspiracy culpability by asserting that there was not one conspiracy but two. The defense maintained that Surratt abandoned the first plot to kidnap after the aborted action on March 17, ignoring the fact that Surratt remained active after that date. The defense then claimed that John Surratt never was in a murder plot.

For a penniless soldier from the Vatican, John Surratt had a formidable team of defense attorneys. There was Joseph Bradley, Sr., the dean of the Washington bar, and his son Joseph Bradley, Jr. In addition, Richard T. Merrick, a sharp-tongued cross examiner, also served as counsel.[11] How Surratt obtained these noted attorneys is somewhat of a mystery, but they may have accepted the case pro bono for the notoriety that it brought. John Surratt was becoming famous, not just because of his mother, now considered a Southern martyr, but also for that leap into the dung heap in Italy. He was a dashing rogue, well dressed in a black suit, six feet tall and slender. He made an impressive appearance. Southern heroes were emerging, and he was one. He was also the only Southern spy and courier of whom the public knew. The others wouldn't come out of hiding for another fifteen years. His attorneys were the A-Team, well coached, with a good game plan, and ready to play. They reserved their opening statement until the prosecution rested, and then they told the jury that they could clear the name of not only John Surratt, but also his mother's.

The first defense witness was a credible doctor from New York City named Augustus Bissell, who testified that on April 14, 1865, he was in Elmira, New York, to track down a witness in his lawsuit against a railroad. He dropped into the Brainard House Hotel to rest awhile in the lounge, and a man sat down beside him. The man noticed Dr. Bissell's bad leg and asked him if he had suffered a wound in the war, but Bissell was suspicious that he was a railroad detective. He cut the conversation short, but he remembered the man. He identified John Surratt as that man. When asked about how he could be certain of the date, he replied that later that evening his wife wired him that their child was seriously ill and asked him to come home. Before he could reach home, the child died.[12] After that, several others testified that they had seen the oddly dressed Surratt on April 13, 14, and 15 in Elmira. Surratt had done his alibi work well. In the first two hours, the defense had destroyed the first three parts of the state's indictment.

The defense then presented the hotel register at the Webster House in Canandaigua, New York, which showed that a John Harrison registered on April 15. The defense used John's sister, Anna, to identify the handwriting. The state objected, saying that anyone could have inserted that name on the register at any time during the last two years. The judge inexplicably sustained the objection.[13] To this author, a former judge, this is an egregious ruling. This exhibit is clearly admissible. If the state wished to attack its credibility, its prosecutors could have done so to the jury at the proper time. With the name John Harrison written in the middle of the page, a claim that space was reserved so that a name could be added later is ridiculous. Almost any jury would laugh an attorney out of a courtroom if they made such a statement.

The judge also excluded the testimony of Gen. Edwin Lee, who testified that he had assigned Surratt to scout the prisoner of war camp during those critical days of April. This was highly unfair of the judge and shows how squalid courts could be in those days. Judge Fisher also excluded the testimony of a priest who claimed to have had a conversation with Louis Weichmann outside the confessional. During that conversation, Weichmann confided that he was in the War Department and relayed information to the Confederacy. Fisher ruled the testimony irrelevant. Judge Fisher made no judicial mistakes in Surratt's favor. It was all one sided. The jury may have seen through all this.

There was a lot riding on this case. The district attorney for Washington, D.C., Edward C. Carrington, stood to face the jury in final arguments. He first attacked the elephant in the room: sectional prejudice.

> I cannot regard this cruel, miserable murderer and assassin as a representative man of the South; and if an attempt should be made . . . by innuendoes . . . to present him to the imagination of this jury as an embodiment . . . of southern honor and southern chivalry, I call upon you to spurn it as an insult to every honest man, born and reared upon southern soil. Southern men do not justify assassination and cold blooded, deliberate, cruel murder. I am aware that I address southern men with southern sympathies . . . loyal men, men true to the laws and the Constitution of our common country. What honorable man, north, south, east or west, will proclaim to the civilized world that he justifies, palliates, sympathizes with a traitor, a spy, and an assassin. . . . Give me a jury of honorable confederate soldiers, give me a jury of young rebels, with arms in their hands, who entered into this fierce and cruel war, under the delusion that they were doing God's service, misled by wicked designing and ambitious politicians, and let me tell the sad story of this cruel murder, and they would hang this wretch as high as old John Brown.[14]

Carrington forgot who he was talking to. Southern soldiers didn't believe they were fighting under a delusion. They did not appreciate the district attorney bad-mouthing their politicians. They also felt that they were back in their common country at the point of a bayonet. But during his two-day summation, Carrington did bring up three points of damning evidence against Surratt. The first was the fact that if Surratt were involved in a conspiracy to assassinate Lincoln, he was guilty no matter how far away he was from Washington, D.C. Second, even if the object of the conspiracy was to kidnap the president and one of Surratt's co-conspirators killed Lincoln without the foreknowledge of and contrary to the other co-conspirators, all conspirators, including Surratt, were guilty. Carrington's final point was that Surratt, so long as he served his role in the conspiracy, whether or not he physically aided or abetted in the murder, was constructively present at Ford's Theatre.[15]

Carrington then went over every piece of state's evidence, both good and bad, and reviewed the evidence against all the conspirators in the assassination trial. Carrington defended Weichmann, denying that he was a conspirator. He went on to state that even if he was a conspirator, Weichmann did the right thing in turning state's evidence against the others. The prosecutor even pursued the bad strategy of retrying Mary Surratt. Rehashing her hanging was like rubbing sandpaper across an open wound. Most Southerners felt that executing her had been wrong, and the president's efforts to shut out her desperate daughter's heart-rending pleas to extend her mother's life just three more days so she could prepare to meet her maker equaled callous indifference to justice. In Carrington's unstructured speech, he finally hit on a good piece of evidence: that of John Surratt delivering the carbines to John Lloyd. One of those weapons had been in the possession of Booth when he was shot to death.[16]

Carrington never mentioned Sainte Marie in his final arguments. The most important testimony of all seemed lost to the consciousness of the prosecution. Sainte Marie could have tied the Confederate government and Surratt directly into the murder plot, but it appears that they didn't even know what they had. When he finally sat down after two days, the jury was bored, confused, and angry.[17] Carrington did not yet know it, but he was about to be out-lawyered.

Merrick followed Carrington. In two days of arguments, he reminded the jury that the North had established a set of conditions at Appomattox, and the South had honored its promise while the North had not. The North pursued a Confederate scout with all of its resources, which included high government officials, spies, detectives, and a limitless treasury. He claimed that Surratt was a penniless young man in this uneven contest, and "the government with its irrelevant evidence, sought to tear open the wounds of war and pour into your minds a torrent of invective calculated to keep alive forever fraternal hatred."[18] "Shame on the United States," cried Merrick as he orchestrated the jury to look down its collective noses at the prosecution.

Merrick then destroyed the fourth part of the indictment by knocking the conspiracy out of it. Merrick correctly noted that in the *Ex Parte Bollman and Ex Parte Swartwout* opinion, arising out of the famous Aaron Burr conspiracy, the Supreme Court had decided that when the indictment alleged a conspiracy in one place but the evidence didn't support the conspiracy in that location, the case had to be dismissed.[19] He reminded the jury that the government in its opening statement promised to prove not only Surratt's complicity in Lincoln's murder but also Surratt's presence in Washington. He then pointed out to the jury that when the prosecution realized the strength of Surratt's alibi, they switched their strategy to conspiracy. The prosecution was giving the jury only a fallback option. Merrick's summation was brilliantly done.

As a final dagger thrust, Merrick talked about the efforts to impeach Andrew Johnson and how Joseph Holt had withheld the clemency plea from the president, thereby allowing the hanging of Mary Surratt. This version of events was false, of course. We know that today, but the jury didn't know it then. Merrick stirred up turmoil not just in the courtroom but in the White House and the War Department too. Andrew Johnson demanded Stanton's resignation that very day.[20] Johnson, a few days later and after examining the papers that Holt claimed to have shown him, stated that he had never seen the clemency plea. A furor began that ended with impeachment proceedings, all started with Merrick's final arguments.

Edward Pierrepont rose for the prosecution and tried to piece together a shattered government case. He did well by organizing the government's proof into cohesiveness for the first time. He made the complex case a simple one for the jury to understand.[21] But it was probably too late. The jury was out for three days and sent a note to the judge that they were hopelessly deadlocked. Judge Fisher tried to put the best face on it for the state by claiming that they were almost evenly split, but in actuality it was eight to four for acquittal. The history books tell us that the jury was comprised of four men for the North and eight for the South, but that's not quite accurate. All twelve jurors were citizens of Washington, D.C., and no one has been able to identify the political leanings of each of the men. One of those for acquittal was born in New York City, so the jury was slanted seven to five if you accept the fact that birthplace was an accurate indicator of the political leanings of the jury. The vote never changed from the first ballot to the last. Not one man was persuaded to change his vote in the jury room.[22]

The end of the trial was bitter. Judge Fisher ordered the name of the senior Joseph Bradley to be stricken from the roles of the Washington bar. It was an arbitrary act of vengeance. Cabinet member Gideon Welles observed, "The judge was disgracefully partial and unjust, I thought, and his charge improper."

The defense hadn't secured an acquittal for John Surratt. He wasn't free, but he had won a major victory. He could go back to his oversized jail space with food catered to him by his friends and read the many books provided. If he wanted, he could contemplate the fate of his not-so-lucky fellow conspirators. Four were dead, including his mother. Four were in the Florida island prison that was turning into a hell hole.

In August 1867, a soldier from Company K at the prison came down with yellow fever. A week later, another soldier from the same company came down with the illness. A third soldier came down with it the next week. Three weeks later, two-thirds of the entire population at the prison had contracted yellow fever. The only physician on the island, other than Mudd, was Dr. Joseph Sim Smith, the prison's doctor. He arrived shortly after the outbreak and enlisted the aid of Mudd. Together, they did what they could for the unfortunates who had come down with the disease. They moved the early patients to another island, but the disease kept spreading.[23] Back then, it was assumed that yellow fever was contagious and carried from person to person. They didn't realize that the carrier was the mosquito that bred in the stagnant pools of water prevalent around Fort Jefferson. Within six weeks, Dr. Smith and his young son were dead of the disease. Mudd was on his own until another doctor, D. W. Whitehurst, arrived from Key West. Both doctors worked night and day to save the hundreds who were stricken. Mudd worked fourteen hours a day for weeks.

On September 17, both Samuel Arnold and Michael O'Laughlen contracted the disease. Six days later, O'Laughlen was dead.[24] Mudd came down with a mild case but survived. The mild form of the disease involves symptoms that include fever, headaches, and nausea. The severe form is deadly and involves high fever, frequent vomiting, severe abdominal pain, and jaundice, which gives the patient a yellow or bronze complexion. Near the end the patient convulses with "black" vomit caused by chronic internal bleeding into the stomach. This bleeding leads to shock and death.

There were about two hundred seventy cases of yellow fever on the island resulting in thirty-eight deaths. As a result of Dr. Mudd's tireless efforts to save patients, prison guards and prisoners alike drew up a petition requesting clemency and Dr. Mudd's release. It was signed by all of the non-commissioned officers. The two commissioned officers opted not to sign.[25] No one knows if President Johnson ever saw the petition, but he must have been aware of it. Dr. Mudd remained imprisoned for another year and a half.

On June 18, 1868, Edward Carrington filed a new indictment against John Surratt. The first count was for conspiracy to aid the rebellion by murdering the president and commander in chief. The second was conspiracy to aid the rebellion by kidnapping Lincoln. The third was conspiracy to aid the rebellion by providing specific material support to the plot to kidnap the president. The fourth count was conspiracy to kidnap Lincoln, and the fifth count was conspiracy to commit assault and battery upon him. This indictment, number 5920, became known as the "rebellion indictment" and significantly included the words "to give aid and comfort" to the said rebellion.[26] Surratt was charged with the new indictment on June 22 and trial was set for June 29. Four men put up the twenty-thousand-dollar bond, and Surratt was set free for the first time since his arrest in Alexandria, Egypt, a year and a half before.

The trial was then postponed. Obviously one week didn't give either side enough time to prepare the case. On September 21, Carrington dismissed the original indictment that had led to the hung jury. The very next day, Surratt's attorneys filed a special defense that the current indictment was barred by the proclamation of amnesty issued July 4, 1868, which pardoned every person who directly or indirectly participated in the late rebellion, excepting persons under indictment for treason or other felonies. Surratt once again got a break. His special defense plea wasn't going to be heard by Judge George Fisher but by Judge Andrew Wylie, the judge who signed the writ of habeas corpus for his mother. Then his attorneys slipped in another defense against Indictment 5920 based on the statute of limitations. The case was dismissed by Judge Wylie, but the state appealed, correctly arguing that the limitations could be extended if the defendant was fleeing from custody. The defense countered, arguing that the state cannot appeal a case it has lost. The appeals court agreed and dismissed the case. John Harrison Surratt was completely free. Once again, he had the better lawyers.

George Alfred Townsend wrote in the *Cleveland Leader* on October 4, 1868, "This Surratt trial ranks like the trial of Aaron Burr at Richmond, a sensation without climax. It seems strange, however, that Mudd, Spangler, and the minor conspirators against Mr. Lincoln, should be parboiling at the Dry Tortugas, while the glove fellow and prime conspirator with Booth goes absolutely free."[27]

But the Dry Tortugas conspirators weren't surrendering without a fight. The determined Dr. Mudd's attorneys filed for a writ of habeas corpus on August 28, 1868, in the district of southern Florida. Judge Thomas Boynton promptly denied the writ, stating that *Ex Parte Milligan* was not the case in point. Lincoln was killed in a military district within a war zone; therefore, he had no problem classing the offense as a military one. Mudd's attorneys appealed the case to the

Supreme Court, where it languished for several months while the court considered other cases. On February 15, Edwin Stanton wrote a letter to President Johnson stating:

> In view of the decision of the Supreme Court in Milligan's case respecting the limits and extent of the jurisdiction of military tribunals, this Department [War Department] is unable to determine what cases, if any, of those mentioned in the aforesaid reports can be acted upon by military authority. I should therefore recommend that they be referred to the Attorney General for his investigation and report to the end that the cases be designated which are cognizant by the civil authorities, and such as are cognizant by military tribunals.[28]

In other words, Stanton was at a loss as to how to proceed in future cases nor could he predict which cases already heard would withstand Supreme Court scrutiny. If the highest court in the land ruled in favor of Mudd, Johnson and his henchmen, Stanton and Holt, were politically ruined. By the time Mudd's appeal reached the Supreme Court, President Johnson had already suffered impeachment, but he had every intention of remaining in politics. Johnson would run for a U.S. Senate seat the same year he left the White House, even though his presidential office had been saved by only one vote. It appears that he lived in fear of an adverse ruling by the court.

Attorney General James Speed's ruling in 1865 permitting the government to try Booth's conspirators by military tribunal had a couple of weaknesses. One was that Speed did not consider the conspirators to be civilians but enemy belligerents. The second deficiency was that they had committed offenses against the laws of war.[29] In 1865 the laws of war, at best, were unwritten doctrine with no defined offenses. They were based on tradition and were intended to exercise control over offenses committed by military personnel on the high seas or on foreign soil. What would later be counted as war crimes, such as running Nazi death camps for example, were spelled out by treaties and international accords negotiated long after the 1860s.

When Speed justified the military commission with the laws of war or laws of nations, he was on shaky ground and subject to second-guessing by the Supreme Court. Stanton should have recognized that. Whether he told Johnson about it cannot be determined—it would be unlike Stanton to admit making a mistake of that magnitude—but someone else could have. What we know is that Johnson, in the final days of his presidency, pardoned Dr. Samuel Mudd on February 8, 1869, before the Supreme Court could rule on his appeal, thus rendering moot any Supreme Court decision.[30] In Mudd's pardon, he cited the doctor's courage and skill in fighting the yellow fever epidemic. For those who believe Mudd was pardoned for his medical work, I have seashore property in Kansas. Johnson pardoned Spangler and Arnold just days later. They didn't do any work in the hospital, but they had appeals pending in the Supreme Court too. For those who say that Johnson pardoned all three just to infuriate the Radical Republicans in Congress, I have seashore property in Nebraska. They were all pardoned to nullify any Supreme Court decision that would have reversed the sentences handed out by the military commission. A ruling for those three also would have nullified the sentences that hung Mary Surratt, Lewis Powell, George Atzerodt, and David Herold. That was something that Johnson could not abide. That would have been his ultimate shame.

Stanton, too, has his demons in this story. In November 1865, he ordered the custodian of the Confederate records, Francis Lieber, to deliver to him the original Dahlgren papers that alleged a plan to assassinate Jefferson Davis and the Confederate cabinet members. Those papers were never seen again.[31] If Stanton had ordered Dahlgren to assassinate when he conducted that raid in 1864, it would have been ruinous to Stanton by the fall of 1865. The South's retaliation on Lincoln would have been seen as Stanton's fault, and rightly so. Stanton knew what he was talking about with his res gestae statement "Damn the rebels! This is their work." He just couldn't prove it. In a conspiracy of this scope, it takes many years for all the facts to come out, but Stanton did know one thing: He started it. Lincoln's death wasn't the result of an egotistical madman of an actor. Ego came into it, yes. But when all the facts are in, it can be said that Lincoln's death was an act of war.

CHAPTER SEVENTEEN

A Story Revised

As noted in the outset of this book, Lincoln's assassination is the most under told story in American history, even as more than fifteen thousand books have been written on the subject. The brief history in schoolbooks reflects only what Lincoln's secretaries knew by 1890, even less when you consider that those men ignored the stories written by George Alfred Townsend in the 1880s. More than one hundred fifty years have elapsed since the tragic event. Getting at the truth with a conspiracy of this scope is like peeling the skin of an onion. It comes in layers. We cannot know what we will find in the next decade or the next century. As recently as 1978, for example, Joan Chaconas of the Surratt Society discovered George Atzerodt's lost confession in the papers of his attorney William Doster. We learned much from this.

By using an unbroken chain of circumstantial evidence, we can draw several logical conclusions regarding events and the roles of certain co-conspirators. An unbroken chain of circumstances will convict someone in a criminal court of law. Thomas Harbin, the Confederate Secret Service agent in north-central Virginia, is one such conspirator who could be convicted in this manner. He meets Booth at the suggestion of Dr. Mudd on December 21, 1864, at a hotel in Bryantown, Maryland. It's obvious that Harbin advised Booth to meet John Surratt, Jr. because two days later, Dr. Mudd arranges a meeting for them in Washington, D.C. Surratt's movements for the next three weeks are known. He was working for

Adam's Express and did not leave the capital during that time. But someone contacted Col. John Mosby to request a muscleman for Booth's kidnapping plot. That someone could have been Harbin. Mosby selected Lewis Powell to infiltrate the Union lines and join Booth's band on January 13, 1865. Two days later, Harbin joined Surratt in Port Tobacco to buy the fifteen-passenger boat and recruit George Atzerodt into the fold. Several months later, Booth meets Harbin while he is on the run after the assassination. Harbin leads Booth to Dr. Stuart and then to the Lucas family. Consideration of all the facts on this matter leads to the correct and logical conclusion that Thomas Harbin was a major co-conspirator.

We also earned that the lowly river guide George Atzerodt, whom Booth despised, knew of the plot to blow up the White House and that the "New York crowd" was heavily involved. We learned that they needed a demolition expert, and the message for one was sent to Richmond via Sarah Slater and/or John Surratt. The book *Come Retribution* taught us about the Confederate Secret Service and the plots to kidnap Lincoln, partly in retribution for the Dahlgren raid and partly as a war goal to regain needed manpower from Northern prisoner of war camps. When the POW exchange was renewed, the Lincoln plot continued with authorization from the top. In hopes of accomplishing what they had been unable to achieve on the battlefields, the plot was coordinated, and scarce resources were used to secure a safe avenue to get the president to Richmond. But page 419 in that book wasn't emphasized enough when it labeled as "obvious" the connection between the visit of the Confederate agents Surratt and Slater and the project mentioned by Atzerodt in his confession.

An unbroken chain of evidence also applies to John Surratt, Jr. The timing of his visit to Benjamin's office, his payment in gold to deliver the message to Canada to transfer the money, the date of his letters from Montreal to home, his use of flamboyant clothes in Elmira, New York, to create a memorable alibi during the assassination, and his admissions to Henri Sainte Marie lead us to unmistakable conclusions.

Surratt knew the contents of his message to Montreal. He knew to establish an alibi far away from Washington. Since Booth did not have his address until he looked at Annie Ward's letter, any message he gave to Booth about killing the president was verbal and could only have been delivered to Mrs. Surratt. Booth probably sent Surratt a letter on April 10 or early on April 11, which would have given Surratt a time range for the event. Surratt received the letter from Booth on April 12 and left for Elmira the same day. Jacob Thompson emptied the bank account five days after Surratt's message was delivered to Gen. Edwin G. Lee. That fact is unmistakable too. The only conclusion that can be drawn from these events is that John Surratt, Jr. was a major co-conspirator in not only the abduction but also the murder. That explains why he hid and then ran.

This book leads the reader to the same conclusion regarding Judah Benjamin. All suspicion, facts, and events point to Secretary of State Judah Benjamin as the main person of interest in this murder mystery. It was Benjamin with whom Surratt and Slater met on March 29 in Richmond with the message from New York. It could only have been Benjamin, head of the Confederate Secret Service, who could have gone to Gen. Gabriel Rains to recruit Thomas Harney, the needed demolition expert, and send him to Col. John Mosby for insertion into the Federal capital to accomplish that goal. It was Benjamin who directed Surratt and Slater back to Montreal with orders to transfer the unused money for his planned use in Europe. This book contains a copy of the disbursal warrant of April 1, 1865, that releases fifteen hundred dollars in gold to Benjamin to pay Thomas Harney to purchase gunpowder and to pay Surratt to deliver his important message to Canada to move the money to Europe. The usual authorization from Jefferson Davis to withdraw these funds does not exist in his log of Secret Service warrants to the Treasury Department.[1]

On their way north, Benjamin's messengers, in all probability, left a ciphered or verbal message for Booth to abandon any kidnap plot and proceed with a new plan to behead the Union government in case the Harney plan failed. We know that Booth had a cipher code device keyed to one in Judah Benjamin's office. This book submits that the message to John Wilkes Booth was carried by John Surratt, who knew its contents. Surratt took too many pains to set up an alibi for him not to have known of the South's plan. Booth also knew that he had been demoted to Plan B, in favor of the Harney demolition plot. The Atzerodt confession adds weight to this inference by depicting Booth as rushing forward with his plan "or the New York crowd will get him first." Many historians have overplayed Booth's ego, but they are correct to a point. Booth yearned to be a hero. To be one of the nation's leading actors wasn't enough.

It is plausible that Benjamin never told Jefferson Davis about the change in plans to assassinate instead of abduct or about his transfer of the Confederate funds from Canada to Europe. Benjamin's lifelong friend, Sen. James Bayard from Delaware, offered financial assistance to get him started in England, but Benjamin declined. He wrote to Bayard that he had purchased six hundred bales of cotton before abandoning Richmond, and one hundred bales had reached England, netting Benjamin twenty thousand dollars.[2] There was no way Benjamin could give a U.S. senator the truth, friend or not. Getting cotton out of the Confederacy in the months after January would have been impossible. There were no ports. His cotton would have been confiscated or stolen. It is a story that fails all credibility tests. Yet Benjamin had enough money to attend a British law school and buy his way into the English bar, perhaps even securing protection from extradition. That would have cost only a fraction of the money formerly in the Canadian coffers of the Confederacy. We don't know what happened to the rest of it, but the chances are strong that Benjamin would have used at least some of the Canadian money eventually.

Perhaps the lawsuit United States vs. Wagner answers that question.[3] The British court's decision in 1867 allowed the Union to move forward with a lawsuit in England, pursuing the notion that the merchant company Fraser, Trenholm & Co. was in possession of former Confederate goods and money. The lawsuit dragged on for years, and Fraser, Trenholm & Co. finally declared bankruptcy after spending a fortune in attorney's fees fighting the suit. The Union recovered virtually nothing.

Benjamin was the only Confederate cabinet member to leave the country and never return. He failed to write memoirs and burned all his papers before he died. Last but not least, John Surratt confessed to someone he thought a Southern ally, Henri Beaumont de Sainte Marie, that the murder was ordered by parties in New York and London who were under the immediate orders of Jefferson Davis. That was a telling statement. That remark by Surratt was an admission of Benjamin's guilt. Benjamin would have known about the laws of presidential succession and how the nation would attempt to move forward if both the president and vice president were killed. Booth likely would not. Before the fateful day of April 14, 1865, Booth had never mentioned targeting any Northern leaders other than Lincoln. This book further argues that Benjamin had private reasons for singling out four victims for assassination. This author argues that the circumstances can only mean one thing: Judah Benjamin ordered the assassination of several, if not all, of the Union leadership.

After the war, Benjamin and Davis seem to have split when they were the closest of confidants during the conflict. This author submits that there could only be two reasons. The first reason was the relationship between Benjamin and his courier, John Surratt. During his imprisonment, Davis had to have learned of Surratt's close relationship with Booth, and it wouldn't have been difficult to figure out that Benjamin sent an assassination order to Booth through "Johnny." He must have resented Benjamin for the actions he took without obtaining his presidential approval. The second reason would have been the Canadian money. Davis desperately needed Benjamin's help with his memoirs, which he was writing to reinforce his own flagging finances. Davis became so angry with Benjamin's refusal that Benjamin is only mentioned once in the memoirs, a deliberate slight. But Benjamin was just as adamant that he maintain as low a profile as possible with the "hated Yankee." He was desperate to direct their attentions elsewhere. He could still be extradited and hanged. All the evidence points in no other direction.

The aftermath of Lincoln's assassination has shown a North in political disarray, making judicial policy mistakes that the nation wouldn't support a year later. While little fault can be found in the verdicts of the military commission, *Ex Parte Milligan* loomed large in scolding the Northern leaders for trying citizens by military tribunal, shaming them for the hanging of Mary Surratt. The hysteria in the wake of the president's murder supported such action, but temperaments quickly changed, putting Andrew Johnson, Edwin Stanton, and Joseph Holt in political peril. Even though they grew to despise each other, they were forced to support one another in this common endeavor for political survival. If Johnson ever had a guilty conscience, it was the callous indifference he showed Anna Surratt in refusing to see her before her mother's execution. That guilty conscience and fear of *Ex*

Barrister Judah Benjamin in wig. Look at me, scot-free. (Public domain)

Parte Milligan led to the pardons of Samuel Mudd, Samuel Arnold, and Edman Spangler.

This book also shines light on Edwin Stanton for destroying the Dahlgren papers. That action speaks volumes about why he sent Ulric Dahlgren to Hugh Judson Kilpatrick in the first place. No commander, even Kilpatrick, would appoint a stranger to be second in command of a major raid, jumping over all his other officers in his division, unless ordered to do so. Now we know the why. If it wasn't for the cover-up, we wouldn't have known the crime.

Finally, we come to John Surratt. While historians as well as contemporaries chastised him for hiding in Canada and forsaking his mother in her time of need, the evidence against her shows us that had he stepped forward to rescue her, there would have been five nooses on that scaffold. After his statements to Sainte Marie, he was careful the rest of his life. In his own mind, he was a soldier/spy with his own set of ethics. He could have turned state's evidence against Benjamin or even Jefferson Davis when he was in legal peril with his life hanging in the balance, but he didn't. He never threw anyone under the bus. Did he lie? Sure, he did. So did a lot of others in this story. Andrew Johnson lied about not seeing Mary Surratt's clemency plea. Joseph Holt covered for all the liars he conjured up for the conspiracy trial. Samuel Mudd lied, as did Samuel Cox, Thomas Jones, and Thomas Nelson Conrad. They were all trying to save their skins. While it's not commendable, at least it's understandable.

Historians are reticent to judge people from past generations by the modern era's practices and political correctness. Lincoln was not considered in the same light as he is today, even by his own people. Benjamin did act in time of war, and after all, was targeted first by the Union in the Dahlgren raid. Perhaps it can be said that he was ahead of his time. By World War II, the assassination of leaders was commonplace. The British, along with the Czech government in exile, assassinated the evil Reinhard Heydrich on Operation Anthropoid in June 1942. Hitler ordered the death of Churchill in the newly discovered "Death by Chocolate" attempt in May 1943.[4] Churchill considered sending agents to the Berchtesgaden to gun down Hitler. U.S. citizens cheered when Osama bin Laden was assassinated by Seal Team Six in May 2011. The participants of this 1865 plot were not much different from people in war a few generations later.

We should not close this book without considering the overall tragedy of Pres. Abraham Lincoln's assassination. The first victim is obviously Abraham Lincoln himself. This poor man labored incessantly to preserve the union of the United States during his presidency. He suffered along with the soldiers of both sides, regretting the loss and bloodshed of those whom he considered Americans, whether rebel or not. He had the empathy to worry about the South's plight after the war and its ability to rebuild. He spoke of binding up the nation's wounds and helping the widows and children of those killed. He worried about the plight of the freed slaves and their ability to adjust to their new freedom and thrive in future generations. Lincoln was a genuine protector of all the nation's citizens. Taking away the years in which he could enjoy his hard-won peace and the privilege of effecting the rebuilding of the devastated nation was the ultimate egregious act.

The second victim of the assassination was the nation as a whole. No one else, especially Andrew Johnson, had Lincoln's natural empathy. Further, no one else had the political skills and the national respect to effect a peaceful reconstruction without the accompanying malice that followed. Lincoln is the only one who could have kept the radical abolitionists at bay to accomplish this. The nation today holds President Lincoln in its highest esteem, as it should. Two of the most important documents in our history were written by the eloquent Lincoln. We still admire him for his resolute determination to save the Union, despite a long sequence of opposition and defeat. Had he lived to finish his second term, the nation would have been much better off, then and now.

The major players in this story lived on after the end of this saga.

The Northerners:	*Date of Death*
Edwin Stanton	December 24, 1869
Andrew Johnson	January 31, 1875
Joseph Holt	August 1, 1894
John Bingham	March 19, 1900
H. L. Burnett	January 4, 1916
James Speed	June 25, 1887
Louis Weichmann	June 5, 1902 (with a deathbed declaration on his lips that he spoke the truth)
John Lloyd	December 18, 1892 (due to a construction accident)

Of the military commission:	
David Hunter	February 2, 1886
Lewis Wallace	February 15, 1905
T. M. Harris	September 30, 1906
August Kautz	September 4, 1895
Robert S. Foster	March 3, 1903
David R. Clendenin	March 5, 1895
James Ekin	March 27, 1891
C. H. Tompkins	January 18, 1915
Albion Howe	January 25, 1897

On the Confederate side:	
Jefferson Davis	December 6, 1889
Judah Benjamin	May 6, 1884
L. Q. Washington	November 4, 1902 (Benjamin's clerk)
Thomas Harbin	November 18, 1885
Thomas Jones	March 5, 1895
Samuel Cox	January 6, 1880
Thomas Nelson Conrad	January 5, 1905
Jacob Thompson	March 24, 1885
George Sanders	August 13, 1873
Beverly Tucker	July 4, 1890
Dr. Samuel Mudd	January 10, 1883
Samuel Arnold	September 21, 1906
Edman Spangler	February 7, 1875
Benjamin Franklin Stringfellow	June 8, 1913
Gen. Edwin Lee	August 24, 1870
Clement Clay	January 3, 1882
Anna Surratt	October 24, 1904
John Surratt, Jr.	April 21, 1916 (What irony. No man in this story outlived John Surratt. But one woman did.)
Sarah Slater	April 20, 1920

Notes

Chapter One

1. Museum of the Confederacy video, March 21, 2014.

2. *Battles and Leaders of the Civil War*, vol. 3 (New York: Castle Books, 1956), 393-96.

3. Shelby Foote, *The Civil War: A Narrative,* vol. 2 (New York: Random House, 1958), 573, 574.

4. Museum of the Confederacy video.

5. *Battles and Leaders*, vol. 4, 95.

6. Foote, vol. 2, 912; and H. Donald Winkler, *Lincoln and Booth: More Light on the Conspiracy* (Nashville: Cumberland House, 2003), 23.

7. Foote, vol. 2, 913-14.

8. Ibid., 914; and Adjutant General's Office, Entry 721 Serial 60, RG 94.

9. Museum of the Confederacy video.

10. www.historynet.com, citing *Military History Quarterly* (Winter 1999).

11. Eli N. Evans, *Judah P. Benjamin: The Jewish Confederate* (New York: Free Press, 1988), 256-57.

12. William Hanchett, *The Lincoln Murder Conspiracies* (Urbana: University of Illinois Press, 1983), 33-34.

13. Foote, vol. 2, 916.

14. Douglas Southall Freeman, *Lee's Lieutenants: A Study in Command*, vol. 2 (New York: Charles Scribner's Sons, 1944), 133.

15. Museum of the Confederacy video.

Chapter Two

1. Foote, vol. 1, 53-54.

2. *Battles and Leaders*, vol. 1, 150.

3. William A. Tidwell, James O. Hall, and David Winfred Gaddy, *Come Retribution: The Confederate Service and the Assassination of Lincoln* (Jackson: University Press of Mississippi, 1988), 62.

4. E. Porter Alexander, *Fighting for the Confederacy* (Chapel Hill: University of North Carolina Press, 1989), 50-51; and Tidwell et al., 80.

5. Tidwell et al., 80-86.

6. Ibid., 66.

Chapter Three

1. Tidwell et al., 174-75; and U.S. Consuls dispatches T-469 reel 10.

2. Tidwell et al., 175.

3. Ibid.; and Investigation and Trial Papers of the Assassination, RG 153, NA.

4. Tidwell et al., 192.

5. Ibid., 175

6. Ibid., 20.

7. Tidwell et al, 173.

8. Ibid., 180, quoting Montreal newspaper dated November 13, 1863.

9. Tidwell et al., 199.

10. John W. Headley, *Confederate Operations in Canada and New York* (1906; repr., Fairfax, VA: Time Life Books, 1984), 258.

11. Tidwell et al., 195.

12. James D. Horan, *Confederate Agent: A Discovery in History* (n.p.: Pickle Partners, 1954), 71; and Tidwell et al, 195.

13. Tidwell et al, 196.

14. Foote, vol. 3, 586-87.

15. Schein, 65-66, 69; and Headley, 376.

16. Tidwell et al., 204-5.

17. Ibid., 204.

18. Evans, *Judah P. Benjamin*, 146-49.

19. Ibid., 116.

20. Ibid., 4.

21. Ibid., 14.

22. Robert Douthat Meade, *Judah P. Benjamin: Confederate Statesman* (New York: Oxford University Press, 1943), 19-20.

23. Ibid., 25.

24. Ibid., 29-30.

25. Evans, 27.

26. Ibid., 35.

27. Ibid., 89.

Chapter Four

1. Tidwell et al., 185.

2. Ibid., 186; and Godfrey J. Hyams statements, April 12, 1865, Attorney General Archives.

3. Tidwell et al., 185-86.

4. Ibid., 186-87.

5. Edward Steers, Jr., *Blood on the Moon: The Assassination of Abraham Lincoln* (Lexington: University Press of Kentucky, 2001), 53-54.

6. Tidwell et al., 187.

7. Ibid., 235-36.

8. Foote, vol. 3, 302.

9. Tidwell et al., 264; and Thomas Nelson Conrad, *The Rebel Scout* (Washington, DC: National, 1904), 120.

10. Tidwell et al., 262-63.

11. Tidwell et al., 263.

12. Headley, 281.

Chapter Five

1. Samuel B. Arnold, *Defense and Prison Experiences of a Lincoln Conspirator* (Hattiesburg, MS: Book Farm, 1943), 18-19.

2. Tidwell et al., 264.

3. Ibid., 265.

4. Ibid., 253.

5. Ibid., 255.

6. Investigation and Trial Papers of the Assassination, reel 4, frames 140-70, and reel 6, frames 1491-96 NA.

7. Douglas Southall Freeman, *R. E. Lee* vol. 1 (New York: Charles Scribner's Sons, 1934), 394-401.

8. Select Comm., S. Rep. on Harpers Ferry No. 278 Serial 1040 (1860).

9. Tidwell et al., 256.

10. Hanchett, 45-46.

11. Ibid., 41.

12. Jefferson Davis Papers, Rice University.

13. Foote, vol. 1, 36-39.

14. Hanchett, 41.

Chapter Six

1. Ray Neff, *Dark Union* (Hoboken, NJ: John Wiley & Sons, 2013), 19.

2. Ibid., 23.

3. Tidwell et al., 333.

4. Ibid., 334.

5. Ibid., 331; and Steers, *Blood on the Moon*, 73.

6. Tidwell et al., 334.

7. Ibid.

8. Ibid., 336-77; Michael W. Kauffman, *American Brutus* (New York, Random House, 2005), 160; and Tidwell et al., 336-37.

9. Hanchett, 45-46.

10. Edward Steers, Jr., *His Name Is Still Mudd: The Case Against Doctor Samuel Alexander Mudd* (Gettysburg, PA: Thomas, 1997), 39-41.

11. Steers, *Blood on the Moon*, 78-79.

12. Winkler, *Lincoln and Booth*, 43.

13. Steers, *Blood on the Moon*, 83.

14. James L. Swanson and Daniel Weinberg, *Lincoln's Assassins: Their Trial and Execution* (New York: HarperCollins, 2008), 64-67.

Chapter Seven

1. Michael Schein, *John Surratt: The Lincoln Assassin Who Got Away* (Palisades, NY: History, 2015), 56; and Tidwell et al., 339.

2. Schein, 56.

3. Ibid., 57-58.

4. Conrad, 140.

5. Tidwell et al., 300, 318.

6. Ibid., 348.

7. Ibid., 307-8, 318.

8. Foote, vol. 3, 770-72.

9. Ibid., 775-78.

10. Ibid., 777.

11. Tidwell et al., 309-18.

12. Ibid.

13. Dorothy Meserve Kunhardt, *Twenty Days* (New York: Castle Books, 1965).

14. Tidwell et al., 346.

15. James O. Hall Papers and John Stanton Papers, 1982, Surratt Society Library.

16. Schein, 67.

17. James O. Hall Papers, *The Lady in the Veil*, July 2, 1975.

18. Hall Papers, 1982.

Chapter Eight

1. "Investigation and Trial Papers Relating to the Assassination of President Lincoln," Microfilm Publication M-599, reel 3, frames 1046-48, NA.

2. Steers, *Blood on the Moon,* 83-84.

3. Ibid.

4. Tidwell et al., 414.

5. Steers, *Blood on the Moon,* 86-87.

6. Schein, 85-86.

7. Hanchett, 223.

8. Neff, 19-26.

9. Tidwell et al., 415.

10. Schein, 93-94.

11. Ibid., 95.

12. Freeman, *Lee's Lieutenants,* vol. 3, 647-52.

13. Foote, vol. 3, 843-44.

14. Ibid., 844.

15. A. A. Hoehling and Mary Hoehling, *The Last Days of the Confederacy* (n.p.: Fairfax Press, 1981), 124.

16. Schein, 99.

17. Steers, *Blood on the Moon,* 313, note 34.

18. Tidwell et al., 419.

19. Ibid.

20. Meade, 336.

21. Duke University Collection, Box 19.

22. Tidwell, *April '65* (Kent, OH: Kent State University Press, 1995), Appendix 1.

23. Evans, 261.

24. Ibid., 208-9.

25. Curt Fields, email message to author.

26. Hoehling and Hoehling, 116.

27. Schein, 117.

28. Ibid., 121.

29. Foote, vol. 3, 846-47.

30. Ibid., 855.

31. Ibid., 854-55.

32. Doris Kearns Goodwin, *Team of Rivals: The Political Genius of Abraham Lincoln* (New York: Simon & Schuster, 2005), 747-48.

Chapter Nine

1. Schein, 119.

2. Ibid., 120.

3. Ibid.

4. Notes on the Ward Department records of John Surratt by D. R. Barbee, 1933, James O' Hall Papers.

5. Schein, 121.

6. John Stanton Papers.

Chapter Ten

1. Steers, *Blood on the Moon,* 139-40.

2. Ibid., 91.

3. Foote, vol. 3, 965-69.

4. Edward Person statement in "Investigation and Trial Papers Relating to the Assassination of President Lincoln," Microfilm Publication M-599, reel 6, frames 16-17, NA.

5. Tidwell et al., 422.

6. Foote, vol. 3, 974.

7. Ibid., 975.

8. Winkler, 79-80.

9. Steers, *Blood on the Moon,* 112.

10. Schein, 141.

11. Steers, *Blood on the Moon,* 117.

12. Ibid., 111.

13. Benn Pittman, "Trial Report," *The Assassination of President Lincoln and the Trial of the Conspirators* (Cincinnati: Moore, Wilstatch and Baldwin, 1865).

14. Steers, *Blood on the Moon,* 130-32.

15. Ibid., 112.

16. Winkler, 70.

17. Steers, *Blood on the Moon,* 313, note 34.

Chapter Eleven

1. Freeman, *Lee's Lieutenants*, vol. 2, 173.

2. Foote, vol. 2, 591.

3. Winkler, 106-8.

4. Steers, *Blood on the Moon,* 126.

5. Winkler, 99.

6. Steers, *Blood on the Moon,* 111-16.

7. Ibid., 116.

8. Timothy S. Good, *We Saw Lincoln Shot* (Jackson: University Press of Mississippi, 1995), 80-81; and Winkler, 103.

9. Steers, *Blood on the Moon,* 121.

10. Ibid., 125-27.

11. Ibid., 128.

12. Ibid., 129.

13. Ibid.

14. Ibid., 130-31.

15. Ibid., 132-34.

16. Hanchett, 61.

17. Winkler, 122-23.

18. Steers, *Blood on the Moon,* 14.

Chapter Twelve

1. Hanchett, 62.

2. Steers, *Blood on the Moon,* 170.

3. Ibid., 175-76.

4. Ibid., 167-69.

5. Winkler, 134.

6. Steers, *His Name Is Still Mudd,* 30.

7. Tidwell et al., 446.

8. Ibid.

9. Ibid., 449.

10. Thomas A. Jones, *J. Wilkes Booth* (Charleston: Forgotten Books, 2016), 93.

11. Steers, *Blood on the Moon,* 164-65.

12. Ibid., 147.

13. Ibid., 153.

14. Roy Z. Chamlee, Jr., *Lincoln's Assassins: A Complete Account of Their Capture, Trial, and Punishment* (Jefferson, NC: McFarland, 1990), 69-72.

15. Schein, 156-57.

16. Ibid., 160.

17. Ibid., 163.

18. Tidwell et al., 483.

19. Ibid., 455.

20. Ibid.

21. Ibid., 455-57.

22. Ibid., 457-58.

23. Winkler, 146-47.

24. Steers, *Blood on the Moon,* 186-87.

25. Ibid., 188; and Winkler, 174.

26. Tidwell et al., 468.

27. Ibid.

28. Ibid., 469-73.

29. Winkler, 179.

30. Ibid., 180-81.

31. Ibid., 183.

32. Ibid., 184.

33. Tidwell et al., 477.

34. Winkler, 187.

35. Ibid., 188.

36. Chamlee, 289-90.

37. Lloyd Lewis, *Myths After Lincoln* (New York: Harcourt, Brace, 1929), 246-58.

38. Ibid., 255-56.

39. Steers, *Blood on the Moon,* 205.

Chapter Thirteen

1. Frederick Hatch, *The Lincoln Assassination Conspiracy Trial and Its Legacy* (Jefferson, NC: McFarland, 2015), 38, 51.

2. Chamlee, 212.

3. Ibid., 216.

4. Ibid., 218-19.

5. Ibid., 218.

6. Ibid., 223.

7. Hatch, 35.

8. Ibid., 36.

9. Ibid., 68-69.

10. Chamlee, 248-53.

11. Hatch, 68.

12. Chamlee, 270.

13. Hatch, 70.

14. Ibid., 71.

15. Ibid., 72-73.

16. Ibid., 73.

17. Chamlee, 439.

18. Richard Mitchell Smoot, *The Unwritten History of the Assassination of Abraham Lincoln* (Charleston: Forgotten Books, 2017).

19. Steers, *Blood on the Moon,* 222.

20. Ibid., 224.

21. Ibid., 225.

22. Chamlee, 309.

23. Ibid., 318; AP account, 35-36; *Philadelphia Inquirer* account, 78-79; and Winkler, 257.

24. Chamlee, 321.

25. Schein, 119.

26. Steers, *Blood on the Moon,* 100-101.

27. Schein, 141, 254, 393.

28. Hatch, 105; and Chamlee, 441.

29. Theodore Roscoe, *The Web of Conspiracy* (Englewood Cliffs, NJ: Prentice-Hall, 1960), 487; and Hatch, 105-6.

Chapter Fourteen
1. Chamlee, 442.
2. Ibid.
3. Hanchett, 110.
4. Chamlee, 444.
5. Winkler, 211.
6. Chamlee, 444.
7. Ibid.
8. *New York Times,* July 7, 1865.
9. Chamlee, 444-45
10. Ibid., 450.
11. Ibid., 452.
12. Ibid., 465-66.
13. Lewis, 206.
14. Chamlee, 452.
15. Winkler, 215-16.
16. Steers, *Blood on the Moon,* 229; and Hatch, 112.
17. Chamlee, 454.
18. Ibid., 461.
19. Steers, *Blood on the Moon,* 228.
20. Winkler, 203.
21. Chamlee, 470.
22. Ibid., 472-74.

Chapter Fifteen
1. Chamlee, 482.
2. Steers, *Blood on the Moon,* 234.
3. Ibid., 234.
4. Steers, *Blood on the Moon,* 236; Nettie Mudd, *The Life of Dr. Samuel A. Mudd* (New York: Neale, 1906), 131-32.
5. Steers, *Blood on the Moon,* 237.
6. Schein, 164.
7. Ibid., 178.
8. Ibid., 179-80.
9. James O. Hall, *Surratt Courier* (February 1982).
10. Schein, 181.
11. Chamlee, 483.
12. Evans, 312.
13. Meade, 320.
14. Personal tour by author.
15. Suman Naresh, "Judah Philip Benjamin at the English Bar," *Tulane Law Review,* 70 (1996).
16. Conrad, 171.
17. Foote, vol. 3, 1009-13.
18. Schein, 186.
19. Ibid., 191.
20. Ibid., 193.
21. Ibid., 196-97.
22. Evans, 329.

23. Hatch, 123; and 71 U.S. 2 (1866).
24. Hatch, 124-25.
25. Schein, 205.
26. Ibid., 207-8.
27. Ibid., 209.

Chapter Sixteen
1. Schein, 213.
2. Ibid., 215; and Capt. De Lambilly report, November 8, 1866.
3. Schein, 225.
4. Ibid., 226-27.
5. Winkler, 294-95.
6. Schein, 245.
7. Ibid., 246.
8. Ibid., 253-254.
9. Ibid., 254-55.
10. Ibid., 256.
11. Ibid., 265.
12. Ibid., 266.
13. Ibid., 275-76.
14. Ibid., 282.
15. Ibid., 283-84.
16. Ibid., 285.
17. Ibid.
18. Ibid., 287.
19. Ibid., 288.
20. Ibid., 298.
21. Ibid., 303.
22. Ibid., 304.
23. Chamlee, 488.
24. Hatch, 118.
25. Steers, *Blood on the Moon,* 240-42.
26. Schein, 313-14.
27. Ibid., 314-15.
28. Hatch, 144.
29. Steers, *Blood on the Moon,* 213.
30. Chamlee, 539.
31. Museum of the Confederacy video.

Chapter Seventeen
1. Duke University Collection, Box 19.
2. Evans, 329.
3. United States vs. Wagner, Law Reports, Chancery Appeal Cases II, 1866-67, pp. 582-95.
4. Lord Victor Rothschild, letter to Laurence Fish, May 4, 1943.

Index

178½ Water Street, 88

Adam's Express Company, 75
Aiken, Frederick A., 162, 164, 184, 186
Alexander, E. P., 28
Allet, M., 202
Anderson, George S., 40
Antonelli, Giacomo, 202
Arnold, Samuel B., 55, 59, 66-67, 86, 88,
     107, 134, 136, 141, 156, 162, 164, 168,
     173, 184, 190, 214, 217, 224, 226
Atzerodt, George, 72, 75, 82, 85, 90, 104,
     115-17, 121, 123, 128, 130, 135, 141-
     42, 156, 162, 164, 174-75, 180, 187-88,
     206, 208, 217-19, 221
Augur, Christopher C., 130

B. Weir Company, 31, 36
Babcock, John, 24
Badeau, Samuel, 100
Baden, Joseph, 144, 146
Bagby, Richard H., 23
Bainbridge, Absolam, 145-46
Baker, Lafayette C., 89, 146-47, 195, 205
Baker, Luther, 147, 149-51
Barnes, Joseph K., 132
Barry, David, 91
Barton, William S., 28
Bateman, George, 166
Bayard, James, 197, 221
Beale, Richard L. T., 23
Beall, John Yates, 40
Beauregard, P. G. T., 109
Beckwith, Samuel, 146
Bell, William, 121
Benjamin, Judah P., 24-26, 37, 40-42, 44-
     47, 89-90, 92-96, 98-99, 108, 110-11,
     117-18, 131, 169-71, 193-95, 197-98,
     201, 219-22, 224, 226

Benjamin, Ninette, 46
Benjamin, Philip, 43
bin Laden, Osama, 225
Bingham, John A., 160, 226
Bingham, Joseph J., 35
Bissell, Augustus, 209
Blackburn, Luke, 50-51
Blair, Francis P., 77-78
Bocking, R. C., 38
Bonaparte, Louis, 32
Bonfals, M. M. See Benjamin, Judah P.
Booth, Edwin, 59, 61, 134
Booth, John Wilkes, 19, 53-55, 57-59,
     61-70, 72, 75, 81-82, 84, 86-90, 94-96,
     99, 102-4, 106-8, 111-12, 114-18, 121,
     123-24, 126-41, 143-52, 154-55, 157,
     160-61, 163, 165-66, 169-77, 179-80,
     190, 196, 218-22
Booth, Junius Brutus, 57
Booth, Junius, Jr., 59
Boucher, Charles, 142, 191-92, 196
Boyd's Hole, 76-77, 80, 142
Boynton, Thomas, 215
Bradford, E. A., 45
Bradley, Joseph H., Jr., 206-8
Bradley, Joseph H., Sr., 206, 208, 213
Branson, Maggie, 72
Breckinridge, John C., 110
Brogden, Harry, 29, 93
Brophy, John, 185
Brown, John, 59-60
Browner's Hotel, 138
Browning, Orville, 164
Browning, William A., 116
Bryan, E. Pliney, 29
Bryant, William, 144
Buchanan, James, 59
Burnett, H. L., 160, 226
Burroughs, "Peanut" John, 124, 126

Butler, Benjamin, 27, 33
Butterfield, Daniel, 152-53

Calhoun, John C., 48
Cameron, Stephen, 84
Campbell, John, 79
Campbell, Robert, 170
Canby, Edward R., 110
Carrington, Edward C., 210-11, 214-15
Carter, Hosea B., 65
Cartter, David Kellogg, 129
Cawood, Charles H., 29, 80, 82, 85
Channing, Matthew, 61
Chester, Samuel K., 59
Chotank Creek, 76, 80-81, 143
Churchill, Winston, 224-25
Clagett, Richard, 146
Clampitt, John Wesley, 162, 165, 186
Clarke, Asia Booth, 57, 59, 61, 67
Clarke, John Sleeper, 59, 67, 134
Clarvoe, John, 132
Clay, Clement, 34-35, 40, 50-51, 54, 65,
    156, 226
Clay, Henry, 48
Cleary, William, 34, 36
Clendenin, David R., 160, 179, 226
Cobb, Silas, 127, 130
Collier, Fredrick H., 160
Comstock, Cyrus B., 160
Conger, Everton G., 147, 149, 151-52, 155
Conrad, Thomas Nelson, 53, 65, 76, 80, 82,
    142-43, 145, 195, 224, 226
Corbett, Boston, 152-55
"court" cipher, 82
Cox, Samuel, 137-39, 142, 146, 224, 226
Cox, Walter, 162
Coxe, Robert E., 32, 34
Crane, Cordial, 54
Crook, William, 114, 118
Custer, George, 20, 22

Dahlgren papers, 23-26
Dahlgren raid, 37
Dahlgren, Ulric, 21-25, 95, 98, 224
Dana, Charles, 169-70
Dana, David D., 130, 135, 139
Davenport, E. L., 87
Davidson, Squire, 167
Davis, Jefferson, 20, 23-24, 28, 34, 37, 39-
    42, 48, 51-54, 62, 76, 78-80, 91-92, 94-
    96, 98, 108-11, 156, 160, 166-67, 179,
    195-96, 200-1, 217, 220-22, 224, 226
Demill & Co., 88-89

Deveney, John, 65
Dimmock Line, 77, 92
Dodd, Levi A., 190
Doherty, Edward P., 147, 149
Doster, William E., 162, 164
Douglas, Adele Cutts, 184, 186
Douglas, Stephen A., 48
Dunham, Charles, 167
Dutton, George, 190-91
Dye, Joseph M., 206

Early, Jubal, 24, 52, 78
Eckert, Thomas, 79, 114, 128-29, 146, 169,
    187
Ekin, James, 161, 179, 226
Ellsler, John, 63
Ewing, Thomas, Jr., 162-63

Farnsworth, Elon J., 20
Farrell, Francis, 136
Fields, Curt, 98
Fisher, George P., 104, 205, 210, 213, 215
Fletcher, John, 116, 129-31
Florence, Thomas, 184
Forbes, Charles, 118, 124
Ford, John, 59, 115
Ford's Theatre, 123-24
Fort Monroe, 79
Foster, Robert S., 160-61, 179, 226
Fowle, James, 85
Frazier, Trenholm & Co., 197

Gamble Plantation, 193
Gardiner, Alexander, 81, 188
Gardner, George, 135
Garrett, Jack, 150
Garrett, Richard, 145, 148-50
Gillette, A. D., 187, 189
Goldsborough, Louis M., 204
Gordon, John B., 91
Gouldman, Izora, 146
Gouldman, Julia, 149
Grant, Julia, 100, 112
Grant, Ulysses S., 49, 77-79, 91-92, 96, 98-
    101, 112-14, 129, 179
Greek Fire, 37-40
Greenhow, Rose, 185
Gullickson, Ira, 24
Gurley, Phineas, 132

Halbach, Edward, 23
Hale, Charles, 203-4
Hale, Lucy, 155

Halleck, Henry, 167
Hampton, Wade, 22, 52
Hancock, Winfield, 164, 183, 187-88
Harbin, Thomas, 69, 72, 74-76, 135-36,
    142-44, 146, 165, 169, 174, 218-19, 226
Hardy, John F., 136
Harlan, James, 187
Harney, Thomas F., 94-95, 99, 220
Harris, T. M., 160-61, 163, 179, 226
Hartranft, John F., 183, 185, 188-89
Hawke, Harry, 124
Haynes, W. W., 51
Headley, John W., 39
Henry, Michael, 130
Herndon House, 116
Herold, David, 72, 87, 107, 116, 121, 123,
    128-31, 135-39, 143-49, 151, 156, 162,
    164, 168-69, 174, 176, 184, 188
Hess, C. D., 112
Heydrich, Reinhard, 224
Hill, D. H., 119
Hines, Thomas H., 37-38
Hitler, Adolph, 224
Holcombe, James P., 36, 51, 169
Holloway, Lucinda, 155
Holmes, Mary Ann, 57
Holohan, John, 141
Holt, Joseph, 54, 133, 157-58, 160-61, 166,
    179, 181-84, 186-87, 197-98, 207, 212,
    216, 223-24, 226
Hooker, Joseph, 152
Houston, Sam, 48
Howard, Jacob, 21
Howe, Albion P., 160, 179, 226
Howell, Augustus, 82, 84-85, 89-90, 178
Hunter, David, 52, 160, 163, 179, 226
Hunter, Robert, 79
Hyams, Godfrey J., 50-51, 53

Jackson, Thomas J. "Stonewall", 120
Jay Cooke and Company, 66-67
Jeffers, William N., 204
Jett, Willie, 145-47, 149-50
Johnson, Andrew, 81, 96, 98, 104, 115-17,
    121, 123, 130, 139, 141, 158, 160, 175,
    179-88, 196-99, 205, 212, 214, 216-17,
    223-26
Johnson, Bradley T., 52
Johnson, Reverdy, 162-65, 179, 187
Johnson's Island, Ohio, 33, 40
Johnston, Joseph, 100, 109-10, 113, 164
Jones, Thomas, 29, 88, 138-40, 142-43,
    155, 224, 226

Jones, William E. "Grumble", 52

Kane, George P., 32, 62, 65, 169
Kautz, August, 160, 179, 226
Keeler, William F., 190
Keith, Alexander, 31, 36, 50, 65
Kelly, Henry, 191
Kennedy, John, 129
Kennon, Beverly, Jr., 76, 80-81
Kilpatrick, Hugh Judson, 19-22, 24-25, 224
King, Preston, 184, 186
King, Rufus, 200, 202-3, 207
Kirkwood Hotel, 82, 115, 123, 130, 180

Lamon, Ward Hill, 62
Lapierre, Andre J., 192-93, 196
Leale, Charles, 126, 132
Lee, Edwin Gray, 41, 85, 89-90, 93, 99,
    102, 104, 141-42, 170, 192, 209, 226
Lee, Fitzhugh, 23
Lee, John, 130
Lee, Robert E., 20, 23, 25, 30, 41, 59, 62,
    91-92, 98, 108-9, 113, 119-21
Letcher, John, 28
Lieber, Francis "Franz", 25, 128, 217
Lincoln, Abraham, 19-21, 24-27, 30, 41,
    52-53, 57, 61-63, 65, 67, 74, 76-79, 81,
    86-87, 92-96, 98-101, 108, 111-16, 118,
    120, 123-24, 126-29, 132, 158, 160,
    162, 165, 169-71, 173, 175-76, 179-80,
    196, 200, 205-8, 211-12, 214-15, 217-
    18, 222, 224-25
Lincoln, Mary Todd, 100, 112, 114, 118,
    126
Lincoln's Inn, 198
Littlepage, William, 23
Lloyd, John, 90, 107, 114, 165, 168, 177,
    208, 211, 226
Longuemare, Emile, 39
Lopez, Moses, 44-45
Lovett, Alexander, 140
Lucas, William, 144-45

Madison, Dolly, 185
Marie Victoria, 66
Martin, Patrick C., 32, 62, 65-66, 169, 174
Martin, Robert M., 39
Matthews, John, 115, 138
Maury, Dabney H., 110
McCall, W. H., 186
McClellan, George, 40-41, 52, 119-20
McCullough, John, 88
McDevitt, James, 132, 141

McDonald, William L., 51
McEntee, John, 24
McHenry House Hotel, 63
McLeod, H. A., 194
McMasters, James, 39
McMillan, Lewis J. A., 193, 196-97
McNeil, Archibald, 194
McPhail, James, 117, 175, 180, 187
Meade, George, 20-21, 24, 49, 100, 120-21
Mears, Thomas, 63
Mendes, Rebecca, 43-44
Merrick, Richard T., 208, 211-12
Merritt, James B., 54, 166-67
Milford Station, 77
Milligan, James F., 28
Milligan, Lambin, 198
Minor, Robert D., 65
Mitchell, B. W., 119-20
Montgomery, Richard, 166
Moorehead, Charles, 32
Morgan, John Hunt, 36-37
Mosby, John, 24, 72, 81, 94, 142, 145, 153,
     176, 219-20
Mudd, George, 137, 140
Mudd, Samuel A., 66, 68-70, 127-28, 131,
     134-37, 139-41, 156, 162, 164, 168-70,
     174, 190-91, 206, 213-18, 224, 226
Mudd, Sarah Frances, 140, 163
Mussey, R. D., 182

Nanjemoy Creek, 75-76, 87, 128, 143, 208
Napoleon, Louis, 46
National Hotel, 131, 142
Navy Yard Bridge, 116, 127, 129-30
Nichols, W. A., 160
Norris, William, 28
Nothey, John, 107, 177

O'Beirne, James R., 146-47
O'Laughlen, Michael, 55, 67, 86, 88, 134,
     136, 156, 162, 164, 168, 173-74, 214
Ord, C. C., 100
Owens, James, 146

Paine, Lewis. See Powell, Lewis
Parker House Hotel, 53, 55, 57, 62-63, 65,
     68, 127
Parker, John, 118
Parr, Preston, 74, 86
Passapatanzy Creek, 76, 80-81
Payne, Lewis. See Powell, Lewis
Pennington, J. L., 83
Person, Edward, 111

Peterson House, 128
Pierrepont, Edward, 212
Pollard, James, 23
Polley, William, 84
Pope, John, 119
Porter, Horace, 100, 160
Powell, Lewis, 72, 81, 86-87, 89, 103, 108,
     112, 116, 121-23, 128, 134, 156, 162,
     164, 175-76, 183-85, 187-89, 217, 219

Queen, William, 66, 170
Quesenberry, Elizabeth R., 139, 143-44

Rains, Gabriel, 94, 220
Rath, Christian, 186, 188-89
Rathbone, Henry, 123, 126
Reeves, John J., 102
Richards, Almarin C., 141
River Queen, 100
Robinson, George, 122
Robinson, Martin, 22
Roby, Franklin, 138
Rollins, William, 145, 147, 150
Roscoe, Theodore, 179
Rosser, Thomas, 41
Ruggles, Daniel, 145
Ruggles, Mortimer, 145-46, 148

Sainte Marie, Henri Beaumont de, 200-2,
     204-7, 211, 219
Sanders, George, 32, 40, 65-66, 117, 166,
     169, 226
Sanders, Reid, 65
Sandford Conover. See Dunham, Charles
Schein, Michael, 104-5, 201, 207
Seddon, James, 35, 65, 76, 83-84
Sedgwick, John, 22
Seward, William, 48, 62, 78-81, 96, 98,
     112-13, 116-17, 121-23, 128, 132, 139,
     160, 165, 168, 175-76, 187, 202, 206
Sheridan, Philip, 100
Sherman, William T., 49, 91, 98, 100-1,
     109-10, 113, 164
Slater, Rowan, 83, 106
Slater, Sarah, 39, 82-86, 89-91, 93-94, 99,
     102, 106, 117, 131, 134, 141, 165, 170,
     178, 192, 196, 219-20, 226
Slidell, John, 46
Smith, John L., 180
Smith, Joseph Sim, 213
Smoot, Richard, 75, 128, 165-66, 174
Soaper's Hill, 116, 123, 128
Sons of Liberty, 35-36

Spangler, Edman, 115, 124, 126, 141, 156, 161-63, 168, 172-73, 180, 215, 217, 224, 226
Special Order No. 191, 120
Speed, James, 158, 216, 226
Spotswood Hotel, 78, 93
St. Albans, Vermont, 37-39, 65, 83
St. Lawrence Hotel, 57, 64, 102, 141-42
St. Martin, Natalie, 45
St. Nicholas Hotel, 89-90
Stanton, Edwin, 21, 25, 54, 79, 113-14, 128-29, 132-34, 147, 154, 157-58, 161, 164-65, 167, 170-71, 179, 182-83, 187, 190, 197, 199, 205, 212, 216-17, 223-24, 226
Stephens, Alexander, 79-80
Stone, Charles, 130
Stone, Frederick, 75, 162, 164
Stoneman, George, 108, 110
Stringfellow, Benjamin Franklin, 29, 142, 226
Stuart, J. E. B., 59
Stuart, Richard H., 144
Surratt boarding house, 70, 84-86
Surratt, Anna, 175, 184-85, 187-88, 197, 199, 209, 223, 226
Surratt, John H., Jr., 29, 69-70, 72, 74-76, 81, 84-91, 93-95, 99, 102-7, 116-17, 130-32, 134-36, 141-42, 156, 160, 165, 169, 175, 178, 190, 192-93, 196-215, 218-22, 224, 226
Surratt, Mary, 75, 85, 90-91, 107, 114, 132, 134-35, 156, 161-65, 167-68, 176-79, 181, 183-89, 197, 199, 211, 217, 223
Swann, Oswell, 137-38

Taft, Charles, 126
Taltavull Saloon, 124
Tanner, James, 129
Taylor, Zachary, 47
Thompson, Jacob, 34, 36-37, 39-41, 50, 66, 85, 93, 95, 104, 166, 170, 197, 201, 220, 226
Thompson, John Chandler, 66

Thornton, James, 145
Tompkins, C. H., 161, 179, 226
Townsend, George Alfred, 142-43, 215, 218
Trenholm, George A., 96, 109-10
Tresca, Fred, 194
Tucker, Beverly, 40, 65, 226

Vallandigham, Clement, 34
Verdi, F. S., 117, 121, 128
Vesey, Denmark, 44

Wallace, Lewis, 160, 163, 179, 226
Walter, Jacob A., 184, 188
Ward, Annie, 99, 103, 220
Washington, Lucius Quintus, 93, 226
Watson, Giovanni. *See* Surratt, John H., Jr.
Watson, Mary, 29
Watson, R. D., 29, 88-90, 94, 99, 102
Webster House, 209
Webster, Daniel, 48
Weichmann, Louis, 70, 72, 74, 82, 85, 87, 89-90, 104, 107, 115, 132, 134-35, 141-42, 163, 165, 168, 174-75, 177-78, 190, 200, 206-7, 210-11, 226
Welles, Gideon, 128, 132, 187, 213
Wells, H. H., 141
Wheeler, William E., 65, 188
Whitehurst, D. W., 214
Wilding, Henry, 196
Willard Hotel, 112
Williams, William, 138
Wilmer, Parson, 140
Wilson, Dick, 147
Wilson, James, 110
Wise, Henry, 60
Wood, John T., 108
Wood, William P., 195
Woodland, Henry, 138
Wren, George, 59
Wylie, Alexander, 187
Wylie, Andrew B., 215

Young, Bennett, 36, 38
Yulee, David "Levy", 47